CORPORATE GOVERNANCE AND ECONOMIC PERFORMANCE

Corporate Governance and Economic Performance

Edited by
KLAUS GUGLER

OXFORD
UNIVERSITY PRESS

OXFORD

UNIVERSITY PRESS

Great Clarendon Street, Oxford OX2 6DP

Oxford University Press is a department of the University of Oxford.
It furthers the University's objective of excellence in research, scholarship,
and education by publishing worldwide in

Oxford New York

Athens Auckland Bangkok Bogotá Buenos Aires Cape Town
Chennai Dar es Salaam Delhi Florence Hong Kong Istanbul Karachi
Kolkata Kuala Lumpur Madrid Melbourne Mexico City Mumbai Nairobi
Paris São Paulo Shanghai Singapore Taipei Tokyo Toronto Warsaw

with associated companies in Berlin Ibadan

Oxford is a registered trade mark of Oxford University Press
in the UK and in certain other countries

Published in the United States
by Oxford University Press Inc., New York

© Oxford University Press, 2001

British Library Cataloguing in Publication Data
Data available

Library of Congress Cataloging in Publication Data
Data available

ISBN 0–19–924570–3

1 3 5 7 9 10 8 6 4 2

Typeset by Newgen Imaging Systems (P) Ltd., Chennai, India
Printed in Great Britain
on acid-free paper by
Biddles Ltd., Guildford & King's Lynn

Preface

Corporate governance has time and again been the subject of extensive scrutiny and controversy. Much of the debate of the 1960s and 1970s focused on the managerial corporation in the USA and UK, inspired by the seminal work of Berle and Means (1932). The separation of ownership from control has been blamed for spectacular business failures, the build-up of huge excess capacities, and unscrupulous managers expropriating shareholders. Dispersed outside shareholders left managers uncontrolled, and they bought firm after firm in the 'conglomerate merger wave' of the late 1960s, only to be forced to sell off most of these companies shortly thereafter at substantial loss. Corporate governance is concerned with coping with the problems that arise in situations where the one who takes the actions is not (fully) the residual claimant.

Very little is known about how corporate governance functions outside the United States; however, several stylized facts have emerged. In Japan *keiretsus* with extensive cross shareholdings are common. In Continental Europe a concentrated voting control structure is widely observed. Governance is mainly exerted via large shareholdings, and (hostile) takeovers are very rare. Other features are underdeveloped equity markets, group structures such as *pyramiding* (a pyramidal group is a business entity where legally independent firms are controlled by the same family or institution through a chain of unidirectional ownership relations), and controlling stakes of other corporations, families, banks, and the state. In most countries, including the United States, control is not contestable. When control is not exerted through control blocks, anti-takeover devices like poison pills, classified boards and anti-takeover laws limit the scope for control challenges through markets. The United Kingdom, where such challenges are possible, is an exception.

This book is the result of a collective research effort by members of the European Corporate Governance Network (ECGN) to gather information about corporate governance and performance in a large number of countries. The ECGN was founded in 1996 by Fabrizio Barca, Erik Berglöf, Francesco Brioschi, and Colin Mayer. The Network was born of the need to combine the efforts of researchers who are interested in corporate finance and corporate governance in Europe. Especially in the field of corporate governance, comparative empirical research is necessary, since so many different systems are in place all over the world. Lack of hard data has been a major impediment to such research, and the ECGN brings together 'country teams' familiar with the language and corporate culture of their respective countries. Other work by ECGN teams consists of an effort to collect comparable data on voting control structures of listed corporations in Western and Eastern Europe, i.e. data on equity and voting rights. *The Control of Corporate Europe* by Barca and Becht (2001), is one of the results of this research effort.

What ultimately matters for the corporation, policymakers and society alike is whether corporate governance affects economic performance, and if so, how. This book takes this further step by analysing the linkages between corporate governance and economic performance. It contains evidence of these linkages, from both English and the respective local language studies, and covers the countries Austria, Belgium, Germany, France, Italy, Japan, The Netherlands, Spain, Turkey, the United Kingdom, and the United States. The broad picture emerging is one of marked variation of systems even within Continental Europe, underlining the importance of cross-country comparisons.

I am indebted to Theodor Baums and Marco Becht for various discussions, comments and suggestions. I am particularly grateful to all the members of the country teams for their work and their patience with me. Of utmost importance for this project to succeed were the meetings of the country teams in Milan in 1997 and 1998, and the meeting in Brussels in 1998, all gratefully supported by the ECGN through grants from the Directorate General for Industry of European Commission, Fondazione Eni Enrico Mattei (FEEM), and the Politecnico di Milano.

Particular gratitude of all of us goes to the OECD, which sponsored research on earlier versions and portions of this project. Valuable comments and suggestions were received from George Papaconstantinu, Maria Maher, and Thomas Andersson.

Klaus Gugler

Vienna
January 2001

Contents

Contents

List of Figures

List of Tables

Notes on Contributors

Magda Bianco is currently responsible for the corporate finance unit at the research department of the Bank of Italy, where she has worked since 1989. Between 1992 and 1996 she was Professor of Industrial Organisation at the Università degli Studi di Bergamo. She holds a Ph.D. in economics from the London School of Economics, and a Master's degree in economics. Her research interests are in the field of corporate finance and corporate governance. She has published articles on Italian corporate governance, bank–firm relationships, financial structure and development.

Ekkehart Boehmer is assistant professor of finance at the Institute of Banking at Humboldt University, Berlin. He holds an MA in economics and a Ph.D. in finance from the University of Georgia. His main research interests are in empirical corporate finance, with a particular emphasis on corporate governance and corporate law. Recent work analyses the German governance system with a special focus on the role of banks in the German economy.

Rafel Crespí-Cladera is associate professor of managerial economics at the Universitat Autònoma of Barcelona (UAB). Currently he is teaching at the Universitat Illes Balears (UIB) as a visiting professor. His research interests are in the field of corporate governance, mainly in empirical corporate finance, ownership structure and management. He graduated from the Universitat de Barcelona (UB) and holds a Ph.D. from the Universitat Autònoma of Barcelona (UAB). He has also taught at the Universitat Pompeu Fabra (UPF) and has been a visitor at Tilburg University (KUB) at the Centre for Economic Research (CentER).

Abe de Jong is an Assistant Professor of Finance at Tilburg University. He holds a Ph.D. in finance from Tilburg University. His Ph.D. thesis is on Capital Structure Choice. His current research interests are in the area of empirical corporate finance.

Marc Goergen holds an M.Sc. in economics from the Free University of Brussels (ULB) and an MBA in European Business from Solvay Business School, Brussels. He completed his D.Phil. in economics at Keble College, University of Oxford before joining both the School of Accounting and Finance, University of Manchester and the School of Management, UMIST, as a lecturer in 1997. He spent 1998 as a lecturer at the ISMA Centre at the University of Reading. In 1999, he moved back to the School of Mangement at UMIST. His areas of research include initial public offerings, corporate governance, ownership disclosure, and corporate investment. His book, *Corporate Governance and Financial Performance*, was published in November 1998 by Edward Elgar. Marc Goergen teaches corporate finance, investment finance, and financial economics.

Klaus Gugler has been Assistant Professor at the Economics Department of the University of Vienna since September, 1995. He holds a Ph.D. in economics from the University of Vienna. His Ph.D. thesis is on investment spending and ownership structure. His research areas are industrial organization and corporate governance.

Elizabeth Kremp is currently scientific adviser at the Companies Observatory of the Bank of France. She studied at ENSAE (National School of Statistics and Economic Administration) in Paris and obtained her Ph.D. in international economics at the Universtiy of Paris (I). She specialized in panel data studies while she was research economist at the National Bureau of Economic research (NBER). She has published studies on a variety of issues (productivity in French services, trade credit, impact of restructuring of French firms, financing of French firms) and is now mainly focusing on empirical corporate finance studies.

Luc Renneboog is assistant professor in finance at Tilburg University (Netherlands). He graduated from the Catholic University of Leuven with an M.Sc. in commercial engineering and a BA in philosophy, and from the University of Chicago with an MBA. He holds a Ph.D. in financial economics from the London Business School. After some time in industry, working for Proctor and Gamble, he taught at the Catholic University of Leuven and, as a visitor, at the University of Oxford. His teaching consists of courses in corporate finance, investments, and real options. His research focuses on corporate governance and ownership structure, dividend policy, investing in art, and share price anomalies.

Kyoko Sakuma is a Ph.D. candidate at the Department of Political Science, Université Libre de Bruxelles (ULB), in Belgium. She is currently completing an MBA at Solvay Business School, Brussels, to supplement her research framework. Her Ph.D. thesis is on the role of banks in restructuring enterprises in Japan and in Germany.

Patrick Sevestre is Professor of Economics at Paris XII-Val de Marne University, and an associate researcher at the Bank of France Research Centre. He obtained his Ph.D. in econometrics at the University of Paris (I). His main research interest is panel data econometrics, both theoretical and applied. His recent publications concern dynamic panel data models, banks' lending behaviour, company labour demand, and production efficiency. He is currently working on the financial behaviour of firms.

Burcin Yurtoglu is at the Department of Economics at the University of Vienna. He graduated with a BA in economics from the Bogazici University in Istanbul, and holds a Ph.D. from the University of Vienna. His main research interests are in empirical industrial organization and corporate finance, with a particular emphasis on corporate governance and firm-level investment.

PART I

CORPORATE GOVERNANCE AND PERFORMANCE: THE RESEARCH QUESTIONS

1

Introduction, theoretical framework, and chapter contents

1. INTRODUCTION

Spectacular business failures, the build-up of huge excess capacities, unscrupulous managers expropriating shareholders by paying themselves fantastic salaries, and the roles played by the market for corporate control and institutional investors in generating apparently short-term investment objectives, have led to a renewed interest in corporate governance. Zingales (1997) defines a governance system in the spirit of Williamson (1985) as a 'complex set of constraints that shape the *ex post* bargaining over the quasi rents generated in the course of a relationship'. More practically, the questions are: (1) How do suppliers of finance control managers? (2) How do they make sure that they get any of their money back? (Shleifer and Vishny 1996). After all, there is the so-called 'separation of ownership and control' as first proposed by Berle and Means (1932). Why does Adam Smith's invisible hand not automatically provide the solution?

This book tries to give answers. It covers the economic literature concerning the interrelationships between corporate governance and economic performance. The book includes an extensive assessment of the current knowledge on the potential influence of corporate governance on the performance of firms, and points to avenues for future research. Policy implications are derived from this assessment.

The focus of this book is on the interrelationships between the structure of ownership (both ownership concentration and identities of owners) and corporate performance. The key questions are: Does direct shareholder monitoring by large shareholders improve the governance and hence the profitability of the corporation? What are the disadvantages of high ownership concentration? Do banks or other institutional investors improve the performance of companies, or are they too 'passive' in governance?

Furthermore, we focus on the analysis of mechanisms that constrain or give incentives to management other than direct shareholder monitoring, i.e. hostile takeovers, the board of directors, and managerial compensation. Takeovers are commonly a disciplinary mechanism in the USA and UK but less frequently so in Continental Europe and in Japan. The questions here are: Are takeovers a good substitute mechanism for direct shareholder monitoring? Are takeover defences beneficial to shareholders?[1] (3) Does managerial compensation give good incentives to managers or are managers 'paid like bureaucrats' (phrase by Hall and Liebman 1997)? The supervisory board plays a potentially important role in efficient governance. Recently, interest increased in the question of whether board structure affects a firm's performance. While the US discussion focuses on the role of outside directors, some Continental European countries have two-tier board systems and co-determination. The country chapters portray their specific environment, and try to assess the question whether there is a relation between board structure and performance.

The book has seventeen chapters in two parts. Part I reviews the economic literature on corporate governance and performance covering mainly Anglo-Saxon (USA and UK) studies, but also studies from Continental Europe and Japan. Most of the studies so far have analysed the 'classic' owner–manager conflict resulting from the 'separation of ownership and control' in the large public corporation. The recent resurgence of interest in Continental European and Japanese corporate governance has highlighted another major conflict in corporate governance, namely the large–small owner conflict. This book gives special reference to these two conflicts in an internationally comparable manner.

Part I analyses the research areas: Direct monitoring and profitability: Are large shareholders beneficial? (Chapter 2); Beneficial block-holders versus entrenchment and rent extraction (Chapter 3); Takeovers and the market for corporate control (Chapter 4); Managerial compensation (Chapter 5); and The identity of owners (Chapter 6).

Part II (Chapters 7 to 16) contains the country reports for Austria, Belgium, France, Germany, Italy, Japan, the Netherlands, Spain, Turkey, and the United Kingdom. The reports cover the basic research areas of corporate governance using local knowledge and focusing on the domestic literature. The reports are thought of as being self-sufficient entities portraying their respective countries. In addition, each country report describes the governance structure of one of the largest industrial firms in the respective nation.

Chapter 17 concludes and draws up policy recommendations. The appendix to this chapter presents a summary of the answers to our research questions.

2. THE THEORETICAL FRAMEWORK

Table 1.1 presents the theoretical framework of the ECGN (European Corporate Governance Network) with regard to the separation of ownership and voting power, as outlined in the Executive Report by Becht (1997). This table exhibits the basic trade-offs encountered with the dispersion versus concentration of cash flow and control rights.

Much of the existing empirical literature compares firms allocated in Quadrant I with firms in Quadrant IV. In particular, in Quadrant I the classical principal–agent problem[2] may occur. 'If the owner-manager sells equity claims on the corporation which are identical to his ... agency costs[3] will be generated by the divergence between his interest and those of the outside shareholders, since he will then bear only a fraction of the costs of any non-pecuniary benefits he takes out in maximizing his own utility'. (Jensen and Meckling 1976: 312). This citation already includes the two most basic conflicts that occur in corporate governance: the conflict between a large controlling shareholder and outside minority shareholders, and the conflict between a controlling manager and outside dispersed shareholders.

Table 1.1. *Dispersion–Concentration tradeoffs for investors*

DISPERSED OWNERSHIP

Quadrant I	**Quadrant II**
Dispersed voting power	Concentrated voting power
Advantages:	*Advantages*:
Liquidity	Direct monitoring
Diversification opportunities (risk sharing)	Liquidity
Low cost of capital	Diversification opportunities
Disadvantages:	Lower cost of capital than in IV
Lack of direct monitoring (free-riding	*Disadvantages*:
problem, absenteeism)	Cash-flow and control incentives
Implications:	misaligned
'Strong Managers, Weak Owners	Potential collusion (manager–block-
(Roe, 1994)	holder)
Takeovers are possible	Extraction of private benefits
Management Control or Market Control	*Implications*:
(Becht and Mayer 2001)	'Strong Voting Block-holders, Weak
Research questions:	Minority Owners'
Are OC firms more profitable than MC firms?	Takeovers impossible/unlikely
What are the efficiency consequences of	*Research questions*:
(hostile) takeovers?	Is there rent extraction by
Is there management entrenchment?	block-holders?
	Does the identity of investors matter?
	What are the effects of pyramiding?

CONCENTRATED OWNERSHIP

Quadrant III	**Quadrant IV**
Dispersed voting power	Concentrated voting power
Advantages:	*Advantages*:
Some protection of small shareholders from	Direct monitoring
voting right restrictions	Cash-flow and control interests
Disadvantages:	aligned
Cash-flow and control incentives misaligned	*Disadvantages*:
Few means of intervention	Low liquidity
Low liquidity	Low diversification opportunities
Low diversification opportunities	High cost of capital
High cost of capital	Potential rent extraction by
Implications:	majority-owner
Mostly disadvantages	*Implications*:
'Strong Managers, Weak Owners'	'Weak Managers, Weak Minority
Takeovers difficult	Owners,
	Strong Majority Owners'
	Research questions:
	Are OC firms more profitable than MC
	firms?
	Is there rent extraction by large
	shareholders?
	Does the identity of investors matter?

Notes: OC=owner-controlled; MC=manager-controlled.

Underlying sources: Becht (1997); Becht and Mayer (2001).

In Quadrant I of Table 1.1, when ownership is dispersed, the incentives to perform direct monitoring are weak, and when voting power is dispersed the means for performing direct monitoring are not available. Free-rider problems (Grossman and Hart 1980)[4] and absenteeism in general meetings ('exit' instead of 'voice') are the consequences. If other disciplining devices are absent (for instance, if anti-takeover devices are present), managers have considerable discretion and power, and may follow their own objectives ('Strong Managers, Weak Owners', Roe 1994). Opponents to this view (e.g. Fama 1980) argue that managers are effectively constrained from taking actions that do not maximize shareholder wealth. In effect, it is assumed that existing disciplining mechanisms suffice to assure profit maximization despite the presence of a dispersed ownership structure. Among these are the board of directors, the threat of takeover, the managerial labour market, competition in the product market, or the financial structure of the firm. Depending on which effects dominate, control either resides with the manager(s) or is transferred to the market (see Becht and Mayer 2001). Advantages of dispersed ownership include enhanced liquidity of stocks, better diversification opportunities, and presumably lower costs of equity capital.

The problem of 'management control' can be overcome, at least theoretically, by concentrating ownership and voting power (Quadrant IV of Table 1.1). Major shareholders have the incentives and the power to monitor managers, since cash flow and control interests are concentrated and aligned. A large fraction of the benefits of monitoring can be appropriated, and concentrated voting rights equip shareholders with the necessary power to influence the decision-making process. However, there are also disadvantages associated with concentrated ownership and voting power: Firstly, concentrated ownership reduces the possibilities for diversification and the liquidity of stocks. From a social viewpoint, undiversified risk-averse owners may undertake investment projects that are suboptimally risky and yield suboptimal returns. Secondly, concentrating voting power raises the likelihood that large block-holders or majority owners may collude with management to exploit small shareholders. This may raise the cost of equity capital for these firms as rational minority shareholders demand a discount on shares.

It is possible to concentrate voting power without concentrating ownership (Quadrant II of Table 1.1), or vice-versa (Quadrant III of Table 1.1). By concentrating voting power but not ownership, some degree of liquidity and risk-sharing opportunities can be preserved, and, at the same time, direct monitoring is possible. However, since controlling block-holders have a disproportionate stake in the companies' profits, they are even more likely than QIV large shareholders to seek other forms of compensation. The block-holder only bears a fraction of the costs of rent-seeking activities but receives the full benefits. Potential problems arise from a conflict of interests between controlling block-holders and small shareholders. This problem may be particularly severe in the case of small shareholders of listed companies that belong to pyramidal groups. For example, they can be expropriated by block-holders who control the whole group through intra-group transfers (Barca 1997; and Zingales 1994).

Quadrant III of Table 1.1 (concentrated ownership but dispersed voting power, e.g. achieved by voting right restrictions) has mostly disadvantages from a corporate governance perspective. Voting-rights restrictions insulate managers from effective direct monitoring, as well as from hostile takeovers. An advantage may be that small shareholders are better protected from rent-seeking activities of large shareholders, since their voting rights have a disproportionately larger impact.

As we have seen, the theoretical predictions on the relationship between the governance structure of the firm and its performance are generally ambiguous. For example, concentrated ownership might provide monitoring incentives that lead to better performance benefiting everybody. However, concentrated ownership might also lead to the pursuit of goals that lie in the interest of the controlling block-holders, but not in the interest of the minority shareholders. The block-holder might transfer resources, leading to suboptimal disclosed performance of the controlled company. Table 1.1 guides us throughout the book to determine which effects dominate.

3. CHAPTER CONTENTS

Chapter 2 cannot unambiguously answer the question of the sign and the magnitude of the relationship between owner-control and performance. However, the evidence is more on the positive side of direct shareholder monitoring. Large shareholders are active monitors in companies and this entails beneficial effects for corporations. According to Roe (1994), the larger ownership dispersion in the USA relative to most other countries is (also) the result of politics that discourage large holdings. The evidence presented here suggests a greater role and fewer restrictions for large shareholders particularly in the United States.

Chapter 3 generally supports the notion that there are potential conflicts of interest between dominant major insider shareholders and other share/stakeholders. The structure of ownership (Morck, Shleiffer, and Vishny 1988a), but also investor protection rights (LaPorta et al. 1997, 1998) are likely determinants of this conflict. The task of prudent company legislation is to secure the benefits of large shareholders as effective monitors of management and, at the same time, to prevent them from consuming excessive private benefits from control. This would induce small and minority shareholders to invest in companies' stocks, despite the presence of large shareholders. High disclosure and accounting standards could provide the necessary transparency for small shareholders to feel comfortable about investing in equity markets. The policy recommendations of the ECGN (see Becht 1997; or Millstein 1998) apply. Disclosure requirements for pyramidal groups, for the structure of ownership and voting rights, and for legal separation devices should be mandatory and enforcement should be strict.

Chapter 4 analyses takeovers and the market for corporate control. As it turns out, takeovers are an incomplete mechanism for solving the basic agency problem in the large public corporation. Some authors find underperformance relative to targets prior to takeovers, others do not. The takeover premium is about 30–40 per cent, and so only the most obvious abuses of managerial discretion seem to be rectified. It appears that existing managers can squander a third of the firm's value before the threat of displacement becomes truly serious. The market value of acquiring firms shows little positive change, or even a negative change, upon the announcement of a takeover. It is not obvious why, when outsiders eliminate inefficient managers, almost all of the return should go to the shareholders of the mismanaged firm. This raises concerns about the motives of acquirer managers. Growth and size maximization might be one explanation. Therefore, takeovers should be seen in conjunction with other control devices, such as large shareholder monitoring or effective supervisory board oversight. One piece of policy advice would be to strengthen these alternative mechanisms, while not necessarily constraining hostile takeovers by regulation. Extreme views of either prohibiting hostile takeovers, or viewing hostile takeovers as the main device of corporate governance, are too simplistic.

Managerial compensation is the topic of Chapter 5. Rewards that promote good incentives must be indexed to outcomes that managers can alter. Stock-market values and current profits are only partly affected by managerial decisions. General business conditions or just (good or bad) luck beyond a manager's control can also affect the fortunes of a corporation. Relative comparisons increase the signal-to-noise ratio and make managerial incentives more effective and contracts more efficient. The evidence is rather bleak on that point, however. Because boards of directors set compensation contracts in most countries, they play a primary role in designing proper incentives for management. There is the suspicion of many authors that boards—especially when they are insider-dominated—align more with management than with outside shareholders. The question arises as to whether agents (boards) should decide key elements of the contract (compensation shape and level) between the principals (shareholders) and other agents (managers), or whether shareholders themselves should decide proposals for compensation packages, in general meetings.

Chapter 6 is on the identities of owners. Ownership concentration is very high in most countries other than the USA or UK, and the question is whether 'who controls the corporation' matters. The available evidence is consistent with the notion that the identity of owners matters. The effects of close bank–firm relationships and shareholdings of institutional investors on firm profitability are ambiguous, the evidence concerning state ownership is on the negative side. Bank involvement in the governance of corporations appears to alleviate financial constraints and distress. The lack of established evidence regarding the effects of institutional investors is particularly worrying, because institutional investors will gain in importance all over the world.

Part II of the book contains the country reports. Chapter 7, by Klaus Gugler, starts with Austria. Austrian corporate governance can best be characterized by an 'insider system' of finance supplemented by state influence, which is currently still strong. Due to insufficient disclosure and accounting provisions, very little systematic evidence about corporate governance is available to date. Ownership concentration seems excessively high, and the stock exchange is very small and illiquid. Hostile takeovers are unimportant as a disciplinary device. Internal control devices, such as large shareholder monitoring, are the primary means of control. Insufficient protection of small shareholders, as well as specific country factors, such as a low demand for outside (equity) finance and state ownership, may be responsible for a lack of efficient securities markets. The conflict between large and small shareholders appears to be an important problem in Austrian corporate governance.

In Chapter 8, Marc Goergen and Luc Renneboog present evidence regarding corporate governance in Belgium. The main characteristics of the Belgian corporate ownership and equity market can be summarized as follows : (1) few Belgian companies are listed; (2) there is a high degree of ownership concentration; (3) holding companies and families, and to a lesser extent industrial companies, are the main investor categories; (4) control is levered by pyramidal and complex ownership structures; (5) there is a market for share stakes. Properties (1) to (4) imply that Belgium can be portrayed as a German-French 'insider system' rather than an Anglo-American system. However, typical for Belgium is the importance of holding companies which are often part of pyramidal ownership chains and which are used to lever control. There is evidence that, when performance is poor, the structure and composition of the board of directors and the ownership structure are important determinants of board restructuring.

Chapter 9 by Ekkehart Boehmer is on German corporate governance. Firstly, current German transparency legislation (WpHG) is not sufficient to achieve the objective of transparency as stated by the European Commission and the German Parliament. Compared to other developed economies, the German stock market is dominated by large shareholders. However, even after introducing the WpHG in 1995, the ultimately controlling parties are often not disclosed, and transfers from smaller shareholders are legally possible. Secondly, due to proxy votes and board memberships, banks control a substantially higher fraction of voting rights than cash-flow claims. Moreover, banks extend more loan money to the typical firm than they hold as equity. Consequently, it is unclear whether their voting power is used in the interest of shareholders. Empirically, bank involvement appears to have a very limited effect on performance. Several open questions remain to assess the efficacy of the German model in relationship to more market-based systems.

In Chapter 10, Elizabeth Kremp and Patrick Sevestre present evidence about France. In France, concentration of ownership is very high, both in listed and non-listed companies. Family control is most common; when banks, insurance, or holding companies are owners, they often have majority control. Existing empirical studies lead to the conclusion that corporate performance is not correlated with ownership concentration. The influence of ownership type on performance is not clearly established. Some studies suggest no link; others show that independent firms perform better than subsidiaries and heads of groups. Nothing can be said about the impact of bank–firm relationships on performance, mainly due to the general unimportance of bank ownership in France. The lack of data on top managers' compensation, and the rarity of hostile takeovers in the past, make it difficult to obtain any idea about their possible impact on managerial behaviour and firm performance.

Chapter 11 by Magda Bianco is on Italy. The Italian corporate governance system has a number of peculiarities as compared to the more well-known Anglo-Saxon or Continental systems: as opposed to the Anglo-Saxon countries, public companies are extremely rare, and the separation between ownership and control limited. Instead, ownership is extremely concentrated, as in most other European countries. Hence, the main conflict of interest has developed between block-holders and minority shareholders, especially in pyramidal groups. The empirical evidence suggests that the existence of block-holders in Italy may have induced mainly rent extraction rather than aligned incentives of majority shareholders with minority ones. Takeovers do not appear in general to have represented until recently an instrument to solve agency problems or to guarantee that inefficient controlling agents are substituted. However, analyses on more recent data suggest that they might be now more closely related to inefficient behaviour. Again, until recently, Italian capitalism does not seem to be prone to using pay-performance schemes. Finally, there is limited evidence concerning the effects of the identity of owners. Certainly institutional supervision is still rare.

Chapter 12, by Kyoko Sakuma, presents the Japanese model of corporate governance. Japanese corporate governance is described as 'contingent governance', in which a main bank shifts control rights from employees to shareholders if the financial performance of the firm deteriorates. The main bank, being not only the chief lender but also often the largest shareholder, has an incentive to replace a poorly performing management as the firm's performance plunges below the predetermined lowest acceptable level for the bank. Empirical evidence does not suggest that concentrated ownership by financial institutions leads to better performance. However, when combined with concentrated debt-holding, banks seem to provide effective rescue operations to firms in financial difficulties. A more active role of institutional investors in Japanese corporate governance depends on the speed of removal of regulatory and organizational obstacles.

Chapter 13, by Abe de Jong, is on the Netherlands. Corporate governance issues in the Netherlands have been associated with technical takeover defences for years. Firms' managers justified these defences as a protection against (foreign) hostile takeovers, while shareholders were complaining about a lack of influence on the management. Nowadays, academic research and public debate in the Netherlands increasingly recognize the versatility of governance structures. Discussions deal with the ownership structure, the board structure, the capital structure, takeover defences, managerial compensation structure, and the impact of these factors on the performance of firms. Several specific elements make the Dutch setting an interesting field of research. Ownership is relatively concentrated and private persons and financial institutions are important owners in Dutch firms. The financial institutions, and especially the large bank-insurance firms, have several relations with firms. Finally the two-tier board system and the lack of information about compensation give rise to controversies about the efficiency of internal control in Dutch firms.

Chapter 14, by Rafel Crespí, draws a picture of the Spanish corporate governance system and its relationship to company and investor performance. There is evidence of a weak disciplinary role of takeovers for underperforming management. Recent data availability from the CNMV, the Spanish securities commission, allows better knowledge of internal mechanisms of control. The role of the board of directors, its size, composition, turnover, and compensation are related to company performance. Rent expropriation by large shareholders is a major concern.

Chapter 15, by Burcin Yurtoglu, analyses the Turkish corporate governance system. Corporate governance in Turkey can be described as an 'insider system' with the insiders being the country's richest families. Ownership is highly concentrated and levered through pyramidal structures, cross-shareholdings, and differential voting rights.

Hostile takeovers are unimportant as a disciplinary device. There are also no signs of a market of large stakes as a substitute for the market for corporate control. Internal control devices, such as major-shareholder monitoring, are the primary means of control. Insufficient protection of small shareholders makes the conflict between large and small shareholders an important problem in Turkey. Lower dividends, lower profitability, and lower market-to-book ratios of firms in the lower parts of a pyramid, provide evidence for rent extraction and entrenchment.

Chapter 16, by Marc Goergen and Luc Renneboog, reviews the evidence on corporate governance and performance in the United Kingdom. The United Kingdom is probably the only country, with the exception of the USA, where one can observe the separation of ownership and control as defined by Berle and Means (1932). The largest average holding in a British company amounts to only 14 per cent of the equity. Given the low ownership concentration, the main agency problem in UK firms is therefore the potential expropriation by the management rather than by a large shareholder. Although the UK has an active market for corporate control, recent empirical evidence suggests that the market for corporate control fails in terms of its disciplinary function. There is a vast pool of empirical studies on the link between ownership and performance. However, the findings from these studies seem to be inconclusive.

Chapter 17 concludes the book with a summary of results. Policy implications are derived from each of the research areas covered.

Notes

1. Examples are Dual-Class Recapitalizations and so-called 'poison pills'. Dual-Class Recapitalizations restructure the equity of a firm into two classes with different voting rights and need the approval of shareholders. Poison pills, which do not require shareholder approval in the USA, are target shareholder rights that are triggered by an event such as a tender offer for control. These rights include, for example, to sell shares to the target at attractive prices. By reducing the probability of takeovers, poison pills may actually *harm target shareholders*.
2. The principal–agent literature is concerned with how the principal (here the owner of the firm) can design a compensation system (a contract) which motivates his agent (here the manager) to act in the principal's interest. A principal–agent problem arises when there is asymmetric information either concerning what action the agent has undertaken or what he should undertake. Prior to the emergence of the principal–agent literature, managerialist theories of the firm directly questioned the profits maximization assumption: Baumol (1959) hypothesized that managers maximize sales; Williamson (1963) added staff and emoluments to the manager's objective function, Marris (1963, 1964) and Grabowski and Mueller (1972) postulated growth maximization by managers.
3. Agency costs are the total costs of structuring, administering, and enforcing the contracts written in a principal–agent setting.
4. The basic free-rider problem of monitoring arises because a monitoring shareholder exerts a positive externality on other (non-monitoring) shareholders, diminishing their incentives to monitor. As the full costs of monitoring are borne but only a fraction of the total benefits are appropriated, less than an optimal monitoring level is attained.

2

Direct monitoring and profitability:
Are large shareholders beneficial?

1. INTERNATIONAL COMPARISON OF OWNERSHIP/
VOTING CONCENTRATION

One natural question from Table 1.1 is whether manager-controlled (MC) firms (QI) are less profitable than owner-controlled (OC) firms (QIV) because of the presence of the separation of ownership and control and the resulting absence of direct monitoring. Before we try to answer this question, Table 2.1 presents an overview over the potential severity of the problem of the separation of ownership and control in Europe, Japan, and the USA. Concentrated holdings of common stock potentially reduce agency problems among shareholders and managers; the larger ownership (and voting power) concentration, the higher the incentive and ability of shareholders to monitor management. This reduction in the 'free-rider problem' of monitoring is accompanied by a 'convergence-of-interest' effect if managers hold large blocks of shares.

Concentrated holdings of voting blocks are the primary means of controlling managers in most Continental European countries such as in Austria, France, Germany, Italy, Belgium, the Netherlands, and Spain (see Table 2.1). In these countries the largest shareholder holds on average around 30 to 55 per cent of the voting power. Ownership/voting concentration in the UK and particularly in the USA is substantially lower, and the average equity holdings of the largest shareholders fall below 20 per cent. Roe (1994) partly explains the larger ownership dispersion in the USA relative to most other countries by politics that discourage large holdings.

The high ownership concentration in Continental European countries implies that for these countries the separation of ownership and control is not the biggest problem for efficient governance of companies, except perhaps for the largest companies with widely dispersed equity claims. Conflicts of interest are most likely to arise between majority (or even super-majority) shareholders and minority owners. Before we turn to this large–small shareholder conflict, we assess whether OC firms are indeed more profitable than MC firms. The next section draws mainly from evidence from the USA and UK.

2. THE EVIDENCE

The managerialist hypothesis states that executives of manager-controlled firms are less likely to engage in strictly profit-maximizing behaviour than are executives of

Table 2.1. *International comparison of voting power concentration in listed companies (ultimate voting blocks)*

Country	Companies	Largest voting block		2nd largest voting block		3rd largest voting block	
		Median	Mean	Median	Mean	Median	Mean
Austria	50	52.0	54.1	2.5	7.8	0.0	2.6
Belgium	121	50.6	41.2	0.0	2.7	0.0	0.2
	BEL20	45.1	38.3	0.0	1.0	0.0	0.0
France	CAC40	20.0	29.4	5.9	6.4	3.4	3.0
Germany	374	52.1	49.1	0.0	2.7	0.0	2.5
	DAX30	11.0	17.3	0.0	1.4	0.0	0.6
Italy	214	51.0	48.0	7.6	10.1	3.0	4.1
Japan	734	—	33.0[a]	—	—	—	—
The Netherlands	137	18.2	26.9	—	—	—	—
Spain	193	34.2	40.1	8.9	10.5	5.2	6.0
Turkey	257	41.2	44.7	14.0	14.6	6.1	7.1
UK	250	9.9	14.4	6.6	7.3	5.2	6.0
USA							
NYSE	1,309	0.0	3.6	0.0	1.5	0.0	0.6
NASDAQ	2,831	0.0	3.4	0.0	1.2	0.0	0.6

[a] Five largest owners.

Notes: '0.0' means that there is no owner holding 5 per cent or more. The disclosure threshold in the UK is 3 per cent.

Sources: Barca and Becht (2000); for Japan: Prowse (1992); for Turkey: Yurtoglu (2001).

owner-controlled firms.[1] Table 2.2 presents a summary of the results obtained in the literature so far for the question of whether OC firms are more profitable than MC firms. Although research on the relationship between ownership structure and performance was also conducted before 1960 (e.g. Berle and Means, 1932), since the 1960s and 1970s renewed interest has been present in academic research.

In general, results are ambiguous, but the preponderance of studies point to a profitability-enhancing role of owner control (see also Short 1994, for an excellent survey). Studies that found that OC firms significantly outperform MC firms are Monsen, Chiu, and Cooley (1968); Larner (1970); Radice (1971); Boudreaux (1973); Palmer (1973); McEachern (1975); Stano (1976); Holl (1977, 1980); Steer and Cable (1978); Bothwell (1980); Levin and Levin (1982); Cosh and Hughes (1989); Zeckhauser and Pound (1990); and Leech and Leahy (1991). Studies that found no significant differences include Kamerschen (1968); Sorensen (1974); Holl (1975); Round (1976); Jacquemin and Ghellinck (1980); Demsetz and Lehn (1985); Holderness and Sheehan (1988); Murali and Welch (1989); Prowse (1992); Mikkelson, Partch, and Shah (1997); Cho (1998); and Himmelberg, Hubbard, and Palia (1999); Jacquemin and Ghellinck (1980) find for their sample of large French firms that profitability increases with size only for firms under familial control, not for non-familial firms. Ware (1975) and Thonet and Poensgen (1979) find that MC firms significantly outperform OC firms.

The dependent variables in the above studies are all proxies for the performance of the firm, e.g. net income/net worth, rate of return on equity, or Tobin's Q,[2] or the riskiness of returns as e.g. the variance and skewness of profitability. With the exceptions of Round (1976)(Australian); Thonet and Poensgen (1979)(German); Jacquemin and Ghellinck (1980)(French); and Prowse (1992)(Japanese) all studies in Table 2.2 analyse either US or UK large-firm samples. The classification into OC and MC firms is mostly rather arbitrary, using a specific percentage ownership criterion for a single block of voting stock or other concentration measures. Firms are usually classified as MC if there is no single block of equity/voting power that exceeds 5–10 per cent. No explicit differentiation is made between ownership and voting rights, so the implicit assumption is that differences between these two concepts are immaterial, and 'one-share-one-vote' prevails. More recent studies focused less on the distinction between OC and MC firms, and more on ownership concentration and managerial and board ownership. Several studies are worth reviewing more intensely, because these address special methodological and interpretational issues such as arbitrariness of classification, omitted variables, industry effects, reverse causality, or simultaneity between control devices. The following studies are, of course, not exhaustive.

Cosh and Hughes (1989) apply a number of refinements in classifying 160 large UK firms into OC and MC firms. They use additional company-level information, e.g. whether or not there is a challenging holding to board-of-director holdings, and ascertaining whether this challenging holding is held by a family, a financial institution or other OC companies. Additionally, they include information on the managerial remuneration structure (stock income versus fixed remuneration, absolute and relative magnitudes). Analysing different time periods (1968–72; 1975–79; 1968–79), they find that OC firms are somewhat faster growing *and* more profitable, and that OC firms

Table 2.2. *Owner-controlled versus manager-controlled firms*

Study	Period and sample	Control classification	Proportion of MC firms	Dependent variables	Results
Berle and Means (1932)	1929: 200 largest US non-financials	MC <20%	44% 21% legal device	—	—
Gordon (1945)	1937: 200 largest US non-financials	As TNEC (1940) plus rectifying 'shortcomings'	>66%	—	—
Larner (1966)	1963: 200 largest US non-financials	OC ≥10%	83.5% MC <10%	—	—
Kamerschen (1968)	1959–64: 200 largest US non-financials	OC ≥10% MC <10%	84.5%	Return on equity	No significant difference; change in control from OC to MC has significantly positive effect
Monsen, Chiu, and Cooley (1968)	1952–63: 500 largest US industrial	OC ≥10% and active control or OC ≥20%; MC ≤5%	—	Net income/net worth; sales/total assets; net income/sales; long-term debt/capitalization	All ratios higher for OC except long-term debt/capitalization
Larner (1970)	1956–62: 187 of largest 500 US non-financials	OC ≥10% MC<10%	>80%	Profit/equity; variance of profit/equity	MC significantly negative (but small); however, variance higher (insignificant)
Radice (1971)	1957–67: 86 large UK firms	OC >15% MC <5%	48.8%; transitional: 16.3%; legal device: 2.3%	Profit before tax/net assets; growth in net assets	OC higher profit and growth rates, differences across industries

Table 2.2. *Contd.*

Study	Period and sample	Control classification	Proportion of MC firms	Dependent variables	Results
Elliot (1972)	1964–7: 88 S & P Compustat firms	OC ≥ 10% and active control or OC ≥ 20%; MC ≤ 5%	—	Liquidity, growth in owner earnings, leverage, capital investment	No difference, except for liquidity (higher in MC firms)
Boudreaux (1973)	1952–3: 72 of 500 largest US industrials	OC ≥ 10% and active control or OC ≥ 20%; MC ≤ 5%	—	Return on equity	OC higher and more variable
Palmer (1973)	1961–9: 500 largest US firms	SOC > 30% WOC 10–29% MC < 10%	—	Average rate of return on net worth	Significantly lower for MC if firm has monopoly power
Sorenson (1974)	1948–66: 30 OC and 30 MC firms	OC ≥ 20% MC < 5%	—	After tax profits/net worth, stockholder rate of return, dividend payout ratio, growth in sales and net worth	OC outperforms MC, but not statistically significant; but dividend payout ratio higher for MC
Holl (1975)	1948–60: 183 listed UK firms	OC ≥ 20% plus some constraints	69.4%	Pre-tax profit/net worth; growth of net assets; variance and skewness of profitability; dividend payout	No significant differences when industry effects included
Ware (1975)	1960–70: 74 large US firms	OC > 25% (or 15% plus representation on board); MC < 5%	—	Net income/net worth; net sales/no. of employees;	MC more profitable and higher payout ratio

Study	Sample	Definition	%	Measures	Findings
McEachern (1975)	1963–72: 48 large US industrials	OC >4% and management representation; EC >4% and no management representation; MC <4%	—	retained earnings/net income; debt/total assets; Average market rate of return; Beta coefficient; payout ratio; age	OC and EC significantly higher rate of return, OC more market-based risk and lower payout ratio
Round (1976)	1962–4: 289 large Australian firms	CC >15% OC >10% MC <5%	—	Net income/total assets	Insignificantly higher for OC
Holl (1977)	1962–72: 343 out of top 500 US firms	SOC >30% WOC 10–29% MC <10%	65.6%	Stockholder rate of return	OC significantly higher (4.5%) if MC able to evade discipline of market for corporate control
Steer and Cable (1978)	1967–71: 82 of top 250 UK firms	OC >15% or >3% if also manager; MC others	—	Rate of return on equity and long-term debt; profit/turnover	OC firms significantly outperform MC firms; organizational form matters (M-form better)
Thonet and Poensgen (1979)	1961–70: 92 (max.) listed German manufacturing firms	OC >25% (but not state or other institution)	25%	Return on equity, market value/book value; growth of total assets; variance of return on equity	MC significantly higher profitability measures; OC higher growth; variance insignificant

Table 2.2. *Contd.*

Study	Period and sample	Control classification	Proportion of MC firms	Dependent variables	Results
Jacquemin and de Ghellinck (1980)	1970–74: 103 of largest 200 French firms	Case by case division into familial and non-familial control	45.6% (non-familial)	Net cash flow/book value of equity and reserves	No average differences; profitability increases with size for familial control only
Bothwell (1980)	1960–7: 150 US industrials	SOC > 30% WOC 10–29% MC < 10%	—	Risk-adjusted economic profit margin (CAPM); return on equity	OC higher profitability; significant in highly concentrated industries
Schreyögg and Steinmann (1981)	350 largest German firms	MC < 1% plus state firms; OC > 25%; ultimate ownership controlled for	50% (firms) 65% (sales)	—	—
Levin and Levin (1982)	1967–76: 200 largest US firms	OC > 10% MC > 10% FC < 10% plus constraints	—	Rate of return on equity, standard deviation of profits; growth rate of sales	OC significantly better
Demsetz and Lehn (1985)	1976–80: 511 large US firms	—	—	Accounting rate of return	No relationship between ownership concentration and profitability
Morck, Shleifer, and Vishny (1988a)	1980: 371 large US firms	Board ownership; dummy for founder or founding family on board	Mean board stake: 10.6%; 24% run by founder	Tobin's Q	Board ownership positive in (0%, 5%); negative in (5%, 25%) and positive in

Study	Sample	Ownership rules	Ownership percentage	Performance measure	Results
					(25%, 100%); founder good in young, bad in older firms
Holderness and Sheehan (1988)	1979–84: 114 majority-held US firms	MH ≥ 50% and < 95% DH < 20%	—	Accounting rate of return; Tobin's Q	No significant differences; Identity of owner matters
Murali and Welch (1989)	1977–81: 43 closely and 83 widely held US firms	CH > 50%	—	Stock market return; Accounting profit rate; Market value	No significant differences
Cosh and Hughes (1989)	1968–79: 160 large UK firms	MC < 5% and several constraints	28.2% (1970)	Rate of return on net assets; share return; valuation ratio	OC significantly higher profitability and lower growth rates
McConnell and Servaes (1990)	1976 and 1986: 1,173 and 1,093 US firms	—	Insider ownership: 13.9%	Tobin's Q	Significant curvilinear to insider ownership; Institutions have positive influence
Zeckhauser and Pound (1990)	1986–9: 286 US firms	Large shareholder > 15%	66% no large shareholder	Earnings/price ratio	Significantly lower for large shareholder firms in open information industries
Leech and Leahy (1991)	1981–5: 470 UK-listed firms	Fixed rules (OC > 5%, 10%, 20%); variable rules: degree of control using probabilistic voting model	66–8.7% (fixed rule); 86–71.1% (variable rule)	Valuation ratio; trading profits margin; rate of return on shareholder's capital; sales and assets growth	OC significantly higher profit and growth rates; Ownership concentration has net negative influence

Table 2.2. Contd.

Study	Period and sample	Control classification	Proportion of MC firms	Dependent variables	Results
Prowse (1992)	1979–84: 143 large Japanese firms, 85 *keiretsu*, 58 independent	—	—	Accounting profit rate	No influence of ownership concentration
Agrawal and Knoeber (1996)	1987: 383 large listed US firms	—	—	Tobin's Q	Too many outside directors on board (with 2SLS)
Mikkelson, Partch, and Shah (1997)	1980–3: 283 IPOs by US companies	—	—	Return on assets	No relationship to board and management ownership
Cho (1998)	1991: 326 out of Fortune 500	Board ownership MC <5%	52%	Capital expenditures; R&D expenditures; market value of equity	2SLS: Investment affects corporate value, which affects ownership (endogenous)
Himmelberg, Hubbard, and Palia *et al.* (1999)	1982–92: 600 (max.) Compustat firms	—	—	Tobin's Q	No effect of insider ownership if it is controlled for firm fixed effects; insider ownership endogenous

Notes: OC = Owner Control; MC = Manager Control; SOC = Strong Owner Control; WOC = Weak Owner Control; EC = External Control; FC = Financial Control; MH = Majority Held; DH = Diffusely Held; CH = Closely Held.

have more highly valued stock and higher returns per ordinary share. MC firms are twice as large as OC firms. A gradual move towards management-control during the 1970s is witnessed; in 1970, 70 per cent of the sample firms were classified as (eventually) OC, but by 1979 this percentage had dropped to 64 per cent.

While better monitoring and/or incentive alignment may be at work, as the authors claim, larger growth and profit rates are also consistent with the Mueller (1972) life-cycle theory of the firm. In the early stages of the life cycle, investment opportunities are abundant, and high growth and high profit rates result. Concentrated ownership holdings are also more likely in these stages, since firms are still small and ownership stakes not yet diluted. According to this theory, by the movement from QI to QIV in Table 1.1, and the implied greater scope for management discretion, over-investment would be expected in later stages of the life cycle. Investment opportunities start falling behind the internally generated cash flows, and unmonitored managers invest partly in negative net-present-value projects. It would be illuminating to have additional information about the 'position' of the firm in its life cycle (e.g. information on age) and so be able to discriminate accordingly.

The study by Leech and Leahy (1991) potentially provides controls for both problems, omitted variables and the arbitrariness of firm classification into owner- and manager-controlled firms.[3] For a sample of 470 large, listed UK companies across a wide range of industries, the authors find a positive correlation between ownership control and the valuation ratio, the profit margin, and the return on shareholders' capital, as well as higher growth rates of sales and net assets of owner-controlled firms. While higher firm-profitability supports the hypothesis of better governance in owner-controlled firms (and governance failures in manager-controlled firms), ownership concentration significantly reduces the valuation ratio and the trading-profit margin. This can be the result of a discount put on shares of firms in which ownership concentration is high. Considering Table 1.1, both advantages and disadvantages of large shareholder monitoring are present at the same time.

One possible caveat regarding the study by Leech and Leahy (1991) is the simultaneous inclusion of a control type dummy and ownership concentration. As firms are more likely to be classified as OC firms if ownership concentration is higher, there may be problems of multicollinearity. Imprecise estimation of coefficients and even changing signs might be the consequence. The finding that there is a positive correlation between owner control and the valuation ratio, but that ownership concentration reduces the valuation ratio, may be attributed at least in part to multicollinearity.

Zeckhauser and Pound (1990) emphasize different planning horizons and differential effects of corporate governance arrangements in different industries. Their central hypothesis is that managers in firms with major shareholders as monitors are more concerned with maximizing the sum of current and discounted expected future profits, rather than taking a short-term view. The authors draw a sample of 286 US firms across 22 industries, half of which are classified as having high and half as having low asset specificity.[4] Their main finding is that corporations in which there is a large shareholder display, on a cross-sectional basis, a significantly lower (around 10 per cent lower) earnings/price ratio than matched firms without large shareholders only in

industries with relatively low asset specificity (such as machinery and paper prod-
ucts).[5] Consistent with this result, the authors find that dividend payout and leverage
ratios are not statistically significantly different in large shareholder firms, i.e. large
shareholder firms do not need to signal their higher expected earning growth rates to
the market through financial policy or capital structure. However, in industries with
high asset specificity (e.g. computers) large shareholders are not associated with lower
earnings/price ratios.

This suggests that the nature of the firm's investment and production decisions influence the asymmetry of information between principal and agent. When outside
monitoring is difficult—as in high asset-specificity industries—large shareholders as
the only control device might not solve the problem. Considering again Table 1.1,
lower liquidity of stocks and higher costs of capital may outweigh the benefits of large
shareholders when industry assets are specific.

One point of critique of the Zeckhauser and Pound (1990) study concerns a possible omitted variable bias. The authors perform t-tests of the difference in the means of
the variables. This does not control for the influence of other variables affecting the
two factors of earnings/price ratios and the presence of major shareholders. In fact,
large shareholders could well be present more often in smaller firms exhibiting lower
earnings/price ratios because, for example, investment opportunities are more
favourable in younger and smaller firms due to life-cycle effects.

Several problems remain with all the above studies relating ownership and profitability variables. First, the identity of block-holders might make a difference. Some
block-holders may be passive, some may be active monitors. The same percentage
holding of equity may affect monitoring incentives in a different manner dependent
on who owns the shares. This issue is tackled in Chapter 6. Second, the direction
of causality is not clear a priori if managers and founders retain larger stakes in
successful firms. Reverse causality then implies that better performance leads to more
concentrated holdings and not the reverse. Third, there are several mechanisms for
controlling agency problems between managers and shareholders. These mechanisms
may interact (substitutive or complementary) and greater use of one mechanism need
not be positively related to firm performance. Indeed, economic theory predicts that
the various mechanisms should be employed up to the zero marginal-profit condition,
and a cross-sectional regression should find no relation between firm performance
and any one of the mechanisms.

The last two problems are dealt with in the study of Agrawal and Knoeber (1996).
The starting hypothesis is that alternative control devices may be used in a substitutive
manner, 'where one specific mechanism is used less, others may be used more, resulting in equally good performance' (Agrawal and Knoeber 1996: 378). Therefore, results
obtained from regression analysis relating the use of any single mechanism to firm performance may ignore the possible interdependence between mechanisms.

The mechanisms analysed are shareholdings of insiders, institutions, and large block-
holders; the presence of outside directors on the board of directors; the managerial
labour market; the market for corporate control; and debt policy. For a sample of 383
large listed US firms, the results are as follows. Examining each mechanism separately by

ordinary least squares (ignoring possible interdependencies among mechanisms), insider shareholding (positive, but non-linear), outside representation on the board (negative), debt policy (negative), and activity in the corporate control market (measured by the average acquisition probability in the respective 2-digit industry; negative) are all cross-sectionally related to firm performance as measured by Tobin's Q. Institutional shareholdings, block-holdings, and CEO human capital are unrelated to Tobin's Q.

Next, the authors stress that causality could well run the other way: better firm performance could lead to greater insider shareholdings, fewer outsiders on the board, less debt, and fewer takeovers. Accordingly, the authors estimate a simultaneous equations system treating firm performance as well as the different control mechanisms as endogenous dependent variables. The interrelationships among control devices show that a more active market for corporate control is associated with greater shareholdings by block-holders and by institutions. This implies a complementary relationship between direct monitoring and the takeover process. In contrast, a substitutive relationship between shareholdings by block-holders and institutions indicate that institutions and large shareholders are alternative mechanisms for outsider activism. In the Tobin's Q equation, the fraction of outsiders on the board remains the only significant and negative coefficient. This suggests that while firms optimally employ the different control devices they tend to have *too many* outside directors, which—in the view of the authors—presents a puzzle.

3. ASSESSMENT AND POLICY IMPLICATIONS

The question of the sign and the magnitude of the relationship between owner control and performance of the corporation is, theoretically and empirically, not unambiguously answered. By and large, however, the evidence is more on the positive side of direct shareholder monitoring. The evidence supports the hypothesis that large shareholders are active monitors in companies, and this entails beneficial effects for corporations. This is also confirmed by managerial turnover studies. For example, Franks and Mayer (1994) find larger turnover of directors when major shareholders are present in German firms. For US firms, Kaplan and Minton (1994) and Kang and Shivdasani (1995) find a larger sensitivity of managerial replacement with respect to poor performance in firms with large shareholders.

According to Roe (1994), the larger ownership dispersion in the USA relative to most other countries is (also) the result of politics that discourage large holdings. The evidence presented here suggests a greater role and fewer restrictions for large shareholders in the USA. As always, however, several caveats remain. First, we are far from reaching definite conclusions about the interrelationships between control devices. Direct monitoring is but one—albeit effective—device for reducing shareholder–manager conflicts. There are also econometric problems if one assumes exogeneity of ownership structure, when in fact ownership and performance are endogenously determined.

Second, the industry in which the firm operates influences the efficacy of direct monitoring. Other control devices (e.g. takeovers and managerial pay schemes) may be better able to rectify managerial failure in some industries, e.g. in industries where assets are very specific and sunk, and direct monitoring technologies prohibitively expensive.

Third, managers operate under at least two constraints—one from stockholders and one from competition in the product market. Therefore, significant differences in performance between OC and MC firms should only be expected in monopolistic or oligopolistic market structures. Palmer (1973) states:

> If, however, managers of management-controlled firms with a high degree of monopoly power, because of their relative freedom from the rigors of competition, have more discretion in the use of their firms' potential profits than their counterparts in firms with a low degree of monopoly power, such an assumption [i.e. that the effect of separation of ownership and control is the same for all degrees of monopoly power] is incorrect, and an interaction term should be included.

Palmer (1973) interacts control type with a barriers to entry dummy, and obtains significant differences between OC and MC average profit rates only among firms with a high degree of monopoly power.

A policy is thus suggested in which corporate governance legislation is viewed in conjunction with competition and antitrust policy. Bad governance is more likely if the firm is effectively management-controlled *and* if free cash flow is high e.g. due to monopoly power. Corporate governance becomes more important as the firm develops. Corporate control failures and/or bad investment decisions are unlikely in the early stages of the life of the firm if investment opportunities are abundant and (free) cash flow is low or even negative. However, with firm growth, maturing, and firm ageing, investment opportunities fall short of the cash flow available. In conjunction, possible dilution and dispersion of equity stakes enhance the role of corporate governance in assuring good company performance. Corporate control failures are most likely in mature firms and/or in oligopolistic/monopolistic environments.

Finally, the identity of the owner-manager and/or owner-monitor is likely to matter. Judging the 'separation of ownership and control' on the basis of ownership concentration alone is misleading. Holding companies, banks, institutional investors, other non-financial corporations, and family owners may have different business objectives. Managers of corporations under governmental, quasi-governmental, or even under direct state control are likely to have different incentives and behave differently from corporations owned by the private sector. Ownership concentration and identities of owners should be viewed as influencing performance separately. We will return to this topic in Chapter 6.

Notes

1. A second hypothesis states that executives of manager-controlled firms are more likely to exhibit risk-averse behaviour due to asymmetries in managerial reward structures, i.e. they bear the losses of bad states (e.g. dismissal), but do not get the full reward of their decisions in good states of the world. We do not follow this hypothesis here.

2. Tobin's Q is defined as the ratio of the market value of the firm to the net-of-tax replacement cost of existing assets.

3. In their multiple regression analysis, they include as independent variables: ownership concentration (various measures), control type (various definitions of owner versus manager control; application of fixed and variable rules), a proxy for risk (both total risk and systematic—beta—risk), size (logarithm of total sales), a diversification dummy (one or more product groups by SIC three-digit codes), age (number of years since registration to test for life-cycle effects), export intensity of sales, and capital intensity of technology (ratio of capital to employees).

4. Industries with average R&D/sales ratios above 1 per cent are characterized as high asset specificity industries below this limit as low asset specificity industries. Large shareholder firms are those where a single outside shareholder owns more than 15 per cent of total common stock.

5. A lower earnings/price ratio implies a higher market premium indicating a higher level of anticipated future performance relative to presence performance.

3

Beneficial block-holders versus entrenchment and rent extraction?

In the preceding chapter, we saw that large shareholders can improve the supervision of management and thereby improve firm performance. However, large block-holders, by virtue of their increased scope of influence over the company may also have detrimental effects. Quadrant IV of Table 1.1 exhibited the costs and benefits of concentrated voting power and concentrated ownership. The benefits of large shareholders are associated with the alignment of cash-flow and control interests and direct monitoring. They have both the interest and the power to get their money back. The costs of major investors, besides reduced diversification and liquidity, include rent extraction and 'managerial entrenchment'. Morck, Shleifer, and Vishny (1988a: 294) define 'managerial entrenchment' as a 'manager who controls a substantial fraction of the firm's equity may have enough voting power or influence more generally to guarantee his employment with the firm at an attractive salary'. Moreover, expropriation *ex post* can lead to suboptimal investment *ex ante* by stakeholders such as minority shareholders and employees.

Collusion between management and block-holders seems all the more likely if there is a difference between cash flow and voting rights. For instance, a block-holder in QII of Table 1.1 could vote favourably on management-sponsored proposals and be compensated by side payments. This incentive arises because the block-holder only bears a fraction of the costs of these payments (i.e. forgone dividend payments in the proportion of his cash-flow rights) but receives the full benefits.

1. REDISTRIBUTION BETWEEN STAKEHOLDERS

Direct evidence on the degree of expropriation is scarce. One way to measure potential expropriation is to compare returns on common and preferential stock. If shares with superior voting rights trade at a large premium, private benefits of control may come at the expense of minority shareholders. While Bergström and Rydquist (1990) and Rydqvist (1987) for Sweden, and Barclay and Holderness (1989, 1992), and Jarrell and Poulsen (1988) for the USA do not find evidence for substantial expropriation, Zingales (1994) finds large voting premia in Italy, suggesting high private benefits of control.

Barclay and Holderness (1989) find that, on average, large blocks trade at a 20 per cent premium which, overall, amounts to 4 per cent of the firm's value. Barclay and Holderness (1992) reveal that managerial turnover is exceptionally high (33 per cent) after the trades. The increase in firm value is at least partly attributable to the specific skills and incentives of the block-holders, since increases in firm value only materialize when the new block-holder gains control over the firm. This implies that the 4 per cent premium is likely to be an upper bound on expropriation by large block-holders in the USA. This is also confirmed by Jarrell and Poulsen (1988). They examine 94 cases of dual-class recapitalization in the period 1976–86 and find significantly negative average price effects of only −0.64 per cent at the announcement date. The largest wealth losses occur for those firms with insider holdings in the 30 to 55 per cent range, indicating possible entrenchment motives.

Zingales (1994), in contrast, obtains extraordinarily high voting premia for Italy (around 80 per cent) and measures the average proportion of private benefits to be around 30 per cent of firm value. In a case study of an intra-group transfer in Italy,[1] Zingales (1994) estimates a dilution of minority property rights equal to 7 per cent of the value of the equity owned by outside shareholders. His conjecture is that these private benefits of control are so large in Italy because the legal system is very ineffective in preventing exploitation of a control position. This problem may be particularly severe in listed companies that belong to pyramidal groups (Barca, 1997).

Somewhat more indirect evidence is obtained from studies relating firm performance to insider ownership (management or director holdings). A negative relationship over some range of insider ownership is interpreted as evidence for rent extraction and/or managerial entrenchment.

For a sample of large US firms, Morck, Shleifer, and Vishny (1988*a*) find a positive relationship between board ownership and Tobin's Q in the 0 to 5 per cent ownership range, a negative relationship between 5 and 25 per cent, and again a positive influence of management ownership on Q beyond the 25 per cent level.[2] Morck, Shleifer, and Vishny (1988*a*) conclude that the 'convergence of interest' and the 'entrenchment' hypotheses are responsible for their findings of a non-linear relationship between management ownership and Q. The initial rise in Q as insider ownership rises reflects managers' greater incentives to maximize firm value and/or the incapability to become entrenched with this small stake. Then, between 5 and 25 per cent, entrenchment outweighs convergence-of-interest, and beyond 25 per cent convergence-of-interest again dominates.

In a refinement, the authors find that among older firms (those incorporated before 1950), the presence of the founding family on the board reduces Tobin's Q on average by 0.147 (t = 1.91), whereas among younger firms (incorporated after 1950), the presence of the founding family raises Q on average by 0.47 (t = 2.02). This indicates that founders (or their descendants) in 'old' firms are too entrenched to be removed, despite having lost their entrepreneurial role.

Similar results are obtained by McConnel and Servaes (1990). In addition, the results of McConnel and Servaes (1990) suggest that there is a need for large stock concentration before shareholders are able to influence management decision-making. They find a significant curvilinear relation between Q (and the return on assets) and the fraction of shares owned by corporate insiders. Tobin's Q first increases (1976 one-to-one, 1986 three-to-one!) with insider ownership, then decreases but does not recoup. In 1976, the point of inflection (the maximum Q) is reached at 49.4 per cent insider ownership, in 1986 at 37.6 per cent. In both years institutional ownership increases the inflection point (to 60.9 per cent in 1976 and 43.2 per cent in 1986), suggesting a value-enhancing role of institutions.

2. ADVERSE INCENTIVE EFFECTS

Expropriation by large investors can be detrimental to other stakeholders not only through direct wealth redistribution but also through adverse effects on the incentives of managers, employees, and minority shareholders. If a large investor cannot credibly commit herself to not extracting rents *ex post, ex ante* incentives are adversely affected. This reduces firm-specific investments. For instance, if large shareholders expropriate minority shareholders, the latter have reduced incentives to provide outside (equity) finance in the first place. Small and illiquid public equity markets are the consequences.

One piece of macroeconomic evidence is given in Figure 3.1, plotting stock-market capitalization to GDP ratios across 14 OECD countries in 1994. La Porta *et al.* (1997) argue that investors are best protected in English common-law countries, less so in Scandinavian and German codes, and most vulnerable in countries of French origin. The Scandinavian code is second best following the English code with respect to

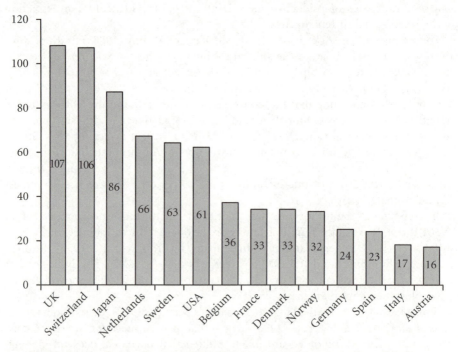

Figure 3.1. *Stock-market capitalization in relation to GDP in 1994 across 14 OECD countries (percentages of GDP)*
Source: 'The Austrian Financial Markets: A Survey of Austria's Capital Markets',
Oesterreichische National Bank, 1996

anti-director rights.[3] Figure 3.1 suggests that stock markets play a much larger role in countries where investor protection is high, like the UK, Switzerland, Sweden, or the USA, than in countries where minority shareholder protection is weaker, such as Austria, Italy, Spain, and Germany. When expropriation of minority shareholders is limited by law, investors anticipate higher returns and are ready to pay more for shares, which in turn induces controlling shareholders to reduce their stakes and/or give up control (La Porta *et al.* 1998).

Small and illiquid stock markets may not be of primary concern if (1) substitutive sources of finance (internal or external) lead to an optimal level and mix of investments, and (2) other monitoring devices substitute for market supervision (e.g. large shareholders). However, doubt has been expressed as to whether debt financing (e.g. bank loans) is a well-suited substitute for equity finance for all types of investments. In particular, investment in the technological stock (e.g. R&D investment) might be adversely affected if the main source of outside finance is debt.

Reasons include: (1) Asset specificity and low resale value may prevent the owner of the R&D asset from receiving a fair price for the asset in the event of insolvency. (2) Bankruptcy costs render capital structure relevant for real investment decisions. (3) Increased riskiness and greater asymmetry of information of R&D projects in comparison to fairly standard capital investment prevent new firms from issuing debt or obtaining bank loans. (4) Cash flows may set in in many periods from the financing of the project and insufficient interest payment coverage leads to early liquidation. (5) A large fixed-cost component of R&D expenditures makes diversification difficult. (6) A suboptimal attitude towards risk is expected if the creditor does not participate in high-return states (as opposed to equity holders), and prefers low-risk, low-return (i.e. interest rate-covering) investments.

Indeed, studies by Long and Malitz (1985) and Bradley, Jarrel, and Kim (1984) find a negative correlation between leverage and R&D activity at the firm level. Figure 3.2 presents additional evidence at the macroeconomic level. It depicts the relationship between stock market capitalization and R&D spending (each variable normalized by GDP) for 14 OECD countries in 1994. A simple ordinary least-squares regression of the R&D/GDP ratio on the stock market capitalization to GDP ratio (STOCK/GDP) gives the following results (t-statistics are in parentheses below coefficient estimates).

$$R\&D/GDP = 1.46 + 0.012*STOCK/GDP$$
$$(t = 5.59) \qquad (t = 2.79) \qquad R^2 = 0.39 \qquad n = 14$$

Stock-market capitalization has a significant positive influence on the R&D/GDP ratio ($t = 2.79$). According to this OLS regression, 'deepening' of a country's stock market by 10 percentage points increases the R&D ratio by 0.12 percentage points. The cross-sectional variation in stock market capitalization explains 39.3 per cent of the variation in R&D intensities across countries. It appears that countries with liquid equity (and possibly venture capital) markets (can) invest more in new technology, future productivity, and growth.

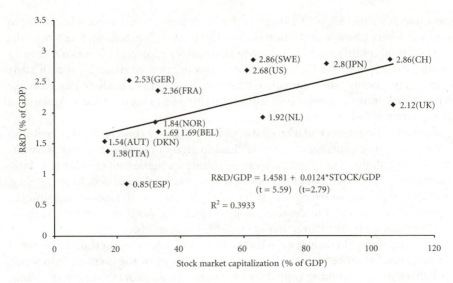

Figure 3.2. *Stock-market capitalization and the R&D/GDP ratio*

3. ASSESSMENT AND POLICY IMPLICATIONS

The literature generally supports the notion that there are potential conflicts of inter-est between dominant large insider shareholders and other share/stakeholders. The structure of ownership (Morck, Shleifer, and Vishny 1988*a*) and also investor protec-tion rights (La Porta *et al.* 1997) are likely determinants of this conflict. Microeco-nomic evidence suggests private benefits of control of up to 30 per cent of firm value in some countries. From a macroeconomic standpoint, potential wealth losses due to expropriation of property rights are harder to evaluate. Investments that have not been made in the first place are, per definition, unobservable. An indication of forgone investments in the technological stocks of some countries with poor investor protec-tion was presented in Figure 3.2, where a significant relationship between stock market capitalization and the R&D/GDP ratio was established.

The question is how company law and governance rules should be designed to se-cure the benefits of large shareholders as effective monitors of management (providing a public good) and, at the same time, to prevent them from consuming excessive private benefits from control to induce small and minority shareholders to invest in companies' stocks. Thus, in evaluating e.g. the costs and benefits of different separation devices, this trade-off is crucial.

As an example, non-voting stock is both a low-cost method of remaining in control and raising outside equity capital, as well as a separation device that potentially leads to diluted incentives and shareholder expropriation. Therefore, the best policy response appears to be to (restrictively) allow the issue of non-voting stock, but at the same time give minority shareholders effective judicial means and powers to claim due compensation if expropriation occurs. As a legal right of redress, one may enable minority shareholders to mount class-action suits, as is possible in the USA.

Likewise, high disclosure and accounting standards could provide the necessary transparency for small shareholders to feel comfortable investing in equity markets. Here, the policy recommendations of the ECGN (see Becht, 1997: 56–64) or Millstein (1998) apply. Disclosure requirements for pyramidal groups, for the structure of ownership and voting rights, and for legal separation devices should be mandatory, and enforcement should be strict. Recent legislation changes in some European countries move into this direction of enhanced minority shareholder protection.

Notes

1. IRI sold its majority stake (83.3 per cent) in Finsiel to STET, controlled by IRI as well, at allegedly too high a price.
2. The coefficients on board ownership are 0.062 (0–5 per cent), −0.016 (5–25 per cent) and 0.008 (above 25 per cent). All coefficients are significantly different from zero. The results for the profit rate are generally less significant, but indicate a positive relationship in the 0–5 per cent range and a negative thereafter.
3. La Porta *et al.* (1997) rank investor protection according to a number of dimensions of shareholder and creditor protection. These include: One share, one vote?, Proxy by mail allowed?, Shares blocked before a general meeting?, Cumulative voting ?, Oppressed minorities mechanism?, Percentage of shares needed to call an extraordinary shareholders meeting, Anti-director rights index, and Mandatory dividends?

4

Takeovers and the market for corporate control

Like a lot of people, you may still think of the 1980s as the era of merger mania. Well, wake up: Today's mergers and acquisitions make the '80s look small-time. The global M&A market broke all records last year at $1 trillion and at its current pace will hit $ 1.3 trillion this year. (The biggest year of the '80s was 1989: $600 billion.) The reasons aren't mysterious. Technological change, deregulation, and globalization are driving many industries consolidate; perhaps most important, with equity markets booming, CEOs are comfortable using their stock to pay what they might in other times consider ridiculously full prices.

(*Fortune 500*, 27 October 1997)

In 1997, there were 23,328 mergers and acquisitions worldwide with a record level of value of $ 1.6 trillion.

(*Der Standard*, 18 May 1998)

According to a study of the US-based consulting corporation Mercer Management Consulting two-thirds of all mergers result in a debacle for shareholders. According to consulter McKinsey only one fourth of all analysed firms have recouped their costs of mergers.

(*NEWS*, 14 May 1998)

From 1985 through 1999, the dollar value of world mergers increased at an average annual rate of 21 per cent, reaching a value of 2.3 trillion dollars in 1999.

(Pryor 2000)

1. INTRODUCTION

The efficiency of takeovers as a disciplinary mechanism is a hotly debated and an unresolved issue. This means of disciplining management is especially in use in 'market'-based systems of corporate finance and governance like the USA and UK.[1] Contrary to what Jensen (1993) complained of, namely that regulatory restrictions hindering mergers and acquisitions would delay necessary corporate restructuring, 'merger mania' as *Fortune 500* calls it was on the rise again in the 1990s. The questions are: Are takeovers a good substitute mechanism for direct shareholder monitoring to control management? What are the efficiency consequences of takeovers/mergers?

Before we turn to these questions, a definition of concepts seems to be necessary. The terms 'mergers', 'acquisitions', and 'takeovers' are all part of the M&A parlance. In a merger, the corporations come together to share their resources to achieve common objectives. As such, it does not greatly concern the rectifying of managerial failure. However, the difference from strictly control-oriented transactions is—at least empirical— rather diffuse. Takeovers and acquisitions are more of an arm's-length deal. In a typical takeover, a bidder makes a tender offer to the dispersed shareholders of a target firm. Conditional on acceptance of this offer, the bidder acquires control of the target. Hostile takeovers are most relevant in a market with corporate control perspective, since target firm management opposes the deal and, if the deal is successful, is likely to be replaced. We will focus on hostile takeovers as a means of correcting managerial failure. Nevertheless, we also present the evidence on mergers and other acquisitions. Firstly, we assume that, when judging the overall welfare implications of hostile takeovers, it is relevant to have knowledge of how combined entities perform on average. Secondly, many studies are not clear-cut about the hostility of deals. Whenever the studies make the discrimination between hostile and other takeovers or mergers, we will report that.

In terms of Table 1.1, most takeovers imply a move from QI to QIV by concentrating cash flow and voting rights. Therefore, in principle, a hostile takeover is a powerful mechanism for disciplining management, since it allows someone who identifies an underperforming company to obtain a large reward. Provided it buys all shares of the target company, a raiding company can reap all the gains of its action. In effect, a takeover is a mechanism for concentrating ownership and voting power in companies where at least 50 per cent of the shares are in free float. There are two main caveats: (1) there may be too few value-improving hostile takeovers, and (2) there may be value-reducing takeovers.

Concerning (1), there are a number of reasons why bidders may reap less than the full benefits of their actions, with the result that takeovers are a suboptimal mechanism for constraining management. (A) There is a free-rider problem (Grossman and Hart 1980). Small shareholders who believe that their decision to sell does not affect the likelihood of success of a bid have an incentive not to tender to a raider, since they may be able to gain from the post-takeover improvement in firm value. (B) The raider may face competition from other bidders driving up the price of the target and reducing its incentive to make a bid. (C) The raider may face defensive actions from incumbent management.

Concerning caveat (2), there are the following reasons to believe that not all takeovers are value enhancing: (A) Bidders may face their own agency problems, and their main objectives may not be profit maximization. Acquiring another firm is certainly the fastest way to grow (Mueller 1969), consistent with managerialist theories of the firm emphasizing the size and growth objectives of managers. (B) Although there may be improvements in productive efficiency, takeovers may worsen dynamic efficiency by reducing firm-specific investment of various stakeholders (employees, incumbent management, suppliers, etc.). (C) There may be distributional consequences. A priori it is not clear that the gains of some stakeholders (e.g. target shareholders) always outweigh the losses of others (e.g. acquirer shareholders, workers, suppliers) and whether the losers are compensated.

The question of whether hostile takeovers keep an eye on the main disadvantages associated with being in QI, Table 1.1, at a reasonable cost, is an empirical one. There are two approaches to analysing the effects of takeovers (and mergers). One is to analyse

ex post accounting data. If takeovers are indeed an effective means of rectifying inefficient management or business strategies, the post-takeover performance of the
combined group should be better than the weighted performance of the acquiring and
target firm prior to the takeover. The second is to examine the share-price reaction of
target and acquiring firms around the announcement date of the takeover. Both
approaches have their problems: accounting data may be unreliable, event studies
assume stock-market efficiency (see Scherer 1988). Keeping these difficulties in mind,
let us consider the facts that have emerged.

2. EVENT STUDIES

2.1. *Target shareholders*

Target shareholders earn, on average, positive returns from tender offers. Jarrell and
Poulsen (1987) estimate premia for 663 successful tender offers in the USA to average
19 per cent in the 1960s, 35 per cent in the 1970s, and 39 per cent in the 1980s. Many
other studies confirm these figures or report even higher target shareholder gains from
takeovers.[2]

There are higher announcement period returns and higher post-takeover returns in
tenders than in mergers (see Servaes (1991) and Agrawal, Jaffe, and Mandelker (1992)).
Higson and Elliott (1998), for a near-exhaustive sample of takeovers between
UK-quoted companies over the 1975–90 period (830 takeovers), find announcement
period cumulative average abnormal returns (CAAR) to target shareholders of 37.5
per cent. In 87.7 per cent of the cases the returns were positive. The authors define a
hostile takeover as one in which the first bid was rejected by the target management.
According to this definition, 15 per cent of the deals were hostile. The hostile takeovers
exhibit announcement period abnormal returns of 42.7 per cent against 36.6 per cent
for friendly transactions. Similarly, Franks and Mayer (1996) find 30 per cent for
hostile bids but only 18 per cent for accepted bids.

Thus, there is considerable agreement that target shareholders are among the
winners of takeover contests, particularly when the bids are hostile.

2.2. *Bidder shareholders*

Bidder shareholder abnormal returns are on average close to zero. Some studies find
small gains, others small losses. Bradley, Desai, and Kim (1984) report significant positive excess returns of 1 per cent for bidders' shareholders over the period 1963–84
in the USA. This average fell from a positive 4.1 per cent in 1963–68 to a negative 2.9
per cent in 1981–4.

Franks and Harris (1989) present similar evidence for 1,900 successful UK takeovers. Although these authors provide evidence that the joint market-value increase of
bidder and target is on average positive, bidder shareholders lose in 53 per cent of
the cases. Higson and Elliott (1998) find essentially zero abnormal returns for bidders

in the UK. Moreover, in 11 out of the 16 years under study, average returns to bidder shareholders over 24 months were negative. Hostile takeovers, in contrast, exhibit significant post-takeover returns of $+24.8$ per cent over 24 months compared to -1.14 per cent for the complete sample. Roughly half of the hostile acquirers have positive post-takeover returns as compared to only 41.4 per cent for friendly takeovers.

Abnormal returns for hostile takeovers are generally higher than for other acquisitions, which is also confirmed in the USA. Agrawal and Knoeber (1996) find significant positive hostile takeover returns of 12.8 per cent over 24 months for US takeovers.

For mergers, results are worse, and can be seen to deteriorate in the long term. The worst results for the post-merger performance of acquiring firms are reported by Agrawal, Jaffe, and Mandelker (1992) for the USA. Their sample consists of 937 mergers and 227 tender offers between 1955 and 1987, representing nearly the entire population of acquisitions of NYSE and AMEX firms by NYSE firms in this period. For mergers, the cumulative average abnormal return for the five year period following the event is -10.3 per cent (t $= -2.37$) and negative in all yearly subperiods. After 5 years, 56 per cent of the cases show negative CAARs. In contrast, for tender offers, Agrawal, Jaffe, and Mandelker (1992) do not find significantly negative CAARs, and CAARs are positive for hostile takeovers. Other studies finding negative effects of mergers are Asquith (1983) and Magenheim and Mueller (1988). Studies that do not find significant underperformance after the acquisition are e.g. Malatesta (1983), Bradley and Jarrell (1988), and Franks, Harris, and Titman (1991).

3. *EX POST* STUDIES

What ultimately matters in evaluating the desirability of acquisitions is whether takeover gains of largely target shareholders are social gains or rather reflect wealth transfers from other economic agents.

Hostile takeovers improve firm value if corporate governance deficiencies are rectified, i.e. if takeovers make deficient management shape up. Jensen (1993) particularly emphasizes the role of hostile takeovers in reducing excess capacity. This goal would not have been realizable in the face of resisting incumbent management and/or other constituencies of the firm such as employees and communities. As an example, Jensen (1993) mentions the tyre industry in the USA, where 37 plants were shut down between 1977 and 1987, and employment fell by over 40 per cent. The means by which this restructuring was achieved were mainly hostile takeovers.

Second, hostile takeovers (and other forms of acquisitions) are socially desirable if some other kind of efficiency gains result, for instance economies of scale or scope, the savings of transaction costs, or the sharing between activities of 'lumpy' or intangible multi-use assets.[3] The following studies review the current state of knowledge concerning the efficiency effects of acquisitions using mainly *ex post* accounting data.

The evidence on hostile takeovers is more on the positive side, although some authors (e.g. Ravenscraft and Scherer (1987a) and Franks and Mayer, (1996)) express doubt that the takeover process is a very effective means of disciplining management. Generally, mergers do not appear to improve productive efficiency and most studies even come up with detrimental effects on efficiency, particularly in the case of unrelated or conglomerate mergers. We first review the evidence about hostile takeovers and then about mergers.

Ravenscraft and Scherer (1987*a*) analyse the post-takeover performance of 95 US firms in the period 1950–76. While the pre-takeover performance (operating income relative to assets) was only 8 per cent worse, lines of business subject to tender offer-induced acquisition were 23 per cent less profitable on average than otherwise comparable lines not involved in tender offers. While the underperformance of targets prior to takeovers is consistent with the notion that takeovers aim at correcting managerial failure, the ensuing failure to actually achieve improvements in performance is not. Although hostile takeovers did not exhibit the same deterioration in profits as mergers, there were also no significant efficiency gains.

While Morck, Shleifer, and Vishny (1988*b*) find that hostile takeovers in the USA are targeted towards troubled industries and firms, the UK is different: Franks and Mayer (1996) do not find underperformance of targets relative to size and industry peers prior to takeovers (80 hostile bids in the UK in 1985 and 1986).

The verdict on mergers is even more negative. The majority of studies does not find significant improvements of firm performance following a merger, or find even a negative development. Ravenscraft and Scherer (1987*b*) report substantial deterioration of profitability of businesses acquired in mergers. Caves and Barton (1989) find that technical efficiency in US 4-digit manufacturing industries in 1977 decreased substantially with the extent of corporate diversification, the main end product of conglomerate mergers. Mueller (1985) compares market shares of 123 US companies that acquired 209 firms with a control sample of unacquired firms between 1950 and 1972. Unacquired businesses, on average, retained 88 per cent of their 1950 market share in 1972, while an acquired business retained only 18 per cent. Mueller and Sirower (1998) reject synergistic gains for 168 US mergers during the period 1978–90. On the contrary, they find support for managerial discretion (i.e. managers maximize their utility and utility rises with the size of the firm they control) and/or hubris (see Roll (1986); managers believe they are better than others and can improve firm value sufficiently to justify high bid prices). Again, effects are worst for mergers involving unrelated businesses. Cowling *et al.* (1980) study productivity changes occurring after largely horizontal mergers in the UK, but none of the 9 mergers that were studied intensively exhibit substantial gains in efficiency. The studies by Mueller (1980) find no increases in post-merger growth rates of merging firms relative to non-merging firms in five countries: Belgium, West Germany, France, Sweden, and the UK. In the Netherlands and the USA, post-merger efficiency even declined.

One of the few studies finding positive effects of mergers is Healy, Palepu, and Ruback (1992). For 50 large mergers between US public industrial firms, they attribute the 3.2 per cent (statistically significantly different from zero) rise in industry-adjusted operating cash-flow return during the 5 years following a merger to increased asset productivity. In particular, mergers involving firms with a high business overlap increase post-merger performance by 5.1 per cent relative to mergers of firms with low or no business overlap.

In conclusion, *ex post* studies indicate that acquirers improve—if at all—only moderately firm efficiency after a merger/takeover. Results are most negative for unrelated and conglomerate mergers, and ambiguities remain also with hostile takeovers. This raises serious concern about the effectiveness of hostile takeovers as the primary means of rectifying poor management. To rely on hostile takeovers as the only or the main disciplinary device does not appear to be optimal.

4. ARE THERE WEALTH TRANSFERS IN TAKEOVERS?

One of the clearest lessons of the recent period is that, whatever the social gains generated by mergers and acquisitions, large redistributions are occurring simultaneously. (Auerbach and Reishus 1988: 1.)

We have assessed that the market for corporate control is not a very effective way to discipline management. If target shareholders win, bidder shareholders break even or lose, and furthermore, efficiency gains are quite low; who pays the bill?

Do labour's losses finance takeovers?

Large public concern has been expressed about the influence of merger and takeover waves on the welfare of employees. Do they lose from (hostile) takeovers?

Shleifer and Summers (1988) express the concern that hostile takeovers can lead to a 'breach of trust'. Focusing on implicit long-term contracts[4] between labour and target management they point out that (in particular) hostile takeovers may involve an *ex ante* inefficiency (i.e. before firm-specific investments are made) associated with the reduced ability of a firm to participate in long-term implicit contracts with its stakeholders. A raider may break implicit contracts if it is in its interest *ex post* (i.e. after firm-specific investments have been made). If stakeholders anticipate that hostile takeovers increase the probability that they are expropriated *ex post*, they provide a suboptimal level of relation-specific investment *ex ante*. 'At least in part, therefore, the gains are wealth redistributing and not wealth creating' (Shleifer and Summers 1988: 42).

The authors themselves present evidence in favour of their theory from two case studies: Carl Icahn's takeover of Trans World Airlines (TWA) in 1985 and the acquisition of Youngstown Sheet and Tube (YST) by Lykes Steamship Company in 1970, and the subsequent acquisition of the latter by LTV Steel in 1979. In the first case, the authors estimate that one and a-half times the takeover premium was transferred to Icahn (and other shareholders) primarily from wage reductions of the 'production' workers. While the authors think that overall efficiency was increased by the takeover,[5] shareholders gained primarily because other stakeholders lost. The second case study demonstrates that not all the stakeholder losses in hostile takeovers are gains to shareholders. Takeovers can have a number of externalities not captured by shareholders or firm stakeholders. For example, YST lay-offs resulted in more than a doubling of bankruptcies in Youngstown, and a plummeting of sale prices of used homes. Sudden redeployments of corporate assets—such as occur in some hostile takeovers—can result in declines of utility of whole cities and regions.

Bhagat, Shleifer, and Vishny (1990) examine 62 hostile takeovers between 1984 and 1986 and find that in 28 of the 62 cases, workers were laid off after the takeover, involving 5.7 per cent of the work forces of these firms. These redundancies account for 10 to 20 per cent of the premium paid.

Do tax payers lose from mergers and takeovers?

Tax motives have long been suspected of causing merger and acquisition activity, and available evidence supports this notion. There are three potential tax benefits associated with the combination of two public corporations: increased utilization of tax loss and tax credit carry-forwards, increased depreciation, and increased interest deductions associated with an increase in the debt/equity ratio of the combined enterprise.[6]

Auerbach and Reishus (1988) find that tax benefits are potentially important. In about 20 per cent of the cases, tax benefits were present with an average value of around 10 per cent of the target's market value. However, the authors assert that tax factors were not the major force behind mergers and acquisitions. Bhagat, Shleifer, and Vishny (1990) single out at least 17 cases (out of 62) where tax advantages represented at least 25 per cent of the takeover premium.

Do bondholders lose from takeovers?

The evidence does not support the notion that sizeable wealth transfers from bondholders to shareholders result from mergers and acquisitions. Denis and McConnell (1986), and Lehn and Poulsen (1987), do not find evidence that the shareholder value created by the acquisitions comes at the expense of preferred shareholders or bondholders.

Do consumers lose from takeovers?

One source of gains to shareholders could be the increased monopoly power resulting from a merger or takeover. Jensen and Ruback (1983) conclude that the evidence rejects this hypothesis. However, Mueller (1996) cites several studies that find increased market power.

Do planning horizons decline due to takeovers?

There has been concern that stock markets may be excessively short-sighted and takeovers might aggravate the problem of 'market myopia'. Jarrell, Brickley, and Netter (1988) report that no empirical evidence has been found to support this theory. For example, a study by the SEC's Office of the Chief Economist (OCE, 1985) of 324 high R&D firms between 1981 and 1984 showed that firms with R&D expenditures are not more likely to be taken over. Moreover, stock prices responded positively to announcements of increases in R&D expenditures.

Hall's (1988, 1990) findings for a sample of more than 1,500 US firms from 1959 to 1987 indicate that most of the takeover activity (580 firms were acquired) is directed towards firms and industries that are relatively less R&D intensive, and towards mature companies with large stable cash flows. Mergers and takeovers themselves do not lead to significant reductions in R&D spending.

5. EFFECTS OF TAKEOVER DEFENCES

Serious concern has been expressed about the presence of defensive measures, particularly for those that do not require shareholder approval. Jensen (1988), in particular, complains about the business-judging rule that gives managers and boards the right to use such devices (e.g. 'poison pills'). Jensen (1988: 43) says, 'In doing so, the courts are essentially giving the agents (managers and the board) the right to change unilaterally critical control aspects of the contract, in particular, the right to prevent the firing of the agents.'[7] Evidence about defensive measures is all the more relevant in the light of Comment and Schwert's (1995) findings reporting a sharp increase in the number of US states adopting anti-takeover legislation and firms adopting poison pills. The percentage of listed firms in the USA that are protected by either control share laws, business combination laws, or poison pills increased from approximately 38 in 1987 to 77 per cent in 1988.

Takeover defences that do not require shareholder approval in the USA include: (1) litigation by the target management; (2) targeted block stock repurchases (greenmail);[8] (3) poison pills; or (4) state anti-takeover amendments. Defensive measures that must be approved by shareholders include: (1) supermajority amendments (i.e. minimum approval required for mergers and other important control transactions); (2) fair price amendments; (3) changes in the state of incorporation; (4) dual-class recapitalization (i.e. creation of classes of equity with differential voting rights); and (5) cumulative voting rights.

Nearly all studies come to the conclusion that the adoption of measures that decrease the probability of takeovers reduces shareholder wealth and possibly social welfare. Jarrell and Poulsen (1987) report significant negative stock-price effects of more than 3 per cent for 104 supermajority amendments since 1980. Jarrell (1985) examines 89 cases involving litigation against a hostile raider. If targets remain independent due to litigation, they lose nearly all of the original premium of 30 per cent. Most studies also find negative stock-price effects of announcements of greenmail, the most comprehensive being OCE (1984). Likewise, by increasing the costs of takeovers and by reducing the probability of takeovers, poison pills may actually harm target shareholders. Malatesta and Walkling (1988) and Ryngaert (1988) present evidence that poison pills harm target shareholders by about 1 to 2 per cent of firm value. Ryngaert and Netter (1987; Ohio anti-takeover law) and Schumann (1988; New York anti-takeover law) present evidence that state anti-takeover amendments have significantly negative effects on potential targets, of 1 to 3 per cent of firm value.

6. ASSESSMENT AND POLICY IMPLICATIONS

Hostile takeovers are an incomplete mechanism for solving the basic agency problem in the large public corporation. Some authors find underperformance of targets prior to hostile takeovers, others do not. The takeover premium is about 30–40 per cent, thus only the most apparent abuses of managerial discretion seem to be rectified. It appears that existing managers can squander one-third of the firm's value before the threat of displacement becomes truly serious. Also, the market value of the acquiring firm shows little positive or even negative change. It is not obvious why, when outsiders eliminate inefficient managers, that almost all of the return should go to the shareholders of the mismanaged firm.

The *ex post* studies of the performance of acquiring firms in the USA and UK at best indicate that even hostile acquirers improve firm efficiency only moderately, if at all. This raises concern about the effectiveness of hostile takeovers as the primary means of rectifying poor management. Even if the main objective behind hostile takeovers is wealth maximization, the finding that efficiency improvements do not significantly materialize presents a puzzle in the face of high takeover premia paid. Franks and Mayer (1996: 180) conclude: 'The market for corporate control does not therefore function as a disciplinary device for poorly performing companies.' To rely on hostile takeovers as the only or even the main disciplinary device is not optimal. In addition, wealth transfers between the various constituencies of the corporation cannot be excluded; many studies identify labour and tax earning losses after mergers and hostile takeovers.

The question remains as to whether state legislation should step in to reduce the probability of (hostile) takeovers occurring. Holmstrom (1988) holds the view that if firms can alter their charters so that they can choose any likelihood of hostile takeover, there is no reason for the government to intervene to limit takeovers. However, there are problems of internal firm decision-making in the face of a dispersed ownership structure. For example, Brickley, Lease, and Smith (1988) report for a sample of 288 management sponsored anti-takeover proposals in 1984 that about 96 per cent passed, despite the potential wealth losses. Whether principals can cope with their agents concerning acquisition activity certainly depends on the ownership and control structure of the firm.

Takeovers should also be seen in conjunction with other control devices. For example, takeovers may serve as a substitute control device for outside directors (Fama and Jensen, 1983). Kini, Kracaw, and Mian (1995) find for 244 successful tender offers in the USA between 1958 and 1984 that, while a significantly inverse relationship exists between pre-takeover performance and post-takeover turnover in the CEO for targets with inside-dominated boards, there is no such relationship for targets with outside-dominated boards. Evidently, takeovers and outside board members serve as substitute control mechanisms. Researchers and politicians certainly should explore these issues in more detail. For example, if one thinks that hostile takeovers are harmful to the economy, but if substitutive relationships exist, one could strengthen these alternative mechanisms while not constraining hostile takeovers by regulation. Extreme views of either prohibiting hostile takeovers or viewing hostile takeovers as the main device of corporate governance are too simplistic.

Notes

1. Franks and Mayer (1990) estimate that 4 per cent of the UK capital stock was subject to ownership changes via takeovers in any one year in the second half of the 1980s.
2. See Jensen and Ruback (1983) and Jarrel, Brickley, and Netter (1988) for surveys; see also DeAngelo, De Angelo and Rice (1984) or Franks and Mayer (1996).

3. The word 'synergy' is often used for this last source of efficiency gain.

4. Shleifer and Summers (1988: 37) describe the value of implicit contracts as follows: 'A corporation is a nexus of long-term contracts between shareholders and stakeholders. Because the future contingencies are hard to describe, complete contracting is costly. As a result many of these contracts are implicit, and the corporation must be trusted to deliver on the implicit contracts even without enforcement by courts. To the extent that long-term contracts reduce costs, such trustworthiness is a valuable asset to the corporation. Shareholders own this asset and are therefore able to hire stakeholders using implicit long-term contracts.'

5. The authors mention the replacement of a bad management, lower costs making more investment projects profitable in the future, and not-incurred social costs of possible bankruptcy in the absence of the takeover.

6. The Tax Reform Act of 1986 reduced two important tax incentives to merge in the USA: the ability to use the accumulated tax losses and credits of acquired companies to shield a company's own taxable income; and the opportunity to step up the bases of depreciable assets for tax purposes without paying capital gains taxes.

7. The concern over poison pills was heightened by the Delaware Supreme Court's 1985 ruling in *Moran* v. *Household International* that poison pills do not require majority voting approval by shareholders.

8. Greenmail occurs when target management ends a hostile takeover threat by repurchasing the hostile suitor's block of target stock at a premium.

5

Managerial compensation

Managerial compensation potentially aligns shareholder and manager interests by maintaining a close relationship between pay and performance. Managerial compensation is a hotly debated issue, particularly in US corporate governance, since the last two decades have witnessed an explosion in the level of managerial pay. For instance, Hall and Liebman (1997) find that total compensation of the mean CEO in a sample of the largest US firms increased by 209 per cent from 1980 to 1994.

When there is a separation of ownership and control, the one taking the potentially value-enhancing actions, and the residual claimant of these actions, are different persons. Where effort is unobservable and/or direct control mechanisms do not function well, incentives are required to induce managers to act in investor's interests. This requires a less than full insurance of managers, that is, managers should bear some of the uncertainty in returns and be made the residual claimants, at least partially. Agency theory therefore prescribes that particularly for firms in QI and QII of Table 1.1, managerial pay should be tied to performance through salaries and bonuses, shareholdings in the firm, stock options, or (as a negative feedback device) dismissal in the case of bad performance.

1. DETERRENCE EFFECTS

Mirrlees (1976) suggested penalties (e.g. loss of job or reputation) as efficient incentives. The diminishing marginal utility of money makes the monetary reward required to induce good behaviour larger than the monetary penalty needed to discourage bad behaviour.

The evidence shows considerable build-up of reputation and accumulation of firm-specific capital among business executives. This implies significant deterrence effects for misbehaviour of managers. Executives at or near the CEO rank in large corporations hold their positions for fairly long intervals, and have been employed by the firm for a very long time. Kostiuk (1989) and Murphy (1985) report that the average CEO is 55–7 years old, has been in the position between 7 and 8 years, and has worked for the company for more than 25 years. Negative feedback mechanisms are better suited for younger executives who need to build up their reputation and who have not yet gained control over much of the firm's resources. Rewards to elicit efficient action in the face of a separation of ownership and control appear to be especially important for CEOs at the top of the hierarchy.

2. THE PAY–PERFORMANCE AND THE PAY–SALES RELATIONSHIPS

The use of incentive devices should manifest itself in a positive relationship between managerial compensation and performance (for a comprehensive survey see Rosen, 1992). Excluding stock option grants, sensitivities are quite small and remarkably constant across studies, methodologies, samples, and time periods. For example, Murphy (1985; 73 US firms, 1969–81) finds a pay–performance elasticity of 0.12–0.16; Coughlin and Schmidt (1985; 40 Forbes firms, 1978–80) an elasticity of 0.1–0.15; and Barro and Barro (1990, 1982–7) an elasticity of 0.17. These elasticities suggest that a 10 per cent rise in firm profitability leads to a 1 to 1.5 per cent rise in CEO compensation.

In contrast, Hall and Liebman's (1997) results suggest that previous sensitivity measures ignored changes in the value of stock and stock options, which account for virtually all of the sensitivity. For a sample of 478 large US companies for the period 1980 to 1994, the authors show that CEO wealth changes by millions of dollars for corresponding changes in firm value. For example, the median total compensation for CEOs (salary and bonus, restricted stock grants, other compensation, stock option grants, changes in the value of stock holdings, and changes in the value of stock option holdings) is about $US 1m. if their firm's stock has a 30th percentile annual return (-7.0 per cent) and is $US 5m. if the firm's stock has a 70th percentile ($+20.5$ per cent) performance. The distribution of elasticities has a mean of about 4.9 and a median of 3.9. While the authors obtain elasticity estimates for salary and bonus that are similar to those in the rest of the literature (around 0.2), stocks and stock options are the driving force behind the close pay–performance relationship in the USA. In addition, a tremendous rise in the pay–performance relationship for US CEOs is reported in the period 1980 to 1994. The median elasticity of CEO compensation with respect to firm value more than tripled, from 1.2 in 1980 to 3.9 in 1994. The authors estimate that roughly half of the increase in sensitivity is due to the increase in the use of stock options, the rest is attributable to the increase in the stock market.

One principle of efficient compensation is that managers should be rewarded for outcomes over which they have control. It is harder for an executive manager to claim that performance is low due to high effort and bad luck if benchmark companies are performing well. Lazear and Rosen (1981) point out that relative comparisons wash out common components of variance among competitors and isolate specific performance-related components. Relative comparisons increase the signal-to-noise ratio and make managerial incentives more effective and contracts more efficient. This would call for compensation that rises with the *relative* performance of the firm, e.g. relative to industry peers or direct competitors. The evidence concerning relative-performance effects is more on the negative side. Murphy (1985), Barro and Barro (1990), and Hall and Liebman (1997) find that relative performance does not matter much for managerial compensation.

The elasticity of executive annual-salary-plus-bonus with respect to sales is in the 0.2 to 0.25 range and relatively uniform across firms, industries, and time periods (see also Baker, Jensen, and Murphy, 1988). While this finding is consistent with value maximization if larger firms employ better-qualified and better-paid CEOs, a mechanical pay–sales relationship provides managers with incentives to behave in a sales-maximizing manner. It is quite puzzling that most studies (e.g. Main, Bruce, and Buck 1994; Conyon and Leech 1993; Gregg, Machin, and Szymanski 1993) find that company size and changes in size are much more significant determinants of executive pay than measures of shareholder performance.

3. ARE CONTRACTS EFFICIENT?

There is considerable debate as to whether compensation contracts are efficiently designed. Do compensation contracts effectively align shareholder and manager interests in the presence of a separation of ownership and control? While the closely related nature of pay and performance (at least in the USA, as shown by Hall and Liebman 1997) points to high-powered incentives achieved by the use of stock options, several questions and concerns remain.

Firstly, as also evidenced by Hall and Liebman (1997), relative pay is not a significant component of CEO compensation packages, although it should be. Stock options with a fixed exercise price are not apt to tie CEO compensation to industry performance. Hall and Liebman (1997) mention that one of the main reasons why options with an exercise price that moves with a market or industry index are rarely used is that these options must be expensed against current earnings under existing accounting rules, while options with a fixed exercise price do not reduce current earnings.

Secondly, while principal–agent theory predicts a positive association between pay and performance, a crucial assumption of this theory is the presence of asymmetric information in the form of hidden action (i.e. the financier cannot observe the actions of the manager) resulting in moral hazard. As outlined in QIV, Table 1.1, if ownership and voting power is concentrated, monitoring is likely to be better and information asymmetry is lower. One would expect that the optimal pay–performance elasticity of CEO compensation for these firms is lower than for firms with a dispersed ownership structure, since direct monitoring substitutes for it. Indeed, Kole (1997) finds for 371 out of the 1980 *Fortune 500* firms that the presence of a family representative either in management or on the board of directors significantly reduces the probability of adopting an equity-authorizing plan or a stock option plan.

A third caveat with a simplistic view of pay–performance elasticity concerns the risk attitude of the controlling manager. Agency theory predicts that optimal piece-rates (i.e. performance-related pay) should decline with the risk-aversion of the agent. If a risk-averse CEO is forced to accept a very high-powered incentive contract, he/she would demand a higher average pay level to compensate for the utility loss resulting from the increased variance of the compensation. Likewise, agency theory predicts that performance-related pay should decline with the total risk in the industry.

Finally, Yermack (1997) finds that the timing of stock option awards coincides with favourable movements in company stock prices. In particular, the author finds for 620 stock option awards to CEOs of *Fortune 500* companies between 1992 and 1994 that stock prices experienced an average cumulative abnormal return of more than 2 per cent in the 50 trading days following CEO option awards. Managers who become aware of impending improvements in corporate performance may influence the board of directors to award more performance-based pay as a low-risk method of capitalizing on investor's expected reactions to news of the operating improvements. Of course, it is not optimal if managers asymmetrically benefit from corporate improvements and avoid the downside risk in compensation.

4. MANAGERIAL COMPENSATION AND OTHER CORPORATE GOVERNANCE DEVICES

Other corporate governance devices may substitute for compensation-based alignment between management and shareholder interests. Direct monitoring by shareholders and boards of directors, and indirect monitoring via the market for control (hostile takeovers) are among the most important devices. Indeed, the optimality of performance-based compensation depends crucially on the assumption that direct monitoring of the agent is either prohibitively costly or undersupplied, due to the free-rider problem of monitoring.

Mehran (1995) confirms substitution between direct monitoring and compensation incentives. In a regression of the percentage of equity-based compensation on the percentage of shares held by all outside block-holders, the negative coefficient underlines substitution between direct monitoring and pay incentives. Indirect evidence in favour of the substitutive hypothesis between direct monitoring and pay incentives is presented in Conyon and Leech (1993) for the UK (294 companies, 1981 to 1986). The authors find that the level of real director pay is lower in companies that have a higher share-ownership concentration or are defined as owner-controlled.

In principle, board monitoring can be a substitute for direct owner monitoring and, if so, reduces the optimal amount of pay-based incentives. However, board members may be agents themselves and agency costs are expected. Supporting this view, Mehran (1995) finds that the presence of outside directors increases the percentage of equity-based compensation which is either inconsistent with a substitutive hypothesis or consistent with outside directors not monitoring well. Conyon and Leech (1993) do not find evidence that separating the roles of chairman and CEO depresses executive compensation levels.

Worldwide institutional investors become more important. However, Cosh and Hughes (1997) do not find evidence that institutional holdings alter the level of remuneration or the pay–performance relationship for 64 UK firms between 1989 and 1994.

5. ASSESSMENT AND POLICY IMPLICATIONS

Rewards that promote good incentives must be indexed to outcomes that managers can alter. Stock-market values and current profits are only partly affected by managerial decisions. General business conditions or just (good or bad) luck beyond a manager's control can also affect the fortunes of a corporation. Relative comparisons increase the signal-to-noise ratio and make contracts more efficient. However, while recent evidence shows a strong relationship between pay and performance for the USA, there is no evidence that relative-performance incentives are used heavily. One reason may be the comparative disadvantage at which stock options with a variable exercise price (e.g. a market index) are put; while money options with a fixed exercise price do not reduce current earnings, options with an unknown exercise price must be expensed against current earnings. A policy recommendation therefore is to harmonize accounting rules concerning stock options with a variable and a fixed exercise price. To promote relative pay incentives and to avoid misrepresentation of the current standing of the corporation, expected per-period costs of stock options should be expensed against current earnings, irrespective of the modalities.

In the UK, the Cadbury Committee recommended in the Code of Best Practice that there should be a remuneration committee which determines executives' pay. This committee should mainly consist of non-executive directors. Information should be provided in a form that differentiates between salary and performance-related pay. While these suggestions are valuable, they are far from being sufficient. Ezzamel and Watson (1997) find asymmetric adjustments of executive pay levels, i.e. executives that were relatively underpaid in the previous period caught up, but the overpaid did not adjust downwards. This is consistent with the hypothesis (and the complaints of shareholder groups) that remuneration committees have the effect of bidding up executive pay rather than strengthening the pay–performance link.

Because boards of directors set compensation contracts, they serve a primary role in designing proper incentives for management. There is the suspicion of many authors, however, that boards align more with management than with (dispersed) shareholders. Theory predicts that abuses are particularly likely in the combination of QI, Table 1.1, and a failure of alternative control mechanisms. The question arises whether agents (boards) should decide on key elements of the contract (compensation shape and level) between the principals (shareholders) and other agents (managers) as it is the case in most countries. The evidence suggests that shareholders themselves may decide on proposals on compensation packages in general meetings.

6

The identity of owners

1. INTERNATIONAL COMPARISON OF IDENTITIES OF INVESTORS

Little evidence exists on the identity of investors and their effects on corporate governance and performance. Table 6.1 categorizes common share holdings into several categories, namely Families, Households, and Individuals; Non-financial Business; Banks; Other Financial Firms; the State; Foreign Holdings; and Pension Funds, Mutual Funds, and Dispersed Holdings.

There are several caveats with this table, allowing only tentative conclusions. Firstly, samples differ in size and composition. We tackle this problem in part by discriminating between samples of purely listed firms and samples including all firms (France and Italy). Secondly, some studies have applied different categorization procedures, as can be inferred from the notes to the table. Thirdly, methods of calculations differ somewhat across countries, i.e. the UK and USA figures are value-weighted figures, whereas the figures for the other countries are unweighted.

Keeping these caveats in mind we make the following tentative conclusions. Firstly, for listed firms only, the category Families, Households, Individuals is much more important in the USA than in Europe and Japan. In Austria, Belgium, Germany, the Netherlands, and Japan, this category holds 10 to 25 per cent of the equity in contrast to the 50.2 per cent in the USA. If one includes unlisted firms, this picture might change (see France; Italy is not comparable since the category 'Families, Households, Individuals' includes also the category 'Pension Funds, Mutual Funds, and Dispersed Holdings').

Secondly, it appears that the non-financial corporate sector is a more important category in Continental Europe and Japan than in the USA and UK. The combined entity 'Non-financial Business' and 'Foreign Holdings' (the owners of which are predominantly foreign non-financial business firms), holds on average around 20 per cent in the USA and UK, but more than 40 per cent in Continental Europe (there are no comparable figures for Belgium and the Netherlands).

Thirdly, banks and the financial sector in general, as shareholders in listed firms, are more important in Europe, and particularly so in Japan, than in the USA. While the combined category 'Banks' and 'Other Financial Firms' holds less than 5 per cent in the USA, this category holds between 10 and 30 per cent of the equity in most other countries, with the possible exception of Italy. Interestingly, financial firms as shareholders in non-financial firms are much more important in the UK than in the USA.[1]

Table 6.1. *International comparison of identities of owners (common stock, percentages)*

	Families, households, individuals	Non-financial business	Banks	Other financial firms	State	Foreign holdings	Pension, mutual funds, and dispersed
Listed firms							
Austria (1996)	22.6	25.9	11.4	n.a.	3.3	17.1	33.4
Belgium (1994)	15.6	10.8	<1%	26.7	<1%	n.a.	44.9
Germany (1996)	15.3	43.1[a]	7.8	4.2	2.4	0.2[b]	27.1
The Netherlands (1996)	10.8	2.4	7.4	25.4	1.1	n.a.	52.9
Japan (1996)	23.6	23.8	25.9	12.3	0.5	9.8	4.3
Spain (1996)	11.0	15.3	6.4	8.4	2.6	8.3	n.a.
Turkey (1996)	7.7	29.2	6.0	n.a.[c]	24.2	7.1	25.8
UK (1989)	20.0	8.0	n.a.[d]	20.0	3.0	9.0	40.0
USA (1990)	50.2	14.1	0.0	4.6	0.0	5.4	25.7
Listed and unlisted firms							
France (1996)	51.2	25.2	2.6	9.3	0.0	2.6	9.1
Italy (1992)	48.0[e]	36.9	0.2	n.a.	4.6	8.1	n.a.

[a] Including foreign companies
[b] Foreign governments only
[c] Included under banks
[d] Prowse (1992) reports 4.3% for 1990
[e] Includes the category 'Pension, mutual funds, and dispersed'.

Sources: Austria: 62 listed companies, Gugler *et al.* (1997). Belgium: Becht and Chapelle (1997). France: all firms, Bloch and Kremp (1997). Germany: Boehmer (1999), all 430 officially listed German corporations. Italy: representative sample of 973 firms of more than 50 employees; Bianchi, Bianco, and Enriques (1997). The Netherlands: 137 listed firms; De Jong, Kabir, and Röell (1997). Japan: Japan Stock Exchange Council (Share Ownership Distribution Report 1996), see also Chapter 12. Spain: Crespí and Cestona (1997), declared significant shareholdings (CNMV). The numbers include the largest voting bloc per category of owner. Turkey: total market values of the securities quoted on the Stock Exchange. Yurtoglu (2000). UK: total market values of the securities quoted on the Stock Exchange; Confederation of British Industry estimates, Charkham (1994). USA: total market values of the securities quoted on the Stock Exchange, Prowse (1992).

Additionally, there are other channels for banks and other financial institutions to exert corporate control, such as proxy voting, representation on the supervisory board, and provision of external financing of non-financial corporations (see also Chapter 9 for an extensive discussion of these channels). Gottschalk (1988) finds that banks accounted for more than 50 per cent of all votes cast at the shareholder meetings in 31 of the largest 100 German firms. Baums and Fraune (1995) analyse AGM participation and voting for those 24 out of the top 100 listed firms that have more than 50 per cent of their shares widely held. Out of the attending votes, banks control 13 per cent due to their own share-holdings, 10 per cent due to dependent investment funds, and 61 per cent due to proxy votes. Gorton and Schmidt (1996) estimate that banks exerted 20 per cent of the voting rights of 57 large German corporations in 1985 via proxy voting. For Germany, the Monopolkommission (1980) found that bank representatives accounted for 9.8 per cent of all supervisory board seats of the 100 largest stock corporations, and banks were present on 61 of these boards. Schroeder and Schrader (1996) find that in 1995 financial institutions held 19 per cent of the seats of shareholder representatives on the boards of the top 100 German corporations (see also Chapter 9 on Germany).

The evidence on external financing is more mixed. In the period from 1970 to 1989, 19 per cent of total gross sources for investment by the non-financial enterprise sector in Germany were loans from financial institutions (mainly banks; see Edwards and Fischer, 1994). This is more than 50 per cent of total external financing needs. However, Corbett and Jenkinson (1996), analysing flow of funds data, find that the importance of bank finance declined in Japan and Germany from 1970 to 1989. While bank finance is higher as a percentage of total funds in Japan (around 30 per cent), the figures for Germany, the UK, and USA are much lower. Strikingly, Germany has the *lowest* dependence on bank finance over the 1970–89 period (11.0 per cent; USA: 16.6 per cent; UK: 19.5 per cent).

The question arises as to whether the identity of the controlling shareholder(s) matters for the performance of the firm.

2. BANK OWNERSHIP AND BANK–FIRM RELATIONSHIPS

While controlling bank-equity holdings were forbidden in the USA until recently, in most other countries banks are allowed to hold debt and equity in the same non-financial corporation. Several theoretical arguments regarding the beneficial effects of bank holdings and control-oriented finance have been developed in the literature: (1) Banks can gain an informational advantage from equity holdings in non-bank firms. Closer lender-borrower ties, i.e. credit ties supplemented by equity holdings, representation on the supervisory board, etc., might result in less asymmetry of information and therefore lead to fewer principal–agent conflicts. (2) Economies of scale and scope in information collection and the exercise of control rights cheapen the supply of loan finance. (3) Bank equity holdings can serve as a hedging device against possible wealth transfers in the presence of principal–agent conflicts with respect to both owners and debtors, and owners and managers. (4) Better information flows between management and creditors might prevent premature liquidation of projects with low short-term returns but long-term viability (see Von Thadden, 1990).

Critical models of the role of banks in corporate governance emphasize the potential costs of banks as controlling institutions, e.g. rent extraction by the bank, given a possible monopoly position *ex post*. Von Thadden (1992) shows that it may be beneficial for the firm to have more than one bank providing external finance. Rajan (1992) sees a rationale for giving collateral to uninformed lenders.

If the benefits of bank involvement in the governance of the firm outweigh the costs, one expects that the cost of capital will be lower, profitability higher, financial distress less and/or better worked out, and cash constraints fewer.

2.1. *The cost of capital and macroeconomic evidence*

McCauley and Zimmer (1989) juxtapose cost of capital measures[2] for the US, UK, German, and Japanese corporate sectors. For 1988, the authors arrive at estimated costs of capital for equipment and machinery of 11.2 per cent in the USA, 9.2 per cent in the UK, but only 7.2 per cent in Japan and 7.0 per cent in Germany. Even more striking are the differences in the cost of capital for research and development expenditures. While the typical R&D project must earn 23.7 per cent in the UK and 20.3 per cent in the USA, a comparable project in Germany only needs a 14.8 per cent and in Japan an even lower 8.7 per cent real rate of return to cover financing costs. While the authors mention a number of reasons for this, for instance differences in taxation, household savings rates, and macroeconomic stability, they emphasize the close relationships between banks and corporations in the 'bank-based' systems of Germany and Japan. In particular, greater integration of industry and banking permitted higher leveraging without raising bankruptcy rates much above those in the USA and UK. However, as already mentioned, Corbett and Jenkinson (1996) find that the importance of bank

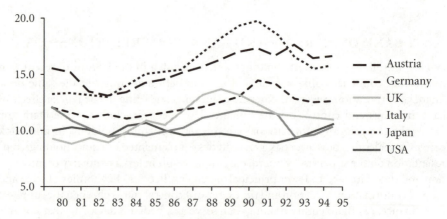

Figure 6.1. *Gross fixed capital formation in 6 OECD countries*
(business sector, percentages of GDP)
Source: WIFO

competitors, after learning from financial difficulties, may act in a way which aggravates financial distress.

To my knowledge, the only study analysing whether close financial links reduce the costs of financial distress is Hoshi, Kashyap, and Scharfstein (1990*b*) for Japan. They find that while financially distressed firms invest and grow less than the industry average, non-group firms invest roughly 75 per cent less than group member firms in the year after the onset of financial distress. Cumulative investment (sales growth) of group firms in the three years following the beginning of financial distress is 46 per cent (58 per cent) higher than for non-group firms. Group firms' capital stocks do not erode, in contrast to non-group firms' stocks. In addition, borrower concentration has positive effects. A 1 per cent increase in the fraction of the lending by the largest bank translates into an increase in investment (sales) for group *and* non-group firms of 0.24 per cent (0.5 per cent). The authors take this as evidence that close bank–firm relationships (i.e. control-oriented finance) reduce the costs of financial distress. Hoshi, Kashyap, and Scharfstein (1990*b*) mention several ways in which financial distress costs might be mitigated in group financing arrangements. As with European style *Hausbanken*, concentrated holdings of credit and equity reduce the free-rider problem and the asymmetry of information. Financial links between suppliers, customers, and distressed firms (e.g. cross-shareholdings) would imply a more stable relationship.

3. STATE OWNERSHIP AND PROFITABILITY

The numerous cases of privatization in Europe in recent years, and the transformation process in the former Eastern bloc countries, have led to increased interest in the performance of the state as a large and controlling shareholder. Managerial discretion and non-profit-maximizing objectives are expected for state firms according to agency theory. Citizens ('principals') can be viewed as very dispersed ultimate 'shareholders' with insufficient incentives and ability to monitor and discipline the state ('agent'). This corresponds to QI of Table 1.1. Moreover, as stressed by Shleifer and Vishny (1996), the *de facto* control rights belong to bureaucrats who typically have goals very different from social welfare, but dictated by their political interests or short-run maximization of employment. Accordingly, most of the empirical studies find negative effects of state control on firm profitability.

Kole and Mulherin (1997) is one of the few studies analysing the effects of government ownership in the USA. Their 17 sample firms were vested by the 'Office of the Alien Property Custodian (APC)' during World War II from enemy nationals. The authors cannot detect any differences in performance between state and private firms. Of course, the small degrees of freedom in this study does not allow for far-reaching generalizations. However, as the authors note, the reasons for their findings might be that there was little evidence of government intervention in investment policy, and competition in the product market constrained the politicization of management often found in government enterprises.

Megginson, Nash, and Randenborgh (1994) compare the pre- and post-privatization operating performance of 61 companies from 18 countries and 32 industries that

finance, while unambiguously higher in Japan, is actually lower in Germany, as compared to the UK and USA.

Figure 6.1 plots the ratio of gross fixed capital formation in the business sector to GDP at market prices for the 'bank-based' systems in Austria, Germany, Italy, and Japan, and for the 'market-based' systems of the USA and the UK. Evidently, Austrian, Japanese, and also German firms invest a higher proportion of GDP in capital formation than do firms in the other countries. Closer interlinkages between banks and firms might be one reason. However, bank-based systems of governance also tend to have weaker investor protection, higher ownership concentration and therefore less-developed capital markets (compare La Porta *et al*. (1997) and Figure 3.1). Given the relationship between stock-market development and R&D expenditures as exhibited in Figure 3.2, there is the suspicion that less risky, debt-holder oriented investment strategies are favoured in 'bank-based' systems of finance.

2.2. *Bank–firm relationships and profitability*

In an influential study, Cable (1985) finds for 48 large German firms in 1970 that all three bank variables employed—bank debt, representation on the supervisory board, and bank voting power—are positively and statistically significantly related to profitability. The author therefore concludes that the findings are consistent with an efficiency-improving role of banks in corporate governance. 'It is bank control as well as bank lending which raises profitability' (Cable 1985: 130). However, in a critique of Cable's (1985) study, Edwards and Fischer (1994) identify a possible simultaneity bias: If banks are better able to screen good risks than other lenders, a positive coefficient for bank debt may reflect the greater ability of banks relative to other suppliers of capital to identify firms with greater credit worthiness and a larger volume of profitable investment projects. This reverse causality implies that firms with higher profitability are able to borrow more from banks, not that banks have superior monitoring capabilities.

Other studies that find positive effects of bank involvement in corporate governance on profitability include Gorton and Schmid (1996) and Lichtenberg and Pushner (1992). Gorton and Schmid (1996; German manufacturing corporations; 88 firms in 1974 and 57 firms in 1985) find that performance is significantly positively related to bank equity holdings only in 1974 (a recession year) but not in the 1985 sample. The authors interpret their findings as consistent with the view that universal banking is a substitute for a stock market providing oversight of firm management. Lichtenberg and Pushner (1992) ask whether the identity of shareholders matters for the efficient governance of companies in Japan. For 1,241 manufacturing firms over the period 1976 to 1989, they find a significantly positive relationship between the ownership shares of financial institutions and total factor productivity.

In contrast, several other studies find either no significant improvement of profitability, or even negative effects of bank–firm relationships. Chirinko and Elston (1995) find for 91 large German firms over the period 1965–90 that bank debt is negatively related to return on assets. Bank equity ownership is unrelated to profitability. Likewise, Weinstein and Yafeh (1998), while attributing superior access of main bank clients to capital resources, find significantly lower profitability and growth rates for firms with a main bank in Japan. The relatively high interest rates paid suggest that banks used their monopoly power to siphon off rents from the industrial sector. Gugler (1998) cannot establish a profitability-enhancing role for controlling banks in Austria.

To summarize, the results obtained in the literature are more consistent with the notion that concentrated holdings of stock yield better performance of the firm (QIV of Table 1.1) than does the role for banks. However, one has to view close bank–firm relationships as the endogenous outcome of missing or illiquid securities markets. Accordingly, evidence on other effects of close bank–firm ties is more on the positive side.

2.3. *Bank–firm relationships and financial constraints*

One strand of literature tests whether there are financial constraints, i.e. whether firms cannot finance all positive net present value projects they have. If firms operate in a Modigliani/Miller (1958) world of financial irrelevance, cash flow should have no say in determining actual investment. A positive and significant cash-flow coefficient then detects the upward sloping cost of funds schedules once internal funds are depleted. Differences in estimated cash-flow coefficients between subsamples of firms (e.g. small versus large firms, young versus old firms, or bank-controlled versus other firms) indicate cash constraints. The advantage of this approach is that even though the individual estimates of the coefficients may be biased (due to the possibility that cash-flow proxies for an important omitted variable, namely the profitability of investment), provided that the bias is the same across sets of firms, the estimated difference in the coefficients should be an unbiased estimate of the true difference.

Kaplan and Zingales (1997) criticize this approach. They find for the low-dividend subsample (49 firms) which Fazzari, Hubbard, and Petersen (1988) view as financially constrained, that in '85 per cent of firm-years, the firms could have increased their investment'. Kaplan and Zingales (1997) conclude this from 10-K reports. In a response, Fazzari, Hubbard, and Petersen (1996) criticize the approach taken by Kaplan and Zingales (1997), mainly on the ground that it relied heavily on statements by managers which may be judgemental. Furthermore, they would mix up the notions of financial constraints and financial distress. We will not judge this ongoing discussion here, but rather present the evidence on investment-cash flow sensitivities in what follows.

For Europe and Japan, most authors find a smaller investment-cash-flow coefficient for firms which have a close and stable relationship to banks than for other firms. This is interpreted as evidence in favour of the hypothesis that closer bank–firm ties reduce the asymmetry of information between borrowers and lenders. Corroborating evidence is presented by Petersen and Rajan (1994) for the USA.

Hoshi, Kashyap, and Scharfstein (1991) divide their sample of large Japanese corporations into 121 affiliated (*keiretsu*) and 24 independent firms. The sample period is 1977 to 1982. The estimated coefficients of both liquidity variables (cash flow and the stock of short-term securities) are much larger for the independent firms than for group firms, namely eight to twelve times as large, and the differences are statistically

significant. In a related paper, Hoshi, Kashyap, and Scharfstein (1990*a*) split th sample into a pre-deregulation period (1978–82) and a post-deregulation perio (1983–5), and find a closer dependence of investment on cash flow in the latter perio only for firms that have loosened their ties to group banks. The authors take this as ev idence that *keiretsu* firms are less cash-constrained than independent firms, due to le asymmetry of information between borrowers and lenders.

Elston (1993), analysing 150 German firms, 27 firms with close bank ties and 1 with weaker ties, finds no differences for the period 1968–72; however, the author reje the hypothesis of a zero cash-flow coefficient for firms with a weak bank tie in t 1973–84 period. Bianco (1996) compares 131 Italian firms where the share of loans the main bank over total loans is greater than 30 per cent, and has been stable over years, with a control sample of more than 2,000 small and medium-sized compar (less than 500 employees). The cash flow variable has a positive and significant imp on investment spending for the whole sample, but not for the subset of firms with a c relationship to a bank. The difference is statistically significant. Gugler (1997, 214 A trian firms, 1991–5) also rejects the cash-constraints hypothesis for bank-contro firms, but finds that family-controlled firms suffer from financing constraints.

Suspected efficiency gains from close relationships between banks and non-finar corporations (*Hausbankenrelationships*) in Continental Europe and Japan led vivid debate in the USA. As already mentioned, US banks were generally prohib from holding common stock in non-financial corporations by the Banking A 1933, which was repealed recently. Petersen and Rajan (1994) find evidence that bank–firm ties reduce the cost of capital and increase the availability of finance i USA. The authors analyse 3,404 US small and medium-sized firms in 1988/9. Borr concentration (measured by the number of banks providing credit) has a signific negative impact on interest rates. This supports the notion that close bank–firm reduce the cost of capital. Moreover, measures of cash constraints are negatively re to measures of bank–firm relationships; Petersen and Rajan (1994) measure cash straints by the percentage of trade credits that were paid after the due date. A t discount scheme offers a discount of 2 per cent if a bill is paid within two weeks going this discount implies an implicit annual borrowing rate of around 40 pe The argument is then that firms are likely to be cash-constrained if they forgo thi gain. This proxy for cash constraints is regressed on several variables measuri closeness of a borrower–lender relationship. The length of the longest relatic with a financial institution exerts a negative influence on this measure of cash straints. In addition, both other proxies for the closeness of a relationship, provision, and concentration of borrowings, are also negative and significant.

2.4. *Bank–firm relationships and financial distress*

There are at least three sources of financial distress costs. Firstly, free-rider pr and negotiation costs rise with the number of creditors, leading to possible investment and inefficient liquidation. Secondly, incomplete and/or asym information is likely to make these problems worse. Thirdly, consumers, suppli

experienced full or partial privatization during the period 1961 to 1990. Mean and median profitability, real sales, operating efficiency, and capital investment spending increase significantly after privatization. In addition, there is no evidence that employment levels fall after privatization. Quite the opposite, 64 per cent of the sample companies employ more workers after transfer to private ownership. Larger performance improvements are reported for the group of firms that experience 50 per cent or more turnover of directors than for the group of companies experiencing less dramatic change in directors after privatization. This points to the importance of internal control mechanisms in constraining management actions, particularly in the absence of competition in the product market.

This is also in line with Yarrow (1986), who argues that competition and managerial accountability are more important than privatization per se in promoting economic efficiency. Likewise, Boardman and Vining (1989) find for the 500 largest non-US mining and manufacturing companies in 1983 that private corporations are both more profitable and more efficient than either completely or partially state-owned companies. Corroborating evidence is provided by Gorton and Schmid (1996) for Germany, and Gugler (1998) for Austria.

4. INSTITUTIONAL INVESTORS AND CORPORATE GOVERNANCE

The increasing importance of institutional investors such as insurance companies, pension funds, or mutual funds as shareholders has led to a debate on their likely impact on corporate governance and performance.[3] The importance of institutions as major equity-holders makes them potentially able to play a key role in the corporate governance system of a country. The questions analysed in this section are: (1) Are institutional investors active investors? (2) Which incentives do they face to maximize shareholder value? (3) What is the evidence with respect to firm performance?

4.1. *Theoretical considerations*

A clear account of the willingness and ability of institutions to intervene in the governance of corporations is given in Short and Keasey (1997) and Romano (1994). There are several reasons why institutions may have insufficient incentives to intervene in the governance of firms. Firstly, the size of institutional holdings in any given firm is likely to be insufficient to provide enough incentives for monitoring. Short and Keasey (1997) report that most institutional holdings rarely exceed the 3 per cent level. Secondly, there could be a reinforced free-rider problem: an institution that undertakes costly actions to intervene in company management exerts a positive externality on other institutions doing nothing.[4] Thirdly, there are conflicts of interest if the institution has other business relationships with the company or suffers from political pressure groups.[5] Finally, and potentially most important, institutional investors are agents themselves. Jenkinson and Mayer (1992: 2) say, 'Why precisely managers of institutional funds are supposed to be so much better at administering non-financial enterprises than the management of these enterprises themselves, or why similar problems of corporate governance do not afflict the funds themselves, are questions that are never very clearly answered.' Indeed, institutional investors are organizations where one expects a large separation of ownership and control, since many are widely held.

4.2. *The evidence*

The evidence by and large reflects the above-mentioned caveats concerning the incentives of institutional investors to efficiently monitor and constrain management.

Pound's (1988) results concerning 100 proxy contests in the USA in the period 1981 to 1985 indicate that institutions do not act as efficient monitors. Institutional ownership significantly increases the probability of management victory over a dissident shareholder's proposal in general meetings. This suggests that institutions either face conflicts of interests and align strategically with the management, or have insufficient motivation to stand up against incumbent management. Passivity of institutional investors is also reported by Cosh and Hughes (1997) for the UK concerning remuneration packages.

In contrast, Brickley, Lease, and Smith (1988) document that 'no' votes on anti-takeover amendments increase with institutional (and other outside) block-holdings. For 288 proposals of anti-takeover amendments by 191 US firms in 1984, absenteeism in general meetings is lower in the presence of institutional investors, and the percentage of outstanding stock voted against the management proposal is positively related to the percentage owned by institutions. To account for the heterogeneity of incentives across institutions, Brickley, Lease, and Smith (1988) place institutions in three categories based upon their (hypothesized) susceptibility to management influence: pressure-sensitive (PS) institutions (insurance companies, banks, and non-bank trusts); pressure-resistant (PR) institutions (public pension funds, mutual funds, endowments, and foundations); and pressure indeterminate (PI) institutions (corporate pension funds, brokerage houses, investment counsel firms, and others). The results support the hypothesis that different classes of institutional investors face different incentives. PR and PI institutions significantly increase the percentage of outstanding stock voted against management, while this is not the case for PS institutions. This implies that more independent institutions are more active monitors, and more readily opposed to management when viewed as necessary.

Direct evidence on the relationship between firm performance and institutional ownership is scarce and conflicting. While Chaganti and Damanpur (1991) find institutional ownership to have a significantly positive effect on the return on equity, the authors do not detect a positive effect on other measures of firm performance (return on assets, price/earnings ratio and total stock return). Smith (1996) analyses 51 firms targeted by the California Public Employees' Retirement System (CalPERS) over the 1987 to 1993 period. Holdings by CalPERS are positively related to the probability of being targeted, although activism does not improve operating performance.

Short and Keasey (1997) also obtain conflicting results concerning the effects of institutional share-ownership in a sample of 225 UK firms over the 1988 to 1992 period.

In all performance equations, the coefficients on the variables representing institutions are insignificant. However, the relationship between the directors' ownership and firm performance is significantly strengthened by the presence of an institutional shareholder. This supports the notion that monitoring is improved by institutional investors. Furthermore, a substitutive relationship between institutional investors and other large shareholders (corporations, charities and families) is detected: if no other large external shareholder is present, institutional investors provide the monitoring (positive effect of institutional share ownership on firm performance), whereas if another large shareholder is present, there is no such relationship.

5. ASSESSMENT AND POLICY IMPLICATIONS

At least for Continental Europe and Japan, the evidence is consistent with the notion that the identity of owners matters. The effects of close bank–firm relationships and shareholdings of institutional investors on firm profitability are ambiguous, the evidence concerning state intervention is on the negative side. Bank involvement is beneficial concerning other dimensions of performance as e.g. financial constraints or distress. The evidence by and large reflects the theoretical ambiguities concerning the proper incentives of institutions to efficiently monitor management. It is not clear what to expect if agents monitor agents, and institutions have conflicting interests in their relationship to incumbent management.

Banks only as lenders may be excessively concerned with low return states and be excessively risk averse. This bias is alleviated by allowing banks to own equity shares to participate also in high return states and to control firm investment decisions. Institutional investors only have proper monitoring incentives when their holdings in individual firms are concentrated. Regulation constraining individual firm share holdings of institutions should trade off safety considerations for the beneficiaries against monitoring incentives of institutional managers.

The lack of established evidence on the effects of institutional investors is particularly worrying, since institutional investors are becoming more and more important worldwide. Research is constrained by the use of publicly available data on institutional ownership. In most countries, the cut-off point of disclosure is 5 per cent. Given the diversification interests of institutional investors and restrictive regulation concerning individual firm shareholdings, many shareholdings are not accounted for in empirical research, and measurement errors are likely. Greater disclosure is called for.

Identities of owners and their connection to corporate governance are an unexplored field of research. The effects of labour unions and/or co-determination are largely unknown. In many European countries, workers have the right to be presented on the supervisory board and exert a considerable monitoring function. In Germany, for example, half of the members of the supervisory boards of the largest corporations are appointed by the council of shop stewards, in Austria this share is one-third (for more details see the country chapters in Part II). Pistor (1998) and Roe (1998) present plausible effects of co-determination. Pistor (1998) emphasizes the potential costs of co-determination, such as increasing the costs of collective decision-making.

Roe (1998) argues that block-holders would not get a fair price for their stock if a diffusion of ownership left firms either with labour-dominated or weak boards. Gorton and Schmid (1998) find that firms with legally mandated equal representation of workers and shareholders on the supervisory board have worse performance but lower risk than other firms (see Chapter 9 for more details).

Stiglitz (1985) emphasizes labour unions. They have the advantage of being intimately involved in the day-to-day functioning of the firm, and they have a strong interest in the survival of the firm. Corporate pension funds and employee stock-ownership plans potentially align the interests of workers and shareholders. Potential drawbacks, however, include delays in necessary firm restructuring, and too little exit and redeployment of resources from declining industries to growth industries. Research should be directed to these questions.

In what follows, Part II portrays the corporate governance systems of Austria, Belgium, France, Germany, Italy, Japan, the Netherlands, Spain, Turkey, and the United Kingdom.

Notes

1. In the USA banks were generally prohibited from holding common stock in non-financial corporations according to the Banking Act of 1933 ('Glass–Steagall Act'), which was repealed in 2000. Banks were allowed to hold only small amounts of non-financial firm equity, and were not allowed to exercise control over commercial companies. For more details, see Pozdena (1991). Until 1991 similar regulations were in place in Italy.
2. The cost of capital is defined as the minimum before-tax real rate of return that an investment project must generate in order to pay its financing costs after tax liabilities.
3. Short and Keasey (1997) find that for a sample of 225 listed UK firms mean institutional ownership increased from 7.7 per cent in 1988 to 15.7 per cent in 1992. The percentage of firms in which a large institution is present increased from 53.3 per cent in 1988 to 83.1 per cent in 1992.
4. For example, should pension funds be active shareholders taking a long-term view (exerting 'voice') or should they simply move funds freely around to find the highest possible return for their beneficiaries (exerting 'exit')?
5. For instance, pension fund managers may be reluctant to oppose the managers of a company with which they want to do business. Romano (1994) mentions political influence on fund managers to support local firms.

References for Part I

Agrawal, Anup and Charles R. Knoeber (1996), 'Firm Performance and Mechanisms to Control Agency Problems between Managers and Shareholders', *Journal of Financial and Quantitative Analysis*, 31/3: 377–97.

—— J. F. Jaffe, and G. N. Mandelker (1992), 'The Post-Merger Performance of Acquiring Firms: A Re-examination of an Anomaly', *Journal of Finance*, 47/4: 1605–21.

Asquith, Paul (1983), 'Merger Bids, Uncertainty and Stockholder Returns', *Journal of Financial Economics,* 11: 51–83.

Auerbach, A. J. and D. Reishus (1988), 'Taxes and Merger Decision', in J. Coffee, L. Lowenstein, and S. Rose-Ackerman (eds.), *Knights, Raiders, and Targets*, Oxford University Press.

Baker, G. P., M. C. Jensen, and K. J. Murphy (1988), 'Compensation and Incentives: Practice vs. Theory', *Journal of Finance*, 43/3: 593–616.

Barca, F. (1997), *Alternative Models of Control: Efficiency, Accessibility and Market Failures, In Property Relations, Incentives and Welfare*, Proceedings of a conference held in Barcelona, by the International Economics Association, ed. J. E. Roemer, New York and London: St. Martin's Press and Macmillan Press Ltd.

—— and M. Becht (eds.) (2001), *The Control of Corporate Europe*, Oxford: Oxford University Press.

Barclay, M. and C. Holderness (1989), 'Private Benefits from Control of Public Corporations', *Journal of Financial Economics*, 25: 371–95.

—— —— (1992), 'The Law and Large Block-Trades', *Journal of Law and Economics*, 35: 265–94.

Barro, J. R. and R. J. Barro (1990), Pay, 'Performance and Turnover of Bank CEOs', *Journal of Labor Economics*, 8/3: 448–81.

Baumol, William, J. (1959), *Business Behavior, Value and Growth*, New York: Macmillan.

Baums, T. and C. Fraune (1995), 'Institutionelle Anleger und Publikumsgesellschaft: Eine empirische Untersuchung', *Die Aktiengesellschaft,* 40: 97–112.

Becht, Marco (1997), 'Strong Block-holders, Weak Owners and the Need for European Mandatory Disclosure', in *The Separation of Ownership and Control: A Survey of 7 European Countries*, Preliminary Report to the European Commission.

—— and A. Chapelle (1997), 'Ownership and Control in Belgium', in *The Separation of Ownership and Control: A Survey of 7 European Countries*, Preliminary Report to the European Commission.

—— and C. Mayer (2001), 'Introduction', in Barca and Becht (eds.), *The Control of Corporate Europe.*

Bergström, Clas and Kristian Rydquist (1990), 'Ownership of Equity in Dual-Class Firms', *Journal of Banking and Finance*, 14: 255–69.

Berle, A. and G. Means (1932), *The Modern Corporation and Private Property*, New York: World Inc.

Bhagat, S., A. Shleifer, and R. W. Vishny (1990), 'Hostile Takeovers in the 1980s: The Return to Corporate Specialization', *Brookings Papers: Microeconomics*, 1–72.

Bianchi, M., M. Bianco and L. Enriques (1997), 'Ownership, Pyramidal Groups and the Separation of Ownership and Control in Italy', in *The Separation of Ownership and Control: A Survey of 7 European Countries*, Preliminary Report to the European Commission.

Bianco, Magda (1996), 'Bank–Firm Relationships and Pyramidal Groups in Italy: Effects on the Availability of Finance', Banca d'Italia, Servizio Studi.

Bloch, Laurence and Elizabeth Kremp (1997), 'Ownership and Control in France', in *The Separation of Ownership and Control: A Survey of 7 European Countries*, Preliminary Report to the European Commission.

Boardman, A. and A. R. Vining (1989), 'Ownership and Performance in Competitive Environments: A Comparison of the Performance of Private, Mixed, and State-Owned Enterprises', *Journal of Law and Economics*, 32: 1–33.

Boehmer, E. (1999), 'Who Controls Germany? An Exploratory Analysis', Working paper, US Securities and Exchange Commission.

Bothwell, James L. (1980), 'Profitability, Risk, and the Separation of Ownership and Control', *Journal of Industrial Economics*, 28/3: 303–11.

Boudreaux, K. J. (1973), 'Managerialism and Risk-Return Performance', *Southern Economic Journal*, 366–72.

Bradley, M. and G. Jarrell (1988), 'Comment', in Coffee, Lowenstein, and Rose-Ackerman (eds), *Knights, Raiders, and Targets*, 252–59.

—— A. Desai, and E. H. Kim (1984), *Determinants of the Wealth Effects of Corporate Acquisitions*, Ann Arbor: University of Michigan.

—— G. Jarrell and E. H. Kim (1984), 'On the Existence of an Optimal Capital Structure: Theory and Evidence', *Journal of Finance*, 39:857–78.

Brickley, James A., Ronald C. Lease, and Clifford W. Smith, Jr. (1988), 'Ownership Structure and Voting on Anti-takeover Amendments', *Journal of Financial Economics*, 20/1–2: 267–91.

Cable, John (1985), 'Capital Market Information and Industrial Performance: The Role of West German Banks', *Economic Journal*, 95/377: 118–32.

Caves, Richard, E. and D. R. Barton (1989), 'Efficiency, Productivity Growth, and International Trade', in D. Audretsch, L. Sleuwaegen, and H. Yamawaki, *The Convergence of International and Domestic Markets: Contributions to Economic Analysis*, Amsterdam: North-Holland: 3–27.

Chaganti, R. and F. Damanpur (1991), 'Institutional Ownership, Capital Structure and Firm Performance', *Strategic Management Journal*, 12: 479–91.

Charkham, Jonathan P. (1994), *Keeping Good Company*, Oxford: Clarendon Press.

Chirinko, Robert S. and J. A. Elston (1995), 'Finance, Control, and Profitability: An Evaluation of German Bank Influence', *Wissenschaftszentrum Berlin für Sozialforschung*, June.

Cho, M. H. (1998), 'Ownership Structure, Investment, and the Corporate Value: An Empirical Analysis', *Journal of Financial Economics*, 47: 103–21.

Comment, R. and G. W. Schwert (1995), 'Poison or Placebo? Evidence on the Deterrence and Wealth Effects of Modern Anti-takeover Measures', *Journal of Financial Economics*, 39: 3–43.

Conyon, M. J. and D. Leech (1993), Top Pay, 'Company Performance and Corporate Governance', Warwick economic research papers, 410 (Warwick University).

Corbett, J. and T. Jenkinson (1996), 'The Financing of Industry, 1970–1989: An International Comparison, *Journal of the Japanese and International Economies,* 10: 71–96.

Cosh, A. and A. Hughes (1989), 'Ownership, Mangement Incentives and Company Performance: An Empirical Analysis for the UK 1968–80', Discussion paper no. 11/89, University of Cambridge.

—— —— (1997), 'Executive Remuneration, Executive Dismissal and Institutional Shareholdings', *International Journal of Industrial Organization*, 15: 469–92.

Coughlin, A. T. and R. Schmidt (1985), 'Executive Compensation, Management Turnover, and Firm Performance: An Empirical Investigation', *Journal of Accounting and Economics*, 7/2: 43–66.

Cowling, Keith, P. Stoneman, J. Cubbin, J. Cable, G. Hall, S. Dornberger, and P. Dutton (1980), *Mergers and Economic Performance*, Cambridge: Cambridge University Press.

Crespí, R. and M. A. Cestona, Cowling *et al.* (1997), 'Ownership and Control of the Spanish Listed Firms', in *The Separation of Ownership and Control: A Survey of 7 European Countries*, Preliminary Report to the European Commission.

DeAngelo, H., L. DeAngelo, and E. M. Rice (1984), 'Going Private: Minority Freezouts and Stockholder Wealth', *Journal of Law and Economics* 27: 367–402.

De Jong, A., R. Kabir, and A. Röell (1997), 'Ownership and Control in the Netherlands', in *The Separation of Ownership and Control: A Survey of 7 European Countries*, Preliminary Report to the European Commission.

Demsetz, Harold and Kenneth Lehn (1985), 'The Structure of Corporate Ownership: Causes and Consequences', *Journal of Political Economy*, 93/6: 1155–77.

Denis, D. K. and J. J. McConnel (1986), 'Corporate Mergers and Security Returns', *Journal of Financial Economics*, 16: 143–87.

Edwards, J. and K. Fischer (1994), *Banks, Finance, and Investment in Germany*, Cambridge: Cambridge University Press.

Elliot, J. W. (1972), 'Control, Size, Growth, and Financial Performance in the Firm', *Journal of Financial and Quantitative Analysis*, 1309–20.

Elston, Julie (1993), 'Firm Ownership Structure and Investment: Theory and Evidence from German Panel Data', WZB, Discussion paper.

Ezzamel, M. and R. Watson (1997), 'Executive Remuneration and Corporate Performance', in K. Keasey and M. Wright (eds.), *Corporate Governance*, New York: John Wiley & Sons.

Fama, E. F. (1980), 'Agency Problems and the Theory of the Firm', *Journal of Political Economy*, 88: 288–307.

—— and M. C. Jensen (1983), 'Separation of Ownership and Control', *Journal of Law and Economics*, 26: 301–25.

Fazzari, S. M., R. G. Hubbard and B. C. Petersen (1988), 'Financing Constraints and Corporate Investment', *Brookings Papers of Economic Activity*, 141–206.

—— —— —— (1996), 'Financing Constraints and Corporate Investment: Response to Kaplan and Zingales', NBER, Working paper no. 5462.

Franks, J. R. and R. S. Harris (1989), 'Shareholder Wealth Effects of Corporate Takeovers: The UK experience 1955–85', *Journal of Financial Economics*, 23: 225–49.

—— and Colin Mayer (1990), 'Takeovers', *Economic Policy*, 189–231.

—— —— (1994), 'Ownership, Control, and the Performance of German Corporations', Working paper, London Business School.

—— —— (1996), 'Hostile Takeovers and the Correction of Managerial Failure', *Journal of Financial Economics*, 40: 163–81.

—— —— and L. Renneboog (1998), 'Who Disciplines Bad Management', mimeo.

——, R. S. Harris, and S. Titman (1991), 'The Post-Merger Share Price Performance of Acquiring Firms', *Journal of Financial Economics*, 29: 81–96.

Gordon, R. A. (1945), *Business Leadership in the Large Corporation*, Washington: The Brookings Institution.

Gorton, G. and F. A. Schmid (1996), 'Universal Banking and the Performance of German Firms', NBER, Working paper no. 5453.

—— —— (1998), 'Corporate Finance, Control Rights, and Firm Performance: A Study of German Co-determination', Working paper, University of Pennsylvania.

Gottschalk, A. (1988), 'Der Stimmrechtseinfluß der Banken in den Aktionärsversammlungen von Großunternehmen', *WSI-Mitteilungen*, 5: 294.

Grabowski, H. G. and D. C. Mueller (1972), 'Managerial and Stockholder Welfare Models of Firm Expenditures', *Review of Economics and Statistics*, 54: 9–24.

Gregg, P., S. Machin, and S. Szymanski (1993), 'The Disappearing Relationship Between Director's Pay and Corporate Performance', *British Journal of Industrial Relations*, 31/1: 1–10.

Grossman, S. and O. Hart (1980), 'Takeover Bids, the Free-Rider Problem, and the Theory of the Corporation', *Bell Journal of Economics*, 11: 42–64.

Gugler, Klaus (1997), 'Investment Spending in Austria: Asymmetric Information versus Managerial Discretion', University of Vienna, Working paper no. 9705.

—— (1998), 'Corporate Ownership Structure in Austria', *Empirica*, 25: 285–307.

—— S. Kalss, A. Stomper, and J. Zechner (1997), 'The Separation of Ownership and Control: An Austrian Perspective', in *The Separation of Ownership and Control: A Survey of 7 European Countries*, Preliminary Report to the European Commission.

Hall, B. H. (1988), 'The Effect of Takeover Activity on Corporate Research and Development', in A. Auerbach (ed.), *Corporate Takeovers: Causes and Consequences*, Chicago: University of Chicago Press.

—— (1990), 'The Impact of Corporate Restructuring on Industrial Research and Development', *Brookings Papers on Economic Activity, Special Issue*: 85–124.

—— and J. Liebman (1997), 'Are CEOs Really Paid Like Bureucrats?', NBER Working paper no. 6213.

Healy, P. M., K. G. Palepu, and R. S. Ruback (1992), 'Does Corporate Performance Improve After Mergers?', *Journal of Financial Economics*, 31: 135–75.

Higson, Chris and J. Elliott (1998), 'Post-Takeover Returns: The UK Evidence', *Journal of Empirical Finance*, 5: 27–46.

Himmelberg, Charles P., R. Glenn Hubbard, and Darius Palia (1999), 'Understanding the Determinants of Managerial Ownership and the Link Between Ownership and Performance', *Journal of Financial Economics*, 53/3: 353–84.

Holderness, Clifford G. and Dennis P. Sheehan (1988), 'The Role of Majority Shareholders in Publicly Held Corporations: An Exploratory Analysis', *Journal of Financial Economics*, 20/1–2: 317–46.

Holl, P. (1975), 'Effect of Control Type on the Performance of the Firm in the UK', *Journal of Industrial Economics*, 23: 257–71.

—— (1977), 'Control Type and the Market for Corporate Control in Large US Corporations', *Journal of Industrial Economics*, 25: 259–73.

—— (1980), 'Control Type and the Market for Corporate Control: Reply', *Journal of Industrial Economics*, 28/4: 443–5.

Holmstrom, Bengt (1988), 'Breach of Trust in Hostile Takeovers: Comment', in Auerbach (ed.), 'Corporate Takeovers: Causes and Consequences': 56–61.

Hoshi, Takeo, A. Kashyap, and D. Scharfstein (1990a), 'Bank Monitoring and Investment: Evidence from the Changing Structure of Japanese Corporate Banking Relationships', in R. G. Hubbard (ed.), *Asymmetric Information, Corporate Finance, and Investment*, Chicago: University of Chicago Press: 105–26.

—— —— —— (1990b), 'The Role of Banks in Reducing the Costs of Financial Distress in Japan', *Journal of Financial Economics*, 27: 67–88.

—— —— —— (1991), 'Corporate Structure, Liquidity, and Investment: Evidence from Japanese Industrial Groups', *Quarterly Journal of Economics*, 106/1: 33–60.

Jacquemin, A. and E. de Ghellinck (1980), 'Familial Control, Size and Performance in the Largest French Firms', *European Economic Review*, 13: 81–91.

Jarrell, G. A., (1985), 'The Wealth Effects of Litigation by Targets: Do Interests Diverge in a Merger?' *Journal of Law and Economics*, 28/1: 151–77.

—— and A. B. Poulsen (1987), Shark Repellents and Stock Prices: The Effects of Anti-takeover Amendments Since 1980, *Journal of Financial Economics*, 19: 127–68.

—— —— (1988), 'Dual-class Recapitalizations as Anti-takeover Mechanisms: The Recent Evidence', *Journal of Financial Economics,* 20/1–2: 129–52.

—— J. A. Brickley, and J. M. Netter (1988), 'The Market for Corporate Control: The Empirical Evidence Since 1980', *Journal of Economic Perspectives*, 2/1: 49–68.

Jenkinson, T. and C. Mayer (1992), 'The Assessment: Corporate Governance and Corporate Control', *Oxford Review of Economic Policy*, 8/3: 1–10.

Jensen, M. C. (1988), 'Takeovers: Their Causes and Consequences', *Journal of Economic Perspectives*, 2/1: 21–48.

—— (1993), 'The Modern Industrial Revolution, Exit, and the Failure of Internal Control Systems', *Journal of Finance*, 48/3: 831–80.

—— and William H. Meckling (1976), 'Theory of the Firm: Managerial Behavior, Agency Costs and Ownership Structure', *Journal of Financial Economics*, 3: 305–60.

—— and R. S. Ruback (1983), 'The Market for Corporate Control: The Scientific Evidence', *Journal of Financial Economics*, 11: 5–50.

Kamerschen, D. R. (1968), 'The Influence of Ownership and Control on Profit Rates', *American Economic Review*, 58: 432–47.

Kang, J. K. and A. Shivdasani (1995), 'Firm Performance, Corporate governance, and Top Executive Turnover in Japan', *Journal of Financial Economics*, 38/1: 29–58.

Kaplan, Steven N. and B. A. Minton (1994), 'Appointments of Outsiders to Japanese Boards', *Journal of Financial Economics*, 36/2: 225–58.

—— and Luigi Zingales (1997), 'Do Investment-Cash Flow Sensitivities Provide Useful Measures of Financing Constraints?', *Quarterly Journal of Economics*, 112: 169–215.

Kini, O., W. Kracaw, and S. Mian (1995), 'Corporate Takeovers, Firm Performance, and Board Composition', *Journal of Corporate Finance*, 1: 383–412.

Kole, S. R. (1997), 'The Complexity of Compensation Contracts', *Journal of Financial Economics*, 43: 79–104.

—— and J. H. Mulherin (1997), 'The Government as a Shareholder: A Case from the United States', *Journal of Law and Economics*, 40: 1–22.

Kostiuk, P. F. (1989), 'Firm Size and Executive Compensation', *Journal of Human Resources*, 25/1: 90–105.

La Porta, R., F. Lopez-de-Silanes, A. Shleifer, and R. W. Vishny (1997), 'Legal Determinants of External Finance', *Journal of Finance*, 52/3: 1131–50.

—— —— —— —— (1998), 'Law and Finance', *Journal of Political Economy*, 106: 1113–55.

—— —— —— —— (1999), 'Corporate Ownership Around the World', *Journal of Finance*, 54/2: 471–517.

Larner, R. J. (1966), 'Ownership and Control in the 200 Largest Non-financial Corporations, 1929 and 1963', *American Economic Review*, 777–87.

—— (1970), *Management Control and the Large Corporation*, New Jersey: Dunellen Publishing Company.

Lazear, E. P. and S. Rosen (1981), 'Rank Order Tournaments as Optimum Labor Contracts', *Journal of Political Economy*, 89/5: 841–74.

Leech, Dennis and John Leahy (1991), 'Ownership Structure, Control Type Classifications and the Performance of Large British Companies', *Economic Journal*, 101/409: 1418–37.

Lehn, K. and A. B. Poulsen (1987), *Sources of Value in Leveraged Buyouts, in Public Policy Towards Corporate Takeovers*, New Brunswick, NJ: Transaction Publishers.

Levin, S. G. and S. L. Levin (1982), 'Ownership and Control of Large Industrial Firms: Some New Evidence', *Review of Business and Economic Research*, 37–49.

Lichtenberg, Frank R. and George M. Pushner (1992), 'Ownership Structure and Corporate Performance in Japan', NBER Working paper no. 4092.

Long, M. and I. Malitz (1985), 'The Investment-Financing Nexus: Some Empirical Evidence', *Midland Corporate Finance Journal*, 3: 53–9.

McCauley, R. N. and S. A. Zimmer (1989), 'Explaining International Differences in the Cost of Capital', *Federal Reserve Bank of New York Quarterly Review*, Summer.

McConnel, J. J. and H. Servaes (1990), 'Additional Evidence on Equity Ownership and Corporate Value', *Journal of Financial Economics*, 27: 595–612.

McEachern, W. A. (1975), *Managerial Control and Performance*, Lexington, Mass.: Lexington Books.

Magenheim, E. B. and D. C. Mueller (1988), 'Are Acquiring Firm Shareholders Better Off After an Acquisition?', in Coffee, Lowenstein, and Rose-Ackerman, (eds.), *Knights, Raiders, and Targets*: 171–93.

Main, B. M. G., A. Bruce and T. Buck (1994), 'Total Board Remuneration', *Managerial and Decision Economics*, 12: 219–29.

Malatesta, P. H. (1983), 'The Wealth Effect of Merger Activity and the Objective Function of Merging Firms', *Journal of Financial Economics*, 11: 155–81.

—— and R. A. Walkling (1988), 'Poison Pill Securities: Stockholder Wealth, Profitability, and Ownership Structure', *Journal of Financial Economics*, 20: 347–76.

Marris, Robin (1963), 'A Model of the 'Managerial' Enterprise', *Quarterly Journal of Economics*, 77: 185–209.

—— (1964), *The Economic Theory of Managerial Capitalism*, Glencoe, Ill.: Free Press.

Megginson, William L., Robert C. Nash and van Matthias Randenborgh (1994), 'The Financial and Operating Performance of Newly Privatized Firms: An International Empirical Analysis', *Journal of Finance*, 49/2: 403–52.

Mehran, H. (1995), 'Executive Compensation Structure, Ownership, and Firm Performance', *Journal of Financial Economics*, 38: 163–84.

Mikkelson, W. H., M. M. Partch and K. Shah (1997), Ownership and Operating Performance of Companies That Go Public', *Journal of Financial Economics*, 44: 281–307.

Millstein, I. M. (1998), *Corporate Governance: Improving Competitiveness and Access to Capital in Global Markets*, a Report to the OECD by the Business Sector Advisory Group on Corporate Governance.

Mirrlees, J. A. (1976), 'The Optimal Structure of Incentives and Authority Within an Organization', *Bell Journal of Economics*, 7: 105–31.

Modigliani, Franco and M. H. Miller (1958), 'The Cost of Capital, Corporation Finance, and the Theory of Investment', *American Economic Review*, 48/3: 261–97.

Monopolkommission (1980), *Hauptgutachten II (1978/79), Fusionskontrolle bleibt vorrangig*, Baden-Baden: Nomos.

Monsen, R., J. S. Chiu, and D. E. Cooley (1968), 'The Effect of Separation of Ownership and Control on the Performance of the Large Firm', *Quarterly Journal of Economics*, 82: 435–51.

Morck, R., A. Shleifer, R. W. and Vishny (1988a), 'Management Ownership and Market Valuation: An Empirical Analysis', *Journal of Financial Economics*, 20: 293–315.

—— —— —— (1988b), 'Alternative Mechanisms of Corporate Control', *American Economic Review*, 79/4: 842–52.

Mueller, Dennis C. (1969), 'A Theory of Conglomerate Mergers', *Quarterly Journal of Economics*, 83: 643–59.

—— (1972), 'A Life-Cycle Theory of the Firm', *Journal of Industrial Economics*, 21: 199–219.

—— (ed.) (1980), 'The Determinants and Effects of Mergers: An International Comparison' Cambridge, Mass.: Oelgeschlager, Gunn & Hain.

—— (1985), Mergers and Market Share, *Review of Economics and Statistics*, 47: 259–67.

—— (1996), 'Lessons from the United States's Antitrust History', *International Journal of Industrial Organization*, 14: 415–45.

—— and M. L. Sirower (1998), 'The Causes of Mergers: Tests Based on the Gains to Acquiring Firms' Shareholders and the Size of Premia', mimeo.

Murali, R. and J. B. Welch (1989), 'Agents, Owners, Control and Performance', *Journal of Business Finance and Accounting*, 16/3: 385–98.

Murphy, K. J. (1985), 'Corporate Performance and Managerial Remuneration', *Journal of Accounting and Economics*, 7/2: 11–42.

OCE (1984), *The Impact of Targeted Share Repurchases (Greenmail) on Share Prices*. Office of the Chief Economist, SEC.

—— (1985), *Institutional Ownership, Tender Offers and Long Term Investment*. Office of the Chief Economist, SEC.

Palmer, J. (1973), 'The Profit–Performance Effects of the Separation of Ownership from Control in Large U.S. Industrial Corporations', *Bell Journal of Economics*, 4: 293–303.

Petersen, M. A. and G. R. Rajan (1994), 'The Benefits of Lending Relationships: Evidence from Small Business Data', *Journal of Finance*, 49/1: 3–37.

Pistor, K. (1998), 'Co-determination in Germany: A Socio-Political Model with Governance Externalities', The Sloan Project on Corporate Governance at Columbia Law School, May.

Pound, J. (1988), 'Proxy Contests and the Efficiency of Shareholder Oversight', *Journal of Financial Economics*, 20: 237–65.

Pozdena, Randall J. (1991), 'Why Banks Need Commerce Powers', *Federal Reserve Bank of San Francisco Economic Review*, Summer.

Prowse, Stephen D. (1992), The Structure of Corporate Ownership in Japan, *Journal of Finance*, 1121–40.

Pryor, F. L. (2000), 'Some Important Economic Impacts of the Worldwide Merger Tsunami, 1985–1999', WZB Economics Seminar.

Radice, H. K. (1971), 'Control Type, Profitability and Growth in Large Firms', *Economic Journal*, 547–62.

Rajan, Raghuram G. (1992), 'Insiders and Outsiders: The Choice Between Relationship and Arms-Length Debt', *Journal of Finance*, 47: 1367–1400.

Ravenscraft, David J. and F. M. Scherer (1987*a*), 'Life After Takeover', *Journal of Financial Economics*, 36.

—— —— (1987*b*), *Mergers, Sell-offs and Economic Efficiency*, Washington: Brookings Institution.

Renneboog, Luc (1997), 'Concentration of Ownership and Pyramidal Shareholding Structures in Belgian Listed Companies', in *The Separation of Ownership and Control: A Survey of 7 European Countries*, Preliminary Report to the European Commission.

Roe, Mark (1994), *Strong Managers, Weak Owners: The Political Roots of American Corporate Finance*, Princeton: Princeton University Press.

Roe, M. (1998), 'German Co-determination and German Securities Markets', *Columbia Business Law Review*, 5: 199–211.

Roll, R. (1986), 'The Hubris Hypothesis of Corporate Takeovers', *Journal of Business*, 59: 197–216.

Romano, R. (1994), 'Public Pension Fund Activism in Corporate Governance', in T. Baums, R. M. Buxbaum, and K. J. Hopt (eds.), *Institutional Investors and Corporate Governance*, Berlin and New York: Walter de Gruyter.

Round, D. K. (1976), 'The Effect of the Separation of Ownership and Control on Large Firm Profit Rates in Australia: An Exploratory Investigation', *Rivista Internationale Di Scienze Economiche e Commercial*, 23: 426–36.

Rosen, Sherwin (1992), 'Contracts and the Market for Executives', in Lars Werin and Hans Wijkander (eds.), *Contract Economics*, Cambridge, Mass. and Oxford: Blackwell: 181–211.

Rydqvist, K. (1987), 'Empirical Investigation of the Voting Premium', Working paper 35, North Western University.

Ryngaert, M. (1988), 'The Effect of Poison Pill Securities on Shareholder Wealth', *Journal of Financial Economics*, 20/112: 377–417.

—— and J. Netter (1987), 'Shareholder Wealth Effects of the Ohio Anti-Takeover Law', *Journal of Law, Economics and Organization*, 4/2: 373–83.

Scherer, F. M. (1988), 'Corporate Takeovers: The Efficiency Arguments', *Journal of Economic Perspectives*, 2/1: 69–82.

Schreyögg, G. and H. Steinmann (1981), 'Zur Trennung von Eigentum und Verfügungsgewalt: Eine empirische Analyse der Beteiligungsverhältnisse in deutschen Großunternehmen, *Zeitschrift für Betriebswirtschaft*, 51: 532–58.

Schroeder, U. and A. Schrader (1996), The Changing Role of Banks and Corporate Governance in Germany: Evolution Towards the Market?', Working paper, Deutsche Bank Research.

Schumann, Laurence (1988), 'State Regulation of Takeovers and Shareholder Wealth: The Case of New York's 1985 Takeover Statutes', *Rand Journal of Economics*, 19/4: 557–67.

Servaes, H. (1991), 'Tobin's Q and the Gains From Takeovers', *Journal of Finance*, 66/1: 409–19.

Shleifer, A. and L. H. Summers (1988), 'Breach of Trust in Hostile Takeovers', in Auerbach (ed), *Corporate Takeovers: Causes and Consequences*.

—— and R. W. Vishny (1996), 'A Survey of Corporate Governance', *Journal of Finance*, 52/2: 737–83.

Short, Helen (1994), 'Ownership, Control, Financial Structure and the Performance of Firms', *Journal of Economic Surveys*, 8/3: 203–49.

—— and Kevin Keasey (1997), 'Institutional Shareholders and Corporate Governance', in Keasey and Wright (eds.), *Corporate Governance*.

Smith, M. P. (1996), 'Shareholder Activism by Institutional Investors: Evidence from CalPERS', *Journal of Finance*, 51/1: 227–52.

Sorensen, R. (1974), 'The Separation of Ownership and Control and Firm Performance: An Empirical Analysis', *Southern Economic Journal*, 41: 145–8.

Stano, M. (1976), 'Monopoly Power, Ownership Control and Corporate Performance', *Bell Journal of Economics*, 7: 672–9.

Steer, P. and J. Cable (1978), 'Internal Organisation and Profit: An Empirical Analysis of Large U.K. Companies', *Journal of Industrial Economics*, 27/1, 13–30.

Stiglitz, Joseph E. (1985), 'Credit Market and the Control of Capital', *Journal of Money, Credit and Banking*, 17/2: 133–52.

Temporary National Economic Committee (1940), *The Distribution of Ownership in the 200 Largest Non-financial Corporations*, Monograph 29, Washington: Government Printing Office.

Thonet, P. J. and O. H. Poensgen (1979), 'Managerial Control and Economic Performance in West Germany', *Journal of Industrial Economics*, 28/1: 23–37.

Von Thadden, E. L. (1990), 'Bank Finance and Long-Term Investment,' mimeo, University of Basel.

—— (1992), 'The Commitment of Finance, Duplicated Monitoring and the Investment Horizon', mimeo, University of Basel.

Ware, R. F. (1975), 'Performance of Manager versus Owner-Controlled Firms in the Food and Beverage Industry', *Quarterly Review of Economics and Business*, 81–92.

Weinstein, D. E. and Y. Yafeh (1998), 'On the Costs of a Bank-Centered Financial System: Evidence from the Changing Main Bank Relations in Japan', *Journal of Finance*, 53/2: 635–72.

Williamson, Oliver, E. (1963), 'Management Discretion and Business Behavior', *American Economic Review*, 53: 1032–57.

—— (1985), *The Economic Institutions of Capitalism*, New York: Free Press.

Wright, M. and K. Robbie (forthcoming), 'Investor Buy-Outs: A New Strategic Option, Long Range Planning'.

Yarrow, George (1986), 'Privatization in Theory and Practice', *Economic Policy*, 2: 324–64.

Yermack, David (1997), 'Good Timing: CEO Stock Option Awards and Company News Announcements', *Journal of Finance*, 52/2: 449–76.

Yurtoglu, B. (forthcoming), 'Ownership, Control and Performance of Turkish Listed Companies', *Empirica*.

Zeckhauser, R. J. and J. Pound (1990) 'Are Large Shareholders Effective Monitors? An Investigation of Share Ownership and Corporate Performance', in Hubbard (ed.), *Asymmetric Information, Corporate Finance, and Investment*: 149–80.

Zingales, Luigi (1994), 'The Value of the Voting Right: A Study of the Milan Stock Exchange', *Review of Financial Studies*, 7: 125–48.

—— (forthcoming), 'Corporate Governance', in *The New Palgrave Dictionary of Economics and the Law*.

PART II

COUNTRY REPORTS:
CORPORATE GOVERNANCE AND
ECONOMIC PERFORMANCE

7

Austria

KLAUS GUGLER

1. INTRODUCTION

Very little systematic research has been done on corporate governance topics in Austria. The system is characterized by centralized ownership of corporations, pyramiding, state, and family ownership, and corporate shareholdings of financial institutions. The universal banking structure encourages the involvement of financial institutions in financing and controlling non-bank firms. There are very few large public corporations with dispersed share ownership, and there is no active market for corporate control.[1] Control is exerted by internal control mechanisms such as boards of directors and large shareholders.

One possible interpretation of Austrian corporate governance is that of an 'insider system' of governance where changes in corporate strategy are triggered by 'committees' rather than the 'market for corporate strategy'.[2] Ownership concentration is tremendous in Austria with the largest owner of the 600 largest Austrian non-financial companies holding around 80 per cent of the equity on average (see Gugler, Stomper, and Zechner, 2000). This potentially gives rise to the conflict between large and small shareholders. Although this conflict has not yet been analysed for large samples of firms, there are some case studies indicating an expropriation of minority shareholders. Although many efforts have been devoted to improving transparency and legal rights of minority shareholders in recent years, there are some legal provisions still in place that may put smaller shareholders at a disadvantage.

There is, for instance, a new takeover law (*Übernahmegesetz*), which has been effective since January 1999, and which stipulates a compulsory offer to minority shareholders in case of a controlling offer. It provides for the installation of an independent Takeover Commission. Amendments to existing laws improving transparency and the legal rights of minority shareholders include the amendment of the Stock Exchange Act (*Börsegesetz*), which, among other things, criminalizes insider dealing and tightens transparency regulations. Section 91 of the Stock Exchange Act implementing the EU's Large Holding Directive (88/627/EEC) specifies the notification thresholds 5, 10, 15, 20, 25, 30, 35, 40, 45, 50, 75, and 90 per cent of the total voting rights of the company. The amendment of the Austrian Stock Corporation Act (*Aktiengesetz*) improves the options for stock corporations to buy back own shares.

However, the legal situation of minority shareholders is far from ideal. If a shareholder, for instance, holds more than 90 per cent of the equity he can 'squeeze out' (under certain conditions) minority shareholders by paying an appropriate consideration (*Umwandlungsgesetz*, or Act on transformation of corporations; see also section 2.1). Likewise, the new takeover law contains some regulations that do not benefit small shareholders. For example, a three-quarters majority at the general assembly can implement an opting-out from the regulations concerning the compulsory offer to minority shareholders. The compulsory offer can be marked down by 15 per cent (see also section 2.2).

In the next section, I review the available empirical evidence concerning our research questions, section 3 presents a short discussion, and the last section concludes.

2. RESEARCH QUESTIONS

2.1. *Are block-holders beneficial or is there managerial entrenchment and rent extraction?*

To my knowledge, the following papers are the only studies that so far have systematically analysed the effects of ownership and voting structure on firm performance using firm level data in Austria.

Hahn, Mooslechner, and Pfaffermayer (1996) for the period 1980 to 1994 find that Austrian subsidiaries of foreign firms with one or two owners invest more and are more productive (higher value added per employee) than Austrian subsidiaries of foreign firms with more than three owners. This is indirect evidence that a more concentrated ownership structure leads to a better monitoring, improving firm performance.

Schmidt (1997) analyses the relationship between ownership structure and performance for 55 Austrian credit unions (co-operative associations) over the period 1991 to 1993. The more members the co-operative has and the smaller the Herfindahl index of voting power concentration, the worse the performance measure return on assets. This is consistent with the management discretion hypothesis. Credit co-operatives can be classified as manager-controlled firms; the average number of members of the co-operatives in the sample was 6,500 in 1991, 6,800 in 1992, and 7,000 in 1993. A large separation of ownership and control is expected, since voting concentration is even more dispersed than ownership concentration: There is the so-called *Kopfstimmrecht* ('one-head-one-vote' instead of 'one-share-one-vote') implying an even distribution of voting rights, although cash-flow rights may be concentrated. In essence, this is a voting cap as in QIII, Table 1.1. The results of Schmidt (1997) are consistent with the theoretical arguments against voting right restrictions.

Gugler (1998, 1999) finds for 214 large Austrian non-financial firms in the 1991 to 1995 period that ownership concentration—measured as the percentage holdings of the largest shareholder—is significantly negatively related to the profit margin. Table 7.1 displays the results. Apart from corporate governance characteristics, this table explains the profits-to-sales ratio through 18 industry dummies at the 2-digit SIC level to control for fixed industry differences such as different barriers to entry, investment

Table 7.1. *The determinants of the profits-to-sales ratio in Austria through 18 industry dummies (1991–1995; t-statistics in parentheses)*

Independent variables	Specification 1	Specification 2
Largest shareholder (% of equity)	−0.04 (3.24)***	−0.06 (3.61)***
Dummy 100% owner	—	0.02 (2.00)**
Dummy bank-control	−0.05 (4.01)***	−0.05 (4.10)***
Dummy state-control	−0.03 (2.70)***	−0.03 (2.89)***
Dummy family-control	−0.03 (3.98)***	−0.03 (4.22)***
Physical investment (% of total sales)	0.05 (2.07)**	0.05 (1.95)*
Financial investments (% of total sales)	0.19 (3.17)***	0.18 (3.10)***
Total assets (in ATS bn.)	0.002 (3.31)***	0.002 (3.37)***
Standard deviation profit-to-sales ratio 1991–1995	−0.56 (3.85)***	−0.56 (3.86)***
R^2	0.25	0.25
Firms	214	214
Observations	1,070	1,070

*** significant at the 1%-level; ** significant at the 5%-level; * significant at the 10%-level.

Notes: Estimation method is OLS with White (1980) heteroscedasticity corrected errors. Bank, state, and family control are defined according to the largest ultimate shareholder criterion (see also Figure 7.1).

intensity (both investment in physical and financial assets), size (measured by total assets), and firm-specific risk (measured by the standard deviation of the profits-to-sales ratio over the 1991 to 1995 period).

The negative effect of the largest shareholder's holdings on performance suggests that ownership concentration is excessive in Austria. This is consistent with the 'entrenchment hypothesis': high ownership concentration may provide the owner with the incentives and the means to entrench himself/herself and/or to divert assets and profits to himself/herself via channels other than the official earnings statements.

Specification 2 in Table 7.1 provides another 'test' of whether there is rent extraction. This specification includes a dummy variable taking the value 1 if the firm has only one owner, and zero otherwise. One might expect that if rent extraction is absent by definition, since there is only one shareholder, performance is better compared to firms where there is potentially rent extraction. The coefficient on this dummy variable is positive and significant, i.e. performance is significantly better in firms with only one owner.[3] This indicates that the influence of ownership concentration on performance is non-linear.

Relative to foreign-controlled firms, control of all three domestic investor classes, banks, the state, and families/individuals, reduces the profitability of the firm. This is also in line with the findings of Hahn, Mooslechner, and Pfaffermayer (1996) and Bellak (1996), who find better performance of subsidiaries of foreign firms than for domestically controlled firms. We will return to the effects of owner identity on firm performance in section 2.4.

The studies above give only indirect evidence as to whether small shareholders might be put at a disadvantage. In what follows, I present cases where minority shareholders were at least partly expropriated by a large and controlling shareholder.

The case that attracted most attention is the sell-off of the majority stake of Creditanstalt AG, which it held in Steyr-Daimler-Puch AG (SDP, 66.8 per cent), to Magna International AG in 1998. After this purchase, Magna International AG made an offer to the other minority shareholders. Most, though not all, of the minority shareholders accepted this offer. Magna held more than 90 per cent of the equity of SDP.

At this point it is useful to recall the so-called *Umwandlungsgesetz* (Act on transformation of corporations). This law provides for the squeeze-out of minority shareholders of up to 10 per cent of the capital.[4] The consequences of the transformation are that firm assets are transferred by universal succession to the main shareholder, and the minor shareholders lose their membership in the company. The minority shareholders must be paid an appropriate consideration (in cash). They cannot rescind the shareholders' resolution on the transformation but they are entitled to have the consideration reviewed in court. This entitlement, and the provision that the costs of the appraisal of firm value has to be borne by the company, have only been in effect since 1996.

Although some minority shareholders voted against their being squeezed out, Magna AG, holding more than 90 per cent of the equity, decided to squeeze out the small shareholders in an extraordinary shareholder's meeting (on 7 September 1998), and to delist SDP AG. Magna did this by 'outsourcing' the minority shareholder claims to a proforma company, Nevia AG, which was founded for this very purpose. Currently, a lawsuit is pending. The 43 remaining shareholders representing around 0.2 per cent of the equity argue that the consideration Magna granted them is 50 per cent below true firm value.

Another case where minority shareholders were squeezed out against their free will is Bau Holding AG. In 1998, the largest and controlling shareholder of Bau Holding AG (an individual) decided to delist Strabag Österreich Beteiligungs AG, majority-held by Bau Holding AG. Bau Holding AG made a compensation offer of 800 ATS per share to the 30 per cent dispersed shareholders. Twelve per cent did not accept this offer. However, by merging Illbau GmbH, also controlled by Bau Holding AG, with Strabag Österreich Beteiligungs AG, the percentage holdings of dispersed shareholders fell below 10 per cent. The minority shareholders were excluded from their options on the new stock! Now, Bau Holding AG held more than 90 per cent of the equity and could squeeze out the minority shareholders that were still present. According to the largest shareholder of Bau Holding AG, these shareholders will get an offer 'which is below the 800 ATS the others got' (*Der Standard*, 7 November 1998).

Other firms which made use of the *Umwandlungsgesetz* and squeezed out minority shareholders in recent years are SCA-Laakirchen AG, Leykam AG, Nettingsdorfer AG, Pharmazent AG, Neumann AG, Montana AG, Meinl AG, and Donau Chemie AG. In nearly all these cases there was the suspicion that the large and controlling shareholder—at least partly—expropriated the minority shareholders.

These cases do not provide dispersed shareholders with the confidence that they are likely to get a fair return on their investment. One has to question these regulations within the *Umwandlungsgesetz*, which denies small shareholders a right of appraisal as regards fundamental property rights. Also, these violations of fundamental property rights are only the most apparent abuses of large shareholder rights. Therefore, outside shareholders may demand a higher rate of return in compensation for the risk of being expropriated by a large and controlling shareholder. In section 3, I argue that this partly explains the observed illiquidity of securities markets in Austria.

2.2. *Takeovers and the market for corporate control*

There is no market for control in Austria. As already mentioned, there are only four listed corporations that can be subject to hostile takeovers in the Anglo-Saxon style because shareholder dispersion is sufficient. Nevertheless, one cannot conclude that control-oriented mergers and acquisitions are negligible in Austria. Trades of large equity blocks are quite common, and in many cases management is turned over by the new owner.

Schmidt (1997), for example, mentions that the number of credit co-operatives decreased by 19 per cent in the three-year period from 1991 to 1993. Most of them were acquired by other co-operatives in the same sector to rectify failure of incumbent management. Bellak (1996) reports around 220 mergers and acquisitions in each of the years 1991 to 1995 in Austria.

Unfortunately, there is no systematic evidence as to the effects of block trades. Given the profitability-enhancing effect of foreign ownership that most authors find, control transfers to foreign investors were likely to be beneficial for the governance and profitability of Austrian corporations. However, Mathis (1989) attributes a market concentration effect to mergers and acquisitions because these increased both the absolute size of corporations and their market shares in Austria.

As already mentioned, a new takeover law has been effective since 1 January 1999. While this new law brings along an essential improvement for small shareholders, some regulations do not treat all shareholders equally. For example, the law provides that whoever acquires a controlling interest directly or indirectly is obliged to issue a public offer for all shares of the company. A controlling interest is defined as a control block of 20 per cent in some cases, usually of 30 per cent. However, the compulsory offer can be marked down by 15 per cent compared to the package price obtained by a major shareholder, which clearly contradicts the principle of equal treatment of all shareholders. Neither the EU Directives nor the British Takeover Code contain such provisions.

2.3. *Managerial compensation*

Systematic evidence on the pay–performance relationship or the question whether compensation contracts are efficiently designed in Austria are not available. This is (also) due to the fact that, as in Germany and other Continental European countries, only aggregate compensation figures of both the supervisory board and the management board must be disclosed in annual accounts.

A study by IPC (1997, International Pension Consultants Ges.m.b.H) shows for 16 Austrian corporations that average pay levels are quite high compared to other European countries (Austrian executives enjoy the second-highest pay level among 16 countries). While all posts of managing directors are eligible for annual incentive payments, only 75 per cent of director posts (lowest per centage among the 16 countries) and 25 per cent of senior manager posts (also lowest) are eligible. Median actual managing director bonus payments are 17 per cent, director bonuses are 14 per cent, and senior manager bonuses 7 per cent of base salary. While these numbers are in line with other Continental European countries, no conclusions are possible as to whether the pay–performance relationship is large or whether it is optimal.

Recently, interest in stock option models has increased. However, most stock-option schemes are strictly regulated and grant Austrian managers additional compensation amounting to an annual salary at most (see *NEWS*, 23 June 2000).

2.4. *Does the identity of the owner matter?*

Corporate governance in Austria is intrinsically connected to pyramiding and to the identity of the controlling owner. As an example, Figure 7.1 is an organization chart of OMV AG as of 1995, the largest Austrian corporation as measured by turnover (around ATS 105b. in 1997, (13.76 ATS = 1 Euro), the number of employees was 8,200). Market capitalization of OMV AG was ATS 47b. in 1997. ÖIAG (Österreichische Industrieholding Aktiengesellschaft) is the controlling owner of OMV AG (49.9 per cent). OMV AG is ultimately controlled by the state, however, since the Republic of Austria owns 100 per cent of the equity of ÖIAG. OMV AG is located in the third layer of the pyramid ('Hierarchy'=3).

OMV AG operates in wholesale distribution of fuels, ores, metals and industrial materials. This industry is currently experiencing substantial deregulation. The first 15 per cent of the equity of OMV AG was placed on the Vienna Stock Exchange in 1987, which marked the beginning of the Austrian privatization programme. Parliament

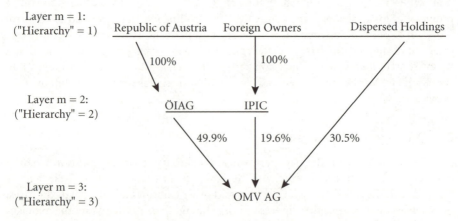

Figure 7.1. *Ownership and control structure of OMV AG in 1995 (Austria)*

re-amended the existing ÖIAG Act at the end of 1993, making it possible for ÖIAG to sell majorities of its industrial interests. Accordingly, subsequent equity issues reduced the amount of equity controlled by ÖIAG in OMV AG to 49.9 per cent in 1995, i.e. below majority control. OMV AG is also listed in Frankfurt, London (SEAQ), Munich, and New York (ADR). Its share in the Austrian Traded Index (ATX) is 16.68 per cent. All shares of OMV AG are voting shares ('one-share-one-vote'). However, OMV AG and IPIC, a company from Abu Dhabi, share a voting pact, which essentially co-ordinates all key corporate decisions. The supervisory board of OMV AG consists of fifteen members (management board: five members), three of whom are nominated by IPIC, five of whom are employee representatives in accordance with §110 Labour Relations Act (see also section 2.5), and seven are nominated by ÖIAG. Two members of the supervisory board are managers of large Austrian banks.

Gugler (1998) classifies firms in the spirit of Figure 7.1 into state, bank, family, and foreign-controlled firms. Figure 7.2 displays the economic importance of these owners in Austria. The sample consists of the 600 largest Austrian companies as of 1995, covering around 30 per cent of economic activity. Nearly 30 per cent of the employees of the 600 largest non-financial companies in Austria are (still) under state control, 35 per cent of the employees are governed by families or individuals, and around 10 per cent are under bank control. In a study of the ownership structure in Austria, Beer *et al.* (1991) found that the state ultimately owned 24 per cent of the equity in the credit sector. Depositary votes by banks are not so important in Austria, since banks have to be authorized specifically in writing by the depositing shareholder to be able to exercise their depositary votes. Foreign firms are very prominent investors in Austria, commanding 26.1 per cent of the employees in the 600 largest non-financial companies.

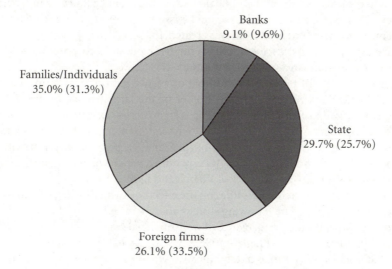

Figure 7.2. *Economic importance of investor classes in Austria (percentages of employees under ultimate control in 1995; percentage of sales in parentheses)*

This suggests that state ownership and foreign direct investment may act as a substitute for domestic private investors and efficient domestic securities markets.

One possible explanation for this ownership and control structure is a historical one. After World War II, two-thirds of industrial production capacity in Austria were in German ownership, and the Allied authorities had the right to confiscate German property for reparation reasons. To avoid this, in 1946 and 1947, two laws for national-ization (*Verstaatlichungsgesetze*) nationalized the largest Austrian companies in the in-dustry, energy, and banking sectors. After some successes and well-known innovations in the 1960s and early 1970s ('Linz-Donawitz-Blasstahl-Verfahren'), the nationalized industries faced a big economic crisis in the mid-1980s, which sparked a privatization programme in 1987. Since then, many former state-owned companies have been pri-vatized in the form of IPOs or sell-offs to domestic and foreign (mostly German) in-vestors. However, many former completely state-owned companies were only partly privatized with the state remaining the largest (and controlling) shareholder as the case of OMV AG demonstrates.

Another peculiarity of the control landscape in Austria is 'ownerless' legal forms mostly in the banking sector. Some legal forms are 'ownerless' in the sense that there are no clearly defined residual owners. Control is not in the hands of any owner and there is complete separation of ownership and control.

Thirty-two per cent of the Austrian banking sector is comprised of savings banks which are, in effect, ownerless.[5] They were founded either by municipalities (*Gemein-desparkasse*) or by savings bank associations (*Vereinssparkasse*). Savings banks have no owners, but they have a special relationship with their municipality or the savings bank association, since these founders are guarantors for the savings bank. While upon foundation the founders have to provide sufficient capital, this capital subsequently belongs to the savings bank and is not paid back to the founder. Since savings banks do not have owners, they cannot raise capital by issuing shares. In order to alleviate this problem, a special hybrid legal form was created, the so-called savings bank stock cor-poration (*Sparkassen-Aktiengesellschaft*). A savings bank stock corporation is a savings bank that owns equity in a stock corporation.

Gugler *et al*. (1997) provide an example of such a hybrid legal form, the largest Austrian bank, Bank Austria AG. The holder of the largest block of more than 40 per cent of the voting rights of Bank Austria is an ownerless association, *Anteilsverwal-tung Zentralsparkasse* (AVZ). The City of Vienna guarantees Bank Austria's liabilities in case of default. Currently, a cross-border merger between the German HVB (*HypoVereinsbank*) and Bank Austria AG is pending, which will terminate the guaran-teeing relationship between the City of Vienna and Bank Austria.

Unfortunately, no systematic studies on the effects of 'ownerless' legal forms on per-formance exist to date. The following studies analyse the effects of the identity of the controlling owner on the performance of non-financial companies.

As displayed in Table 7.1, Gugler (1998, 1999) finds that the domestic owner cate-gories state, banks, and families did significantly worse than foreign owners in the 1991 to 1995 period with respect to the sales to profit ratio. Additionally, rates of return (RoR) calculations suggest that state-controlled firms performed particularly badly over the 1985 to 1994 period; a median real RoR of −3.7 per cent for state-controlled firms compares to a median real RoR of 10.4 per cent for foreign, 8.4 per cent for family, and 5.7 per cent for bank-controlled firms.

Consistently, Hahn, Mooslechner, and Pfaffermayer (1996) find that subsidiaries of foreign firms perform better than their domestic counterparts. Reasons mentioned are that cash constraints are fewer so that all profitable investments can be financed, management and monitoring techniques are better, and technological leadership is more prevalent.

Nemec (1999) analyses 166 listed German and 47 listed Austrian firms. She identifies 43 out of the 213 companies as bank-controlled via supervisory board dominance (bank member is chair or vice-chair of the supervisory board) and 58 companies where banks have influence via an equity stake. Bank-controlled firms are significantly larger than other listed firms, have higher long-term debt ratios, and lower implicit costs of capital (measured by the interest coverage ratio), but have lower profitability (return on assets) and lower growth rates. The majority of differences is only statistically significant when bank control is measured by bank equity stakes. Unfortunately, the small number of degrees of freedom prevents the author from analysing the differences between bank-controlled firms and non-bank-controlled firms only within Austria.

Other institutional investors are nearly absent in Austria due to restrictive legislation up to 1990. The option to form pension funds has only existed since 1990 (see Jud 1993). Corporate control is nearly forbidden by law; shares of an individual stock corporation may only be acquired up to an amount of 5 per cent of the total share capital of that corporation. Investment funds and insurance corporations face similar restrictions and are therefore not large players in Austrian corporate governance. Accordingly, there are no studies assessing their influence on corporate governance and performance. Nevertheless, due to the recent changes in legislation, institutional investors and particularly investment funds have also become more prominent in Austria.

2.5. *Board structure and performance*

Austrian corporate law provides for a two-tier or dual-board system similar to the German system. While a supervisory board for stock corporations (*Aktiengesellschaft*, AG) is obligatory, the establishment of a supervisory board is optional in the case of smaller companies with limited liability, or for partnerships. Amongst other provisions which trigger the need to establish a supervisory board for a company with limited liability (GmbH), such a board is obligatory whenever either the stated capital of the corporation exceeds ATS 1m. and there are more than 50 shareholders, or the annual average number of employees exceeds 300.

Reich-Rohrwig (1993) reports that only 2.3 per cent of Austrian GmbHs maintain a supervisory board. *None* of the companies with limited liability in a 1 per cent random sample drawn by Reich-Rohrwig (1993) voluntarily maintained a supervisory board.

The legal provisions governing the supervisory boards of AGs are §§ 86 to 99 of the Stock Corporation Act. The supervisory board is in charge of appointing, dismissing,

Table 7.2. *Average size of boards by ownership category in Austria*

Control Categories[a]	No. of firms	Supervisory board (s.b.)		Management board (no. of people)
		Proportion with s.b. (%)	Firms with s.b. (no. of people)	
All firms	600	66.2	6.9	3.1
State	89	89.9	9.7	2.9
Banks	39	94.7	7.9	3.5
Family	259	53.4	6.0	3.0
Foreign Firms	213	67.1	5.8	3.2

[a] The controlling category of a company is the category among the state, banks, families, and foreign firms that has ultimately the largest stake in the company (see also Figure 7.1).

Source: Gugler, Stomper, and Zechner (2000). Data Basis: Trend-Verlag.

and supervising the management board. The members of the supervisory board, who are elected by the shareholders, are appointed by a shareholders' resolution at a general meeting. Up to one-third of the members can be nominated by single shareholders or a particular group of shareholders. The holders of one-third of the share capital have the right to elect one supervisory board member.

As in Germany, the Austrian law provides for employee representation on the supervisory board ('co-determination'). For every two members nominated by the shareholders, the council of shop stewards (representing the employees) has the right to delegate one representative of the employees (*Drittelparität*, one-third parity).[6] The participation of employees is governed by the Labour Relations Act (§110).

In general, all members of the supervisory board have the same rights and duties. However, the appointment and removal of the management board and of the chairman and the deputy chairman of the supervisory board require a so-called double majority. Both an effective resolution of the entire supervisory board and the consent of the majority of the shareholder members are necessary. This so-called *Aktionärs-schutzklausel* (clause for the protection of shareholders) makes it impossible for representatives of the employees and/or of minority shareholders to outvote the majority shareholder(s) in these crucial aspects of corporate governance.[7]

The supervisory board must hold at least three meetings per year. The supervisory board may at any time demand reports from the managing directors, and may inspect the books and documents of the company. §95 of the Stock Corporation Act enumerates a list of transactions which should only be undertaken after approval by the supervisory board. These transactions concern main business decisions such as the purchase or selling of interests, real assets, and investments above a certain threshold. Additionally, the supervisory board may file lawsuits against the management by order of the general meeting, but also on its own.

This discussion suggests that the supervisory board potentially has the power to effectively monitor and constrain management. Nevertheless, it is commonly held that supervisory boards are less effective monitors than intended by the law. Reasons include (see Roe, 1998) the large size of the supervisory board, infrequent board meetings, sparse information flow to the board, low incentives to actively monitor management, and co-determination, which gives large shareholders and management incentives to weaken the board. The findings of Reich-Rohrwig (1993) that none of the GmbHs in his sample voluntarily maintained a supervisory board suggests that the costs of establishing the board, and probably the costs of co-determination, outweigh the benefits for large shareholders.

Systematic evidence concerning the effectiveness of boards is sparse, if non-existent. Gugler, Stomper, and Zechner (2000) describe average board size across ownership and control categories for the 600 largest Austrian non-financial companies (see Table 7.2). Average board size is 6.9 people. State-controlled firms typically install a supervisory board, and maintain the largest boards (around ten people). Firms controlled by foreigners and families are less likely to install a supervisory board, and, if they have one, typically maintain smaller supervisory boards (around six people). Bank-controlled firms are in between. These conclusions are unaltered if it is controlled for firm size. In contrast, management boards do not show substantial variation in size across control categories.

Gugler, Stomper, and Zechner (2000) interpret the particularly large board-size of state-owned firms as reflecting a large number of stakeholders trying to influence corporate strategy. Oversized boards are one consequence of heterogenous interests being represented in these 'committees'.

Nemec (1999) finds that 44.7 per cent of the 47 listed Austrian firms in her sample have a bank member as chair or vice-chair of the supervisory board. Unfortunately, this small number of observations does not allow analysing differences across groups of firms.

3. DISCUSSION

Figure 2.1 in Chapter 2 showed that Austrian stock-market capitalization in relation to GDP is lowest among the countries depicted (see also Hopt *et al.* 1998: 1057). The question arises whether poor legal protection of minority shareholders is the force stifling securities markets in Austria. La Porta *et al.* (1997, 1998) argue that where laws are protective of outside investors and well enforced, investors are willing to finance firms, and financial markets are broader and more liquid.

One indicator of the quality of shareholder rights protection is anti-director rights. For Austria, La Porta *et al.* (1998) obtain an anti-director rights index of two, with the index ranging from zero (very poor anti-director rights) to five (best anti-director rights). La Porta *et al.* (1998) find for Austria that (1) cumulative voting is not allowed, (2) an oppressed minorities mechanism is not in place, and (3) shares are blocked before a shareholders' meeting. On the other hand, shareholders are allowed to mail their proxy votes and the minimum percentage of share capital that entitles a shareholder to call in an extraordinary shareholder meeting is less than 10 per cent (namely 5 per cent). For comparison, the USA gets an index number of five, the UK four, Japan three, and Germany only one point. Additionally, creditor rights are substantial in

German civil law countries. This suggests that poorer shareholder rights in Austria than for example in the USA is part of the explanation of why securities markets are illiquid.

Additionally, specific country factors are likely to contribute to the observed illiquidity of securities markets in Austria. The demand for external finance in the form of equity was low in Austria, since state ownership and state intervention substituted for private capital. After World War II, large parts of the basic industries and the banking sector were nationalized, with privatization only beginning in the mid-1980s. There was also the policy of subsidizing all sorts of investments by state funds, with costs of capital presumably less than could be obtained on the external capital market.[8] Additionally, *Hausbanken* made the need for diffuse outside equity participations less pressing.

Austria has also a long tradition of 'social partnership' between employees and employers, and co-determination on corporate boards. Roe (1998) persuasively argues that block-holders would not get a fair price for their stock if a diffusion of ownership left firms either with labour-dominated or weak boards. It is likely that all of the factors above have contributed to the observed illiquidity of securities markets in Austria.

Currently, 17 Austrian firms are listed abroad and take advantage of liquid foreign exchanges (8 on the Neuer Markt in Frankfurt, 7 on the EASDAQ in Brussels, and 2 in Zürich). Most of these listings were IPOs in the last ten years. The demand for equity financing is likely to continue to increase in Austria, since technologies are getting riskier and the state gradually withdraws from running or financing firms.

4. CONCLUSIONS AND ASSESSMENT

The Austrian corporate governance system can best be characterized as an 'insider' system supplemented by a (still) strong influence of the state. Due to insufficient disclosure and accounting provisions, very little systematic evidence is available to date. Ownership concentration is excessively high, the stock exchange is very small and illiquid, and investment strategies are more on the conservative side.

Insufficient protection of small shareholders, as well as specific country factors, such as a low demand for outside (equity) finance and state ownership, are responsible for a lack of efficient securities markets. The conflict between large and small shareholders appears to be an important problem in Austrian corporate governance. Interest in corporate governance is emerging, as the need for reform is being acknowledged. While some proposals and legislative changes point in the right direction, much needs to be done to arrive at a more efficient corporate governance system.

Notes

1. On the Vienna Stock Exchange there are only four corporations in the continuous trading segment with more than 50 per cent of the equity in free float. All other companies have at least one controlling large shareholder, or there are voting pacts among several large shareholders. In 1998, there was one contested takeover and one hostile takeover attempt.

2. Franks and Mayer (1997) characterize an 'insider system' of corporate governance by (1) few listed companies; (2) a large number of substantial share stakes; and (3) large intercorporate equity holdings. Austria is characterized by all of these features.
3. Of course, we cannot determine whether this superior performance of single-owner firms is due to the absence of the large–small shareholder conflict or whether the shareholder–manager conflict is absent (or reduced) by the single owner.
4. Similar provisions are in place in Germany, see Chapter 9.
5. Other 'ownerless' legal forms are private foundations established in Austria in 1993 and mutual insurance associations, for more details see Gugler *et al.* (1997).
6. In Germany, this relationship is one-to-one (see also Pistor 1998). Contrary to German law, an employee representative must be an insider with voting rights for the election of the council of shop stewards in Austria.
7. I am not aware of similar provisions in Germany. Generally, it appears that large shareholders have more legal rights in Austrian than in German supervisory boards.
8. For example, the ERP, BÜRGES, and FGG fund. Additionally there are numerous funds set up by all levels of government (central, federal, and local) for special purposes, e.g. export grants, technology grants, water supply funds, and so on.

References for Chapter 7

Beer, E., B. Ederer, W. Goldmann, R. Lang, M. Passweg, and R. N. Reitzner (1991), *Wem gehört Österreichs Wirtschaft wirklich?* Vienna: Orac Verlag.

Bellak, C. (1996), 'Ausverkauf der Industrie: Entwicklung in Österreich und Konsequenzen für die Interessenvertretung', *Studie im Auftrag der Vereinigung Österreichischer Industrieller*, Vienna.

Franks, Julian and Colin Mayer (1997), 'Ownership, Control, and the Performance of German Corporations', Working paper, London Business School.

Gugler, K. (1998), 'Corporate Ownership Structure in Austria', *Empirica*, 25: 285–307.

—— (1999), 'Eigentümerstruktur und Profitabilität: Eine Analyse österreichischer Unternehmen', *Wirtschaftspolitische Blätter* (June), 583–9.

—— A. Stomper, and J. Zechner (2000), 'Corporate Governance, Ownership, and Board Structure in Austria', *Zeitschrift für Betriebswirtschaft*, Supplement (Jan.), 23–43.

——, S. Kalss, A. Stomper, and J. Zechner (1997), 'The Separation of Ownership and Control: An Austrian Perspective', in *The Separation of Ownership and Control: A Survey of 7 European Countries*, Preliminary Report to the European Commission.

Hahn, F. R., P. Mooslechner, and M. Pfaffermayer (1996), 'Globalisierungstendenzen in der Österreichischen Wirtschaft: Corporate Citizenship als neue wirtschaftspolitische Herausforderung', *Beiträge zur Wirtschaftspolitik*, Arbeiterkammer Wien.

Hopt, K. J, H. Kanda, M. J. Roe, E. Wymeersch, and S. Prigge (1998), *Comparative Corporate Governance: The State of the Art and Emerging Research*, Oxford: Clarendon Press.

IPC (International Pension Consultants Ges.m.b.H.) (1997), *Remuneration of Director's and Managers—Europe*, Vienna: Copyright Monks Partnership Limited.

Jud, W. (1993), 'Institutional Investors and Corporate Governance: The Austrian View', in T. Baums (ed.), *Institutional Investors and Corporate Governance*, Berlin, New York: deGruyter.

La Porta, R., F. Lopez-de-Silanes, and A. Shleifer (1997), 'Legal Determinants of External Finance', *Journal of Finance*, 52/3: 1131–50.

La Porta, R., F. Lopez-de-Silanes, A. Shleifer and R. W. Vishny (1998), 'Law and Finance', *Journal of Political Economy*, 106: 1113–55.

Mathis, F. (1989), *Fusion und Konzentration in der österreichischen Großindustrie*, Vienna: Unternehmer und Unternehmen (Österreichische Gesellschaft für Unternehmensgeschichte).

Nemec, E. A. (1999), 'The Two Faces of Debtholder Control in Bank-Oriented Covernance Systems: Evidence from German Speaking Countries', Working paper, Vienna University of Economics and Business Administration.

Pistor, K. (1998), 'Co-determination in Germany: A Socio-Political Model with Governance Externalities', The Sloan Project on Corporate Governance at Columbia Law School, May.

Reich-Rohrwig, J. (1993), 'Verbreitung und Gesellschaftsstruktur der GmbH in Österreich', in *Festschrift für Walther Kastner*, Vienna: Orac Verlag.

Roe, M. (1998), 'German Co-determination and German Securities Markets', *Columbia Business Law Review*, 5: 199–211.

Schmidt, F. A. (1997), 'Eigentümerstruktur, Agency-Kosten und Unternehmenserfolg: Empirische Evidenz für österreichische Genossenschaftsbanken', mimeo.

White, H. (1980), 'A Heteroscedasticity–Consistent Covariance Matrix Estimator and a Direct Test for Heteroscedasticity', *Econometrica*, 48/4.

8

Belgium

MARC GOERGEN AND LUC RENNEBOOG

1. INTRODUCTION

Belgium is almost prototypical of the Continental European system of corporate governance. Not only are there few companies listed on the Brussels Stock Exchange (only 140 in 1999 on the first market, a reduction compared to 1990 when 182 were listed), but these companies also have a highly concentrated ownership structure. As in France, Italy, and Spain, financial and industrial holding companies hold a voting majority in the average company (Becht and Röell, 1999). As in Germany, industrial firms also hold large shareholdings in other listed and unlisted companies. Usually, complex ownership structures—with holding companies as intermediate investment vehicles—are used to lever control (Goergen and Renneboog forthcoming). The ultimate owner is often a family. This implies that Belgium can be portrayed as a Franco-German 'insider system' rather than an Anglo-American corporate governance system (Crama *et al.* 1999; Becht and Mayer 2001).

The remainder of the chapter is organized as follows. In section 2, we describe ownership and control structures of Belgian firms. Section 3 is about the relationship between the legal basis of the corporate governance system and the degree of development of the capital market. In section 4, we answer the question of whether or not poor corporate performance triggers corporate governance actions. We also look at which corporate governance devices are best suited to dealing with bad performance. In section 5, we investigate whether or not corporate groups facilitate the creation of internal capital markets and the access to bank financing. Section 6 deals with remuneration issues and section 7 concludes.

2. DEVIATIONS FROM THE 'ONE-SHARE-ONE-VOTE' RULE

Renneboog (1997, 1998) analyses the ownership structure of a sample of all listed Belgian companies from 1989 to 1994. Forty-seven per cent of his sample consists of industrial and commercial companies, 13 per cent of financial institutions and insurance companies, and 40 per cent of financial and industrial holding companies. The average ownership concentration—the sum of all share stakes of 5 per cent or more—is high, amounting to 67.2 per cent. Domestic and foreign holding companies own the largest direct shareholdings (32.7 per cent) and the second largest category of owner consists of industrial and commercial companies (with an average equity stake of 14.6 per cent).

However, when one identifies the ultimate shareholders and reclassifies the direct share stakes according to the identity and category of the ultimate shareholder, the percentage of shares controlled by holding companies and industrial firms decreases, as the ultimate owner of some companies are families or individual investors (Becht, Chapelle, and Renneboog 2000). An ultimate shareholder is a family or individual, or a widely held company which directly or indirectly controls a target company via an uninterrupted control chain. At the ultimate level, the most important investors are holding companies, families, and industrial companies. Holding companies now own an average shareholding of 27 per cent, families own 15.6 per cent (compared to only 3.9 per cent of direct holdings) and industrial companies own 10.8 per cent. Control is similar across subsamples of listed holding companies, industrial firms, and financial institutions. In the latter, however, other banks and insurance companies are the major shareholders. Institutional investors hold only relatively small stakes and their stakes are usually below the disclosure threshold of 5 per cent (Cornelis and Peeters 1992). Furthermore, only 20 per cent of the institutions are present at the annual meeting and cast their voting rights (Van der Elst 1999*a*).[1] Banks' shareholdings are relatively small, probably since banks face several conflicts of interest. Firstly, banks are usually also creditors to the company in which they own a (small) share stake. Secondly, banks are usually controlled by large holding companies which may also hold substantial shareholdings in the companies in which banks hold an interest (Verwilst 1992).

In 86 per cent of companies, an investor owns at least a blocking minority (a shareholding exceeding 25 per cent). A shareholder or investor group controls a majority stake in 60 per cent of the companies and in 16 per cent of listed firms a supermajority (a shareholding exceeding 75 per cent) exists. During the 1990s, ownership concentration has increased and the number of intermediate layers of control throughout the ownership cascades has been reduced (Renneboog 1997; Wymeersch 1998). The degree of ownership concentration is in line with most Continental European countries (as shown by the European Corporate Governance Network, Barca and Becht, 2001), but stands in stark contrast to the UK, where only 14 per cent of companies have a large shareholder (Goergen 1998; Franks, Mayer, and Renneboog 1998).

Although ownership and control remain stable over time, it may be that there is an active market in large share stakes. Goergen and Renneboog (2000) report that over the period of 1994 to 1996, in about one-third of the listed companies there were transfers of share blocks of between 5 and 24.9 per cent. The evidence shows that the blocks are not normally dissipated by selling them in the open market. Also, most of the transfers take place outside the stock market. Over the same period, majority blocks were acquired in about 10 per cent of companies and minority blocks were purchased in 10 per cent of listed firms. These changes in shareholdings exclude internal restructuring of equity participation within investor groups as such changes do not entail a change in control. Not surprisingly, ultimate holding companies are the main sellers and purchasers of blocks. A large number of transfers are done by institutional investors, but the transfers usually refer to blocks of less than 5 per cent.

3. THE PROTECTION OF SHAREHOLDER AND CREDITOR RIGHTS

The main agency problem in Belgium, given the observed ownership patterns, is the one between majority and minority shareholders. Consequently, there is a need for strong legislative protection of minority shareholders. La Porta *et al.* (1997, 1999) investigate the protection of shareholder and creditor rights in different legal and regulatory environments. They distinguish between common law and civil law environments. In common law countries law is made by judges whose judgements constitute the legislature. This type of law can be found in the Anglo-American countries (USA, UK, and Ireland) and, to a large extent, in the countries belonging to the Commonwealth. The roots of the civil law system follow the Roman tradition. Such codified law was imposed in most Continental European countries under Napoleonic rule (David and Brierley, 1985), including Belgium. This type of legislation is written by legislators and scholars, and judges interpret this codified law in the courts. Using an index of shareholder rights, La Porta *et al.* (1997) show that the Belgian legislative environment, including enforceability of shareholder rights in courts, offers less protection for both expropriation of shareholders by management and for violation of the rights of minority shareholders by large shareholders.[2]

In Belgium, the legislation has further evolved along the lines of the block-holder system (Wymeersch 1994). The power of the large incumbent shareholders was reinforced with the abolition of automatic voting-right restrictions and the anti-takeover legislation which followed the takeover battle around the Generale Maatschappij van België (Société Générale de Belgique) in 1989, such that hostile takeovers are essentially no longer possible. However, to counterbalance the power of the large shareholder, minority shareholders holding at least 1 per cent of the equity can file a minority claim against the company if the management or the large shareholder are managing the company poorly or are taking advantage of minority stakeholders. However, enforcement of the law is weak, as out of 80 potential violations, only two were brought to court, and these prosecutions were not successful.

La Porta *et al.* (1997) hold historical regulation responsible for the lesser degree of capital-market development in Belgium. However, a number of measures have been taken over the last decade to modernize equity markets and increase their access for both investors and for companies (McCahery and Renneboog 2000). Firstly, improved disclosure requirements and accounting standards have been introduced. Awareness by the general public has grown as the government has promoted small-shareholder ownership in large corporate privatization. Furthermore, protection of minority shareholders has been strengthened via measures such as the abolition of voting restrictions and of dual-class voting rights, and the obligation of granting preferential subscription rights. Globalization of financial markets has created a (slow) trend towards harmonization of corporate governance regimes (Renneboog 1999, Renneboog *et al.* 2001). In Belgium, the number of IPOs grew fast in the second half of the 1990s. In the 6-year period from 1990–5, only nine Belgian companies were floated on the Brussels Exchanges, whereas in the subsequent 4 years, there were 64 Belgian IPOs (mostly on the new stock markets for smaller (high-tech) stocks like Euro.NM, Easdaq, and Nasdaq) (Van der Elst 2000). During the 1990s, equity raised by listed firms has also gradually increased, but still lags (as a percentage of GDP) that of Anglo-American firms.

4. DISCIPLINARY ACTIONS IN THE WAKE OF POOR CORPORATE PERFORMANCE

The average board size is ten directors. Depending on the year, 9–11 per cent of the directors of listed Belgian companies leave the board. These numbers are corrected for normal turnover, which is age-related retirements, deaths, and illness. Only 25 per cent of the average Belgian one-tier board consists of executive directors. The average yearly CEO turnover is 18 per cent. Currently, 80 per cent of companies separate the functions of CEO and chairman. Table 8.1 shows the board structure of a typical Belgian listed company, Glaverbel.

Glaverbel has eleven directors, only two of whom are executives. The majority shareholders appoint just over half of the directors (six), while three directors are independent. Renneboog (2000), and Goergen and Renneboog (2000*a*), investigate whether poor share-price and accounting performance triggers disciplinary actions against the management. In addition, they analyse which governance device (like the board of directors, creditors, large shareholders, or coalitions of shareholders) assumes responsibility for monitoring the corporation. Both studies find that poor past share performance, dividend cuts or omissions, as well as weak past accounting performance, are positively correlated with executive director turnover and with CEO turnover. However, industry-adjusted performance is not correlated with the removal of executive directors. These findings are in line with those of Warner, Watts, and Wruck (1988), and Coughlan and Schmidt (1985), who report that in the USA, CEOs are quickly replaced in the wake of poor financial performance.

Both studies reveal that board structure is crucial for monitoring efficiency. The greater the independence of the non-executive directors, as measured by the proportion of non-executives on the board, the higher is the executive turnover for companies with negative after-tax earnings or with poor share performance. Disciplining of CEOs is facilitated by having a large proportion of non-executive directors on the board, as well as by separating the roles of the CEO and chairman.

Next, Renneboog (2000) and Goergen and Renneboog (2000) investigate whether or not managerial disciplining is related to the presence of large shareholders or a market in substantial shareholdings. They conclude that institutional investors do not initiate board and CEO replacement, even if they hold majority stakes. There is also little evidence of monitoring by holding companies owning large stakes in a poorly performing firm. Only for the subsample of listed holding companies, is there some evidence of a relationship between CEO substitution in the wake of poor performance and the presence of holding companies controlling a voting majority. The presence of share stakes owned by industrial and commercial companies is positively correlated

Table 8.1. *Board of directors and ownership structure of Glaverbel (Belgium)*

A. Board of directors

Total number of directors	11
Executive directors	2
Non-executive directors representing majority shareholder	6
Independent directors	3
Separation of CEO and chairman	Yes

B. Ownership structure

Shareholders	% equity	% votes
Asahi Glass	55.0	60.9
Treasury shares (Glaverbel)	9.6	0.0
Public	35.4	39.1
TOTAL	100.0	100.0

Source: Glaverbel.

with executive and CEO turnover. The relation is only weakly significant for equity stakes held by families. The findings mentioned above are based on equity shareholdings classified into categories of owner, using the identity of the ultimate shareholder. However, when the direct shareholdings by ownership category are regressed on turnover data, no such correlations are detected.[3] The findings endorse the hypothesis that it is the ultimate shareholder—rather than the direct shareholder—who is important in terms of control.

Goergen and Renneboog (2000) also show that the lower the performance, the larger the increases in the ownership by holding companies, industrial companies, and families. If these performance-induced increases in ownership are related to executive turnover in the same or subsequent periods, this market for share stakes could be called a market for partial control. However, these ownership increases are only weakly correlated (at 10 per cent level of statistical significance) with executive and CEO turnover. More specifically, the following conclusions are reported: (1) increases in stakes held by industrial and commercial companies are linked to increased board and CEO turnover in industrial firms when profitability is low; (2) foreign holding companies increase their stakes to remove executive directors or the CEO (but only in listed holding companies); and (3) there is no control relation for institutional investors in industrial companies; but (4) increases in stakes owned by banks and insurance companies are positively related to management turnover in holding companies and financial firms.

All in all, there is some evidence that high concentration of ownership prods shareholders (mainly industrial companies) to monitor and to replace badly performing management. It should be emphasized that the above findings are only valid for listed industrial and commercial Belgian companies, but not for holding companies, nor for financial institutions or insurance companies.

5. THE ROLE OF CORPORATE GROUPS IN FUNDING INVESTMENT PROJECTS

Section 4 has cast doubt on the corporate governance role of holding companies, as little empirical evidence was found that they engage in corporate control activities when the companies they control perform poorly. Deloof (1998) discusses the advantages of creating investor groups. A corporate group consists of companies which are related through cross-ownership. He finds evidence that the holding structures in Belgium have been developed to create an internal capital market which acts as a substitute for the poorly developed Belgian capital market. The internal capital market helps a company to avoid financing constraints on its investments. A vast pool of empirical evidence shows that firms depend significantly on internal cash flows to finance their investment choices. The investment cash-flow sensitivity is alleviated for companies which are part of a corporate group, as members of the group can transfer internal surpluses of funds to other group members with deficits of funds.

Deloof and Jegers (1996, 1999) study the effect of intragroup relations on the level of trade credit received and taken. They show that, besides the financial links, there are also substantial trading relationships between group members. Trade between group members is likely to have weaker informational asymmetries than trade between unrelated companies. Therefore, suppliers with surplus cash extend credit more readily to companies in which they hold shares than to companies in which they do not have any equity interests.

6. REMUNERATION

The Commission for Banking and Finance has encouraged companies to disclose more details of managerial remuneration. In 1998 the Commission on Corporate Governance of the Brussels Stock Exchange recommended that salaries of executive directors should depend on corporate performance. In addition, the corporate governance commission 'Santens' and the Association of Belgian Corporations (VBO) have emphasized that the remuneration of non-executive directors should guarantee their independence and should also reflect their attendance at board meetings and internal committees. Thus, a non-executive director should be paid by the company and not paid by shareholders or other stakeholders. As in most Continental European countries (with the notable exception of Sweden), Belgian companies are not obliged to disclose information on remuneration received by individual managers. Only the total remuneration of the board of directors is provided, in table XIX of the notes to the annual reports.[4] The table gives information about the combined directors' direct and indirect remuneration as well as pension payments. The gross remuneration reported for the whole board also comprises 'tantièmes', which may be paid out of the after-tax profit. The statutes of some companies may limit the disbursement of 'tantièmes' and hence may reduce the relation between managerial compensation and profit.

Publicly available remuneration data do not capture internal additional corporate pension claims, corporate perquisites (such as company cars and club membership), option or warrant schemes. However, several surveys cited in Van der Elst (1999*a*, 1999*b*) show that stock options in listed Belgian companies are relatively rare: none of the non-executive directors received stock options and only 15 per cent of the executive directors had stock options. Van der Elst (1999*b*) investigates the evolution of total board remuneration for the companies forming the Bel-20 stock index of the Brussels Exchange. Over the period of 1988 to 1995, the average remuneration of the board has increased by 44 per cent from about BEF 50m. to BEF 72m., which is an increase in real terms of about 20 per cent. It should be noted that the size of the board of directors in these top 20 companies has not changed significantly over this period with an average of 17.1 in 1988 and of 17.0 in 1995. Whereas no relation is found between directors' pay and corporate performance, remuneration depends strongly on corporate size. However, the economic significance of this relation is limited: an increase of BEF 1 b. (£15.5m.) increases total board remuneration by only BEF 151,000 (£2,340). Larger companies seem to rely more on 'tantièmes' to compensate their directors, but there is no evidence that these are related to profits.

The comparatively modest growth in remuneration in Belgian Bel-20 companies, as well as the reliance on fixed compensation, stands in stark contrast with the USA and UK, where performance-related pay, such as bonuses and share options, constitute the larger part of the total managerial compensation, and where the increase in total compensation packages has been much stronger (Conyon and Murphy 2000*a*, 2000*b*).

7. CONCLUSION

A low ownership concentration, as found in Anglo-American countries, brings about high stock liquidity, so that investors can pursue a short-term return-maximizing portfolio strategy. As a consequence, the agency conflicts between management and shareholders may be substantial. When voting power is dispersed, free-riding on monitoring efforts might occur, as a single shareholder bears all the costs of control, but benefits only pro rata of his share stake. Hence, the disciplining of underperformance is left exclusively to the market for corporate control (see QI, Table 1.1). As a result, in this type of environment, legislation and codes of conduct should focus on shareholder value, shareholder activism, stock options and performance-related pay for management, accountability and independence of the board of directors, fiduciary duties of directors, and (hostile) acquisitions.

In contrast, Belgium offers a very different environment, as corporate ownership is highly concentrated. The fact that large blocks of shares are held by few investors, combined with the opportunity to install anti-takeover defences, almost completely precludes a hostile-acquisitions market. High control power has the advantage that it reduces managerial discretion and the danger of expropriation of investors' money by the managers. However, this reduction of agency conflicts between management and shareholders has an important drawback: it requires an investment of a large proportion of shareholder wealth and a long-term commitment, due to reduced stock liquidity. The major shareholder's investment is to some extent 'locked up' in the company. However, throughout Continental Europe, several devices (e.g. dual-class shares) have been created to maintain control, while allowing a reduction in cash-flow rights. One of these devices is widely used in Belgium and consists of setting up a pyramid of ownership. Whereas pyramids of share stakes require a smaller investment (smaller cash-flow rights), the large shareholder still keeps control over his target company.

The costs of reduced liquidity for a large Belgian shareholder may be more than compensated for by the value of control, as control can allow a large shareholder to extract private benefits from the company. Examples of expropriation of the rights of minority shareholders (sometimes also called 'tunnelling') are given in Johnson *et al.* (2000): investment in assets subsequently sold or leased to a controlling shareholder, transfer pricing advantageous to the controlling shareholders, loan guarantees granted to the controlling shareholder, or expropriation of corporate opportunities, are seldom penalized by courts. An example of expropriation of corporate opportunities is the case of Tractebel in 1999–2000. Tractebel, a large utilities firm, pursued an aggressive international growth strategy, expanding in the energy sectors of the former Soviet Union and Latin America. The main shareholder, Suez/Lyonnaise des Eaux, a French holding company with a strong utilities division, tried to curb Tractebel's international expansion in order to limit competition between Tractebel and Suez/Lyonnaise des Eaux' energy subsidiaries. Tractebel's recalcitrant CEO, who intended to continue Tractebel's international expansion, was subsequently dismissed by Suez/Lyonnaise des Eaux. This example shows that private benefits of control could lead to another kind of agency costs for the minority shareholders, as the major shareholders could adopt a corporate policy at the detriment of the minority.

Consequently, legislation against the expropriation of small shareholders is needed. Current legislation protects minority shareholders against price discrimination in the case of takeovers: when a shareholder has bought a substantial (controlling) share stake, he is obliged to make a tender offer to all shareholders at a price at least equal to that of the large share block. Minority shareholders, owning 1 per cent of the equity capital, can also introduce a 'minority claim' at the courts if they believe that the company is not being run for the benefit of all shareholders (e.g. in the case of large shareholder expropriation). Provided that sufficient minority protection is in place, a control-oriented system can provide some advantages. Firstly, the share stakes of the large shareholders are relatively illiquid, but the presence of share blocks may avoid short termism. Secondly, small shareholders can take a short-term investment strategy and can afford to rebalance their portfolios frequently.

By analysing the relationship between poor corporate performance and board restructuring in the presence of large shareholdings, some studies conclude that there is little evidence of significant large-shareholder monitoring when performance is poor. Both poor share price and accounting performance will lead in subsequent years to higher executive board turnover (corrected for retirements, deaths and illness) and to disciplinary CEO turnover. Institutional shareholders or holding companies owning large equity stakes in poorly performing companies do not seem to discipline underperforming management, but industrial and commercial companies do appear to discipline executive directors. Although poor performance triggers some changes in ownership, this market in share stakes is only weakly related to board restructuring.

An important factor in reducing agency conflicts between management and share-holders is board structure. A large percentage of non-executive directors, as well as the separation of the functions of CEO and chairman, facilitates dismissing bad management. The recent codes of conduct for good corporate governance proposed in 1998 by the stock exchange, the commission for banking and finance, and the employers' organization, all emphasize the need for independent boards. Still, the positive relation between executive director turnover and the percentage of non-executive directors may reflect large shareholder monitoring, because it is the large shareholders who *de facto* nominate their representatives to the board, or at least have some say over nominations.

Given that there is no evidence that holding companies do monitor the companies in which they hold large equity participations, one could question the role of holding companies in corporate governance. The fact that holding companies do not seem to use their control power may justify the discount that financial markets place on the value of the holding companies (compared to the sum of market values of all sub-sidiaries and controlled companies). Still, some evidence was found that holding companies create an internal capital market and relieve some liquidity constraints of the companies they control.

Linking top-management pay to corporate performance is one way of aligning managers' incentives to those of shareholders. However, such a relation is currently not present in Belgian companies. Only recently have managerial stock options been introduced, and the fixed remuneration is strongly related to corporate size. There is currently still a need for more disclosure of the whole remuneration package of top management, and, more specifically, of the stock option or warrant packages offered to management.

Since the main potential agency conflict is between the majority and minority share-holders, strong minority protection is needed, as is enforceability of minority rights in court. In an international context, it seems that the protection of shareholder rights is significantly lagging behind that provided in Anglo-American countries.

Notes

1. In contrast, Goergen and Renneboog (2001*a*) point out that shareholder activism is rising in the UK, with the majority of insurance companies and investment and pension funds casting their voting rights.

2. First, they investigate the extent to which a country adheres to the 'one-share-one-vote' rule. Second, a shareholder protection index is constructed. The index measures whether proxy voting by mail is allowed, whether minority protection mechanisms are in place, and whether a minimum percentage of share capital entitles a shareholder to call for an extraordinary general meeting. Third, the creditor rights are aggregated into an index which is higher when the creditor can take possession of the company in case of financial distress, when there are no re-strictions on workouts and reorganizations and when absolute priority of creditors is upheld. Finally, the Rule of Law index produced by the rating agency International Country Risk indicates the country risk and the degree to which laws are enforced.

3. A similar conclusion was drawn for a sample of French listed companies in Dherment and Renneboog (2001).
4. Since the Royal Decree of 6 March 1990, large companies are obliged to publish consolidated accounts. In terms of remuneration disclosure, the consolidated report is not an improvement over the unconsolidated reports, because the former only states the total remuneration of all directors including that of directors of subsidiaries.

References for Chapter 8

Barca, F. and M. Becht (2001), *The Control of Corporate Europe*, Oxford: Oxford University Press.

Becht, M. and A. Röell (1999), 'Blockholdings in Europe: An International Comparison', *European Economic Review*, 1049–56.

—— and C. Mayer (2001), 'The control of corporate Europe', in Barca and Becht (eds.), *The Control of Corporate Europe*.

—— A. Chapelle, and L. Renneboog (2000), 'Shareholding Cascades: Separation of Ownership and Control in Belgium', in Barca and Becht (eds.), *The Control of Corporate Europe*.

Conyon, M. J. and K. J. Murphy, (forthcoming *a*), The Prince and the Pauper? CEO pay in the US and UK, *Economic Journal*.

—— —— (forthcoming *b*), 'Stock-based Executive Compensation', in Renneboog *et al.* (eds.), *Convergence and Diversity of Corporate Governance Regimes and Capital Markets*.

Cornelis, L. and J. Peeters (1992) 'De gemeenschappelijke beleggingsfondsen envennootschappen', in L. Cornelis *et al.* (eds.), *De Nieuwe Beurswetgeving*, Leuven: Jan Ronse Instituut-K.U. 302–20.

Coughlan, A. T. and R. M. Schmidt (1985), 'Executive Compensation, Managerial Turnover, and Firm Performance: An Empirical Investigation', *Journal of Accounting and Economics*, 7: 42–66.

Crama, Y., L. Leruth, L. Renneboog, and J. Urbain (1999), 'Corporate Governance Structures, Control and Performance in European Markets: A Tale of Two Systems', CentER Discussion paper, Tilburg University.

David, R. and J. Brierley (1985), *Major Legal Systems in the World Today*, London: Stevens and Sons.

Deloof, M. (1998), 'Internal Capital Markets, Bank Borrowing and Financing Constraints: Evidence from Belgian Firms', *Journal of Business Finance and Accounting*, 25: 945–65.

—— and M. Jegers (1996), 'Trade Credit, Product Quality and Intragroup Grade: Some European Evidence', *Financial Management*, 25: 33–43.

—— —— (1999), 'Trade Credit, Corporate Groups and the Financing of Belgian Firms', *Journal of Business Finance and Accounting*, 26: 945–966.

Dherment, I. and L. Renneboog (2001), 'Share Price Reactions to CEO Resignations and Large Shareholder Monitoring in Listed French Companies', in Renneboog *et al.* (eds.) *Convergence and Diversity of Corporate Governance Regimes and Capital Markets*.

Franks, J., C. Mayer, and L. Renneboog (forthcoming), 'Who Disciplines the Management of Poorly Performing Companies?', *Journal of Financial Intermediation*.

Goergen, M. (1998), *Corporate Governance and Financial Performance: A Study of German and UK Initial Public Offerings*, Cheltenham: Edward Elgar.

—— and L. Renneboog (2000), 'Insider Control by Large Investor Groups and Managerial Disciplining in Belgian Listed Companies', *Managerial Finance*, 26/10: 22–41.

—— and L. Renneboog (2001*a*), 'Strong Managers and Passive Institutional Investors in the UK', in Barca and Becht (eds.), *The Control of Corporate Europe*.

Goergen, M. and L. Renneboog (2001*b*), 'Prediction of Control Concentration in German and UK IPOs', in Renneboog *et al.* (eds.), *Convergence and Diversity of Corporate Governance Regimes and Capital Markets.*

Johnson, S., R. La Porta, F. Lopez-de-Silanes, and A. Shleifer (2000), 'Tunnelling', NBER Working Paper, 7523.

La Porta, R., F. Lopez-de-Silanes, A. Shleifer, and R. Vishny (1997), 'Legal Determinants of External Finance', *Journal of Finance*, 52: 1131–50.

—— —— —— —— (1999), 'Corporate Ownership Around the World', *Journal of Finance*, 54: 471–517.

McCahery, J. and L. Renneboog (2000), 'Perspectives sur la diversité et la convergence des régimes du gouvernance des entreprises', *Gouvernance*, 1: 51–84.

Renneboog, L. (1997), 'Shareholding Concentration and Pyramidal Ownership Structures in Belgium', in M. Balling, E. Hennessy and R. O'Brien (eds.), *Corporate Governance, Financial Markets and Global Convergence*, Boston: Kluwer Academic Publishers.

—— (1998), 'Corporate Governance Systems: The Role of Ownership, External Finance and Regulation (part I)', *Corporate Governance International*, 1: 37–48.

—— (1999), 'Corporate Governance Systems: The Role of Ownership, External Finance and Regulation (part II)', *Corporate Governance International*, 2: 4–20.

—— (2000), 'Ownership, Managerial Control and the Governance of Poorly Performing Companies Listed on the Brussels Stock Exchange', *Journal of Banking and Finance*, 24: 1959–95.

—— J. McCahery, P. Moerland, and T. Raaijmakers (eds.) (2001), *Convergence and Diversity of Corporate Governance Regimes and Capital Markets*, Oxford: Oxford University Press.

Van Der Elst, C. (1999*a*), 'Corporate governance en institutionele beleggers in Belgie en West-Europa', Working paper 1999-9, Financial Law Institute, University of Ghent.

—— (1999*b*), 'De remuneratie van de raad van bestuur van de Bel-20 vennootschappen', Working paper 1999-11, Financial Law Institute, University of Ghent.

—— (2000), 'The Equity Markets, Ownership Structures and Control: Towards An International Harmonisation?', Working paper 2000-4, Financial Law Institute, University of Ghent.

Verwilst, H. (1992), 'Aandelenbezit door banken', *Bank- en Financiewezen*, 367–71.

Warner, J. B., R. L. Watts, and K. H. Wruck (1988), 'Stock Prices and Top Management Changes', *Journal of Financial Economics*, 20: 431–60.

Wymeersch, E. (1994), 'Elements of Comparative Corporate Governance in Western Europe', in M. Isaksson and R. Skog (eds.), *Aspects of Corporate Governance*, Stockholm: Juristförlaget. 83–116.

—— (1998), 'De Belgische initiatieven inzake corporate governance en Belgische institutionele beleggers en corporate governance', in Instituut voor Bestuurders (ed.), *Corporate Governance: Het Belgisch perspectief*, Antwerp: Intersentia, 55–86, 183–215.

9

Germany

EKKEHART BOEHMER[1]

1. INTRODUCTION

Corporate governance is currently a topic of great worldwide interest to academics, legislators, and practitioners. In addition to several academic articles, it has prompted active involvement of the OECD, the EU, the German Monopolkommission, the Bundestag, and several other institutions.[2] Especially in comparison to the Anglo-American system, German corporate governance is characterized by lesser reliance on capital markets and outside investors, but a stronger reliance on large inside investors and financial institutions to achieve efficiency in the corporate sector.[3] Since data on German corporations have become more easily available in recent years, the discussion has lately become more scientific and started to focus on studying the benefits and costs of the German system.

The empirical results presented in this survey focus on the relationship between ownership structure and firm performance in Germany. I summarize several empirical studies on this topic and put them into the context of the institutional and legal environment in Germany. Due to data restrictions on unlisted firms, most results are based on corporations trading in official markets, representing the first-tier stock market in Germany. These firms have to publish large block-holdings exceeding 25 per cent in their annual reports. While this type of ownership data has been accessible for several years, information on voting control has only become available with the 1995 transposition of the European Union's Large Holdings Directive into national law (*Wertpapierhandelsgesetz*, WpHG).[4]

Germany is characterized by a low stock-market capitalization relative to other developed economies. Prowse (1995) reports that market capitalization corresponds to 51 per cent of GDP in the USA, 90 per cent in the UK, 71 per cent in Japan, and only 29 per cent in Germany. Adjusted for crossholdings, the figures are 48 per cent in the USA, 81 per cent in the UK, 37 per cent in Japan, and 14 per cent in Germany. Using more recent data, Wenger and Kaserer (1997) estimate a relative capitalization of 21 per cent for Germany. Besides reducing true market capitalization, these substantial cross-holdings have implications for the governance of companies which are discussed below.[5]

This review is organized as follows. Section 2 summarizes important features of the legal and institutional environment of German companies. Then I discuss descriptive statistics and background information on ownership structure, voting control, and the identity of owners in section 3. Section 4 describes the disciplining mechanisms that can potentially sanction management. The extant empirical evidence on the relationship between ownership structure and performance is discussed in section 5. The final section concludes and suggests open questions for future research.

2. LEGAL AND INSTITUTIONAL BACKGROUND

This section provides a brief overview on the legal and institutional background in Germany relevant to the discussion below. First, I discuss basic characteristics of legal forms for businesses. Next, I focus on corporations and discuss their governance structure, voting procedures, and the different types of equity securities available.

2.1. *Organizational forms*

German commercial laws define several ways to organize firms with limited or unlimited liability for owners. Table 9.1 lists the basic characteristics of the most important legal forms of German firms. The most relevant legal distinction is between AGs and GmbHs (*Kapitalgesellschaften*), which provide limited liability to owners, and other legal forms. All limited-liability firms are heavily regulated, while other forms have considerable freedom in designing company statutes and contractual relations between owners and other stakeholders. I try to describe the extent of this freedom by a subjective assessment of how imperative the legal rules are (last column). It should be noted that some relatively non-imperative forms are of substantial importance in Germany, most notably *Vereine* (unions) and *Stiftungen* (foundations). *Vereine* (unions) sometimes appear as organizational forms of large enterprises. (For example, the largest German automobile association (ADAC) is organized as a *Verein*, and so are all soccer clubs. Currently, the larger clubs contemplate following the British model and converting to corporations.) *Stiftungen* often appear as dominant stakeholders or sole owners of the largest companies. Herrmann and Franke (1996) analyse the financial performance of companies led by *Stiftungen*. Other forms like the GbR or the *stille Gesellschaft* play only minor roles among larger firms.

2.2. *Regulation of share corporations (Aktiengesellschaften)*

AGs are the only legal form that may list on a stock exchange (except for the less common KGaAs), and I discuss their features in more detail below. Despite the dominance of AGs of the equity markets, understanding other legal forms is very important for investors and other market participants. Since most German AGs have large block-holders, the organizational form of the block-holder can have substantial effects on how well the listed firm is monitored. For example, an individual with unlimited liability (OHG, KG) may have stronger incentives to actively monitor than the employee of a limited-liability GmbH. Moreover, several listed firms are nested into a group structure that may involve several different types of companies, each subject to different

Table 9.1. *Important legal forms of private companies in Germany*

	Limited liability	Minimum capital ('000 DM)	Smallest number of founders	Smallest number of managers	Degree of imperativeness of the legal rules
Aktiengesellschaft (AG)	Yes	100 (§ 7 AktG)	1 (§ 2 AktG)	1 (§76 I AktG)	High
Gesellschaft mit beschränkter Haftung (GmbH)	Yes	50 (at least 0.5 per owner, § 5 I GmbHG)	1 (§ 1 GmbHG)	1 (§ 6 I GmbHG)	High
Kommanditgesellschaft auf Aktien (KGaA)	General partners: No Shareholders: Yes[a]	100 (§ 7 AktG)	5 (§ 280 AktG)	1 (§ 76 I AktG)	High
Kommanditgesellschaft (KG)	General partners: No Limited partners: Yes[b]	—	2[c]	1	Medium
GmbH (or AG) & Co. KG[d]	Yes	50	1	1	Medium
Offene Handelsgesellschaft (OHG)	No	—	1	1	Medium
Eingetragene Genossenschaft (e. G.)	Usually[e]	0	7 (§ 4 GenG)	2 (§ 24 II GenG)	Medium
Gesellschaft bürgerlichen Rechts (GbR)	No	—	1	1	Low
Stille Gesellschaft[f]	Yes (§232 II HGB)	—	—	—	Low
Eingetragener Verein (e. V.)	Yes	0	7 (§ 56 BGB)	1 (§ 26 I BGB)	Low
Stiftung[g]	Not applicable	—	—	—	Low
Banks, any legal form except sole proprietorship	Depends on legal form	ECU 5 Mio.[h]	Depends on legal form	2 (§ 33 IV KWG)	Very high

[a] § 278 I AktG. General partners are referred to as *Komplementäre*, shareholders as *Kommanditaktionäre*.
[b] § 161 I HGB. General partners are referred to as *Komplementäre*, limited partners as *Kommanditisten*.
[c] At least one general partner and at least one limited partner, § 161 I HGB.
[d] This represents a hybrid form where the general partner of a KG is a (limited-liability) GmbH. While the GmbH & Co KG is the most widely used hybrid form, the (unlimited-liability) general partner may also be an AG, and the enclosing form may also be an OHG. If a GmbH or an AG is involved, all regulations affecting these forms still apply.
[e] The e. G. is generally a limited-liability company (§ 2 GenG). Company statutes may deviate from this rule (§ 6 III GenG): In case of bankruptcy, members may be obligated to pay, in addition to their initial investment, a limited or an unlimited amount to creditors.
[f] This is not a stand-alone organization, but rather a way to participate in any other organizational form.
[g] More precisely, this refers to "rechtsfähige Stiftungen bürgerlichen Rechts" that operate a business.
[h] § 33 I KWG, net of securities that have a cumulative preferential dividend.

requirements regarding disclosure and accounting. Without a sound understanding of each part of the group, it is difficult to appropriately value the listed corporation. See Boehmer (1999) for an empirical analysis of voting control over listed firms in Germany and a discussion of the incentives of various block-holder types.

2.2.1. *Shareholder meetings and board structure*

The AG has three governing bodies: the annual general meeting (AGM) of shareholders (*Hauptversammlung*), a supervisory board (*Aufsichtsrat*), and a managing board (*Vorstand*). Hopt (1998) discusses the history of the German two-tiered board system and critically analyses the potential and efficacy of the supervisory board. Baums (1999) provides a description of management and supervisory boards, their respective functions, and related recent legislation.

In the AGM, shareholders generally decide by simple majority, although the law or statutes may require different voting rules (§133 AktG). The supervisory board must have at least three, and at most 21, members (§95 I AktG) and includes worker representatives for all but the smallest AGs (§96 AktG). The supervisory board elects the managing board that must have at least one member. (§ 76 II AktG, except for insurance companies, where the managing board must have at least two members, §34 VAG.) No supervisory-board member may be on the managing board or in a position of similar executive power (§105 AktG). In practice, however, the boards of affiliated firms generally share several members. For example, a subsidiary's supervisory board generally includes members of the parent company's managing board. Table 9.2 summarizes selected features of AGMs and boards for German AGs.

To call an irregular AGM, at least 5 per cent of capital is necessary, although company statutes may specify a smaller percentage. In Germany, no individual compensation package of board members must be published. Aggregates are included in the annual reports. Similarly, since 1995 executives' trading in their firm's shares can be traced by the securities supervisory office (BAWe), but is not made public. Both potentially beneficial disclosure requirements would be in conflict with Germany's strong legal protection of personal data.

There is some evidence that supervisory boards have become larger, less effective, and less powerful since the 1976 Co-determination Act that mandated labour representation on the boards of large corporations. For example, Schroeder and Schrader (1998) find that supervisory board decisions after 1976 are largely limited to those that are legally mandated. Before 1976, the range of issues decided by the board was much broader than the legal minimum. Gorton and Schmid (1998*a*) find that firms with legally mandated equal representation of workers and shareholders on the supervisory board have worse performance but lower risk than other firms. They further find that equal representation also results in greater pay-to-performance sensitivity of compensation to supervisory board members. Thus, it is not clear, whether equal employee representation is good or bad for shareholders.

Hopt (1998) cites earlier studies that find average supervisory sizes of 7 in 1975, and 13.25 in the 1990s (see Korn/Ferry 1996; and Schiffels 1981). He also finds that committees are of little importance in German boards.

Table 9.2. *Shareholders' meetings and boards of stock corporations in Germany*

	% of capital to initiate an irregular AGM	Depositing of shares before the AGM	Maximum term of appointment	Disclosure of executive compensation	Disclosure of information upon request of individual shareholders	Disclosure of executive trading in shares of their company	Legal actions by shareholders against executives
Aktiengesellschaft (AG)	5[a]	3 or 10 days[b]	Management board 5 years, renewable (§ 84 I AktG); supervisory board: 4 years, renewable (§ 102 I AktG)	Aggregates for both boards, respectively[c]	Since 1993: stakes in other firms >10%, or DM 100 Mio market value and the identity of large owners[d]	No	Yes[e]
Additional requirements or special rules for listed companies	None	None	None	None	None	No[f]	None

[a] § 122 I AktG. Company statutes may specify a smaller percentage.

[b] § 123 III, IV AktG. Company statutes may require that shareholders deposit their shares with a notary or a financial institution (under discretion of the shareholders) at least 10 days before the AGM. Company statutes may further require that shareholders register for the AGM at least 3 days before the meeting.

[c] § 285 IX HGB. The aggregate must include all compensation and other benefits to board members that have accrued during the past financial year. Companies are exempt from this rule, if publishing this information allows the public to identify compensation paid to a specific individual (§ 286 IV AktG).

[d] § 131 AktG and KG, 26.8.93 – 2 W 6111/92, ZIP 1993, 1618. This ruling was the result of a successful suit of E. Wenger against Siemens AG. The court argues that since the EU Large Holdings Directive requires disclosure of 10 per cent stakes to the public, at least the same right should apply to shareholders of the firm. Thus, Schneider (1995) expects that after 1996, when the transposition of the Large Holdings Directive becomes effective, stakes exceeding 5% must be disclosed to shareholders. According to Schneider, it is not clear, however, whether this only applies to stakes in listed firms or to stakes in any firm. Schneider's argument that large owners must be disclosed upon request follows the same reasoning.

[e] If executives violate their fiduciary duty according to § 93 AktG, they are generally personally liable for damages to the company. Shareholders representing at least 10 per cent of capital can initiate legal proceedings against executives.

[f] § 17 WpHG explicitly specifies for AGs listed in an official market that data related to specific individuals must be deleted unless it is relevant to a currently prosecuted insider-trading violation. In no instance must this information be published before publicly accessible court proceedings.

Very revealing with respect to shareholders' rights are several suits advanced by Ekkehard Wenger for disclosure of stakes in other firms and hidden reserves.[6] For example, in *Wenger* vs. *Siemens AG* (see Table 9.2) the court compared a shareholder's request for disclosure of stakes held by the firm to the information provided to the general public as intended by the EU Large Holdings Directive. It ruled that shareholders should have at least the information that is soon available to the public. Observers expect similar rulings on related issues in the future (see Schneider, 1995). The fact that a court ruling is necessary to reassure this basic right of shareholders illustrates well the German tradition of preserving the incumbents' power by issuing as little information about the firm's activities as possible.

The corporate code also provides for legal suits by shareholders against executives. §§93 and 116 AktG define the fiduciary duty of the members of both boards and make executives personally liable for damages they have caused to the company by violating these duties.

Finally, there are few differences in the regulatory framework for listed and unlisted firms. While corporations going public have to disclose information on their security holdings in the listing firm on some markets, there are no ongoing reporting requirements in this regard.

2.2.2. *Proxy rules*

§135 AktG governs how shareholders can name proxy agents as their representatives at the AGM (see Table 9.3). Any organization, bank, or other agent of the shareholder may cast the proxy vote. The shareholder has the option to reveal his name, regardless of whether he provides explicit instructions on how to vote his shares or not. Typically, shareholders remain anonymous, deposit their shares with banks, and grant general power of attorney to that bank with respect to all shares in their portfolio. For more discussion on proxy votes see section 4.4 below.

Table 9.3. *Proxy rules in Germany*

	Can company employees exercise proxy votes?	Can banks exercise proxy votes?	Can other individuals or organizations exercise proxy votes?
Aktiengesellschaft	Yes[a]	Yes	Yes
Additional requirements or specific rules for listed companies	None	None	None

[a] §135 AktG. All proxy votes are exercised anonymously in the sense that the owner of the votes is not named publicly (§129 II, III AktG).

2.2.3. *Share types*

Information on different share types is presented in Table 9.4. AGs must issue common stock (*Stammaktien*) with one vote per share. In addition, up to 50 per cent of total capital can be preferred stock (*Vorzugsaktien*), where each share receives a cumulative, preferential dividend (§ 189 AktG). The preference can be defined, for example, in terms of seniority to the dividend claim of common stock or in terms of a larger dividend. Given the preference, these shares may be issued without the right to vote.

Table 9.4. *Important types of limited-liability equity securities in Germany*

Type of share	Issuing legal form	Exchange listing	Voting rights	Requirements for new issues
Stammaktie (common stock)	AG, KGaA	Possible	Always; generally one per share	75% AGM vote[a]
Vorzugsaktie (preferred stock)	AG, KGaA	Possible	Generally no, unless the required cumulative preferential dividend is not paid in two consecutive years, and in special matters of interest to preferred-stock holders[b]	75% AGM vote[c]
Genußschein (participation right)	All	Possible	No	75% AGM vote[d]
Geschäftsanteil (cooperative share)	e. G.	No	Generally one vote per member, independent of stake size[e]	Membership request and management approval[f]
Geschäftsanteil (GmbH share)	GmbH	No	Votes proportional to stake size (§ 47 II GmbHG)	75% AGM vote[g]

[a] § 182 AktG. The company statutes may stipulate more or less restrictive requirements.

[b] §§ 139–141. AGs may only issue shares without votes if they have a cumulative preferred-dividend claim attached.

[c] § 182 AktG. The company statutes may stipulate only requirements that are more restrictive. A different situation arises if a company has already preferred stock outstanding. It that case, old preferred stock-holders must approve new preferred share with equal or better preference with a 75 per cent majority (not adjustable by company statutes and in addition to the AGM approval, §141 II, III AktG). This additional vote is not required if further issues of preferred shares have been explicitly approved before the first preferred issue.

[d] For AGs and KGaAs: § 221 AktG. The company statutes may stipulate more or less restrictive requirements. For all other forms, issuance generally requires 75 per cent majorities.

[e] § 43 III GenG. The statutes can grant a maximum of three more voting rights to specific members.

[f] § 15 GenG. Increasing the share of existing members requires a 75 per cent AGM majority (§ 16 II GenG).

[g] A seasoned equity offering by a GmbH requires a change of statutes and thus a 75 per cent majority (§§ 3 I, 53 II GmbHG).

Strictly speaking, however, these shares do have a (dormant) vote; §140 II requires that each preferred share has a vote if the preferred dividend is not paid for two years in a row. In addition, preferred shareholders may have the right to vote in matters of special interest to them (§141 AktG).

In addition, firms may issue *Genußscheine* (participation rights), that are very similar to US-type preferred stock. These rights have no voting rights attached and may be designed sufficiently debt-like to make dividends tax deductible, or sufficiently equity-like to be included in banks' equity capital. Although *Genußscheine* can be listed on stock exchanges, banks primarily use them (one prominent exception is family-owned Bertelsmann AG, whose only listed securities are *Genußscheine*). New issues of equity securities generally require a 75 per cent majority at the AGM.

3. OWNERSHIP AND CONTROL STRUCTURES OF LISTED CORPORATIONS

Germany is characterized by highly concentrated share ownership and substantial deviations from the 'one-share-one-vote' paradigm. Among the different shareholder types, banks and insurance companies play an important role in controlling listed firms. In this section, I discuss the institutional background and descriptive statistics relating to the control over German corporations. Before that, I present an example of control structures in Germany, VEBA AG.

3.1. *An example of corporate control in Germany*

Germany has many examples of cross-holdings or listed firms that share the same large shareholders. To illustrate control structures in Germany, however, I believe it is more instructive to look at the role played by the proxy-voting system. Since proxy votes are not reported within the disclosures mandated by the *Wertpapierhandelsgesetz* (WpHG), they play the curious role of potentially making control rights anonymous. Moreover, shareholder representatives on the supervisory board often have no obvious relation to actual block-holders. Rather, they frequently represent banks that exercise large blocks of proxy votes. Both of these features are illustrated in the following example of VEBA AG, using data from 1996 (see Table 9.5).

Veba's 1996 BAWe disclosures show that Allianz AG Holding controls 11.46 per cent of VEBA AG's voting shares. No further block-holders controlling more than 5 per cent are reported. Thus, Veba appears to be a widely held company with one block-holder, who controls a minority stake. Interestingly, the attendance list of the 1996 annual shareholder meeting (supplied by VEBA) tells a different story.

The 1996 AGM was attended by 49.96 per cent of the voting rights. Ranked by the percentage of attending votes, the largest block-holders were Dresdner Bank (33.3 per cent) and Deutsche Bank (9.3 per cent). Various investment companies voted about 18 per cent, other banks about 31 per cent. Out of the bank votes, less than 1 per cent was derived from equity actually owned by the participating bank. All other bank votes

Table 9.5. *Exercised votes at Veba AG's annual general meeting, 23 May 1996 (Germany)*

Voting share-holders	Own shares voted	Other directly controlled shares	Deposited shares	Total shares voted	Per cent of attending par value	Per cent of total par value
Total attending				1,219,423,255	100.00	49.96
Total not attending				1,221,472,445		50.04
Total par value				2,440,895,700		100.00
Dresdner Bank	0	0	405,939,535	405,939,535	33.29	16.63
Kapitalanlage-gesellschaften	0	219,512,250	0	216,715,250	17.77	8.88
Deutsche Bank	0	0	113,401,145	113,401,145	9.30	4.65
Other German private banks	0	400,000	112,129,320	112,529,320	9.23	4.61
Other companies	3,200	93,552,800	0	93,556,000	7.67	3.83
WestLB	0	0	42,820,065	42,820,065	3.51	1.75
Chase Bank	0	0	36,202,560	36,202,560	2.97	1.48
Other state banks	75,000	0	34,702,220	34,777,220	2.85	1.42
BHF-Bank	0	0	24,426,855	24,426,855	2.00	1.00
Commerzbank	0	0	22,793,400	22,793,400	1.87	0.93
Other credit unions	0	0	18,244,415	18,244,415	1.50	0.75
Bayerische Hypobank	0	0	16,782,800	16,782,800	1.38	0.69
DG Bank	0	0	14,982,660	14,982,660	1.23	0.61
NordLB	0	0	14,615,585	14,615,585	1.20	0.60
Bayerische Vereinsbank	0	0	13,968,900	13,968,900	1.15	0.57
Vereins-u. Westbank	0	0	13,387,755	13,387,755	1.10	0.55
Bankgesellschaft Berlin	5,780,800	0	2,197,795	7,978,595	0.65	0.33
Foreign banks	0	0	6,410,420	6,410,420	0.53	0.26
Small shareholders	n.a.	n.a.	n.a.	4,019,820	0.33	0.16
Shareholder associations	0	1,258,950	1,815,005	3,073,955	0.25	0.13
Allianz Kapital-anlagegesellschaft	0	0	2,797,000	2,797,000	0.23	0.11

Note: n.a.=not available.

Sources: Based on Becht and Boehmer (1999) and VEBA AG.

(about 70 per cent of the votes present) were derived from proxies. Companies controlled about 8 per cent, and the small remainder was exercised by other parties.

Most notably, Allianz voted only 0.23 per cent of the attending voting rights, and no other company officially controlled by Allianz appeared on the attendance list. Therefore, assuming that Allianz has an interest in the value of its sizeable stake, it must be the case that Allianz has deposited its shares with a bank (and instructs the bank how to vote) or has it under management by a related investment company.

The shareholder representatives of the supervisory board are consistent with the major voting blocks. On 23 May 1996, the chairman of the supervisory board was Hermann Josef Strenger, chairman of the supervisory board of Bayer AG, Leverkusen (Allianz AG reported to control 5 per cent of Bayer AG). Allianz AG is represented by its CEO Dr Henning Schulte-Noelle. Dresdner Bank AG is represented by the managing board member Dr Bernd Voss and Deutsche Bank AG by its then-CEO Hilmar Kopper, although neither bank has any equity interest in VEBA.

The VEBA example illustrates a few important features of corporate control in Germany. First, control structures can be opaque despite of the disclosures mandated by the 1996 WpHG. In our example, it remains unclear how the only major block-holder exerts its influence. In contrast, banks effectively control the company, although neither of them had to disclose that fact publicly. Second, the proxy-voting system allows controlling shareholders to remain anonymous. Third, proxy voting rights are sufficiently important to allow the respective banks seats on the supervisory board. Holding no significant equity positions in VEBA, these board seats are likely representing creditors and not, as legally mandated, shareholders.

3.2. *Concentration of ownership*

Mella and Jähnke (1996) and several other papers report descriptive statistics on the concentration of ownership. Franks and Mayer (1996, 1997) document that out of 171 large corporations, 85 per cent have a shareholder owning more than 25 per cent, and 57 per cent have a shareholder owning more than 50 per cent of the equity. Boehmer (2000) provides evidence that these figures are representative for all listed firms over the period from 1985 to 1997. He also finds that in 1996, 77 per cent of the median firms' voting rights associated with officially traded shares are controlled by large shareholders (holding more than 5 per cent), corresponding to 47 per cent of gross market capitalization.

3.3. *Ownership versus voting rights*

German law allows various devices that detach control rights from cash flow rights. First, shares may have limited but not multiple voting rights. Corporate law (*Aktiengesetz*, AktG) explicitly allows non-voting shares up to the amount of ordinary shares outstanding (§139 II AktG). Non-voting shares are a potentially powerful mechanism for doubling the relative voting power of ordinary shares, but are primarily used by relatively small, family-owned companies. Since the securities law (*Wertpapierhandelsgesetz*, WpHG) does not require disclosing the ownership of non-voting shares, their dormant voting rights can represent a potentially important pool of hidden voting power.

In contrast, multiple voting rights per share or voting caps are illegal. Multiple voting rights could be authorized by state authorities until 1998 (§12 AktG), but are currently being phased out by most listed companies due to new legislation in 1998

(KonTraG). Similarly, § 134 I AktG used to allow voting caps. They too are currently being phased out due to the 1998 KonTraG.

Company statutes may further impose voting caps that limit the percentage of votes by individual shareholders. Other important devices for exerting control are group structures involving cross-shareholdings, contractual arrangements, personal interlocking of management and supervisory board members, and pyramids. Cross-holdings effectively imply (potentially illegal, §71, 71d AktG) holdings of own shares and increase the voting power of any existing block-holder.[7] In addition, they promote 'voting cartels' where involved management teams vote in favour of each other at the respective annual general meetings (AGMs). Contractual arrangements delegating control are widely used within German groups. Pyramids with outside equity on various levels may concentrate highly leveraged control at the top layer. See Baums (1993), Adams (1994), or Wenger and Kaserer (1997) for sample cases and discussions.

Probably the most important source of voting rights deviating from ownership is the German proxy-voting system (summarized in Table 9.3). Typically, shareholders remain anonymous, deposit their shares with banks, and grant general power of attorney to that bank with respect to all shares in their portfolio. Since disclosure of proxy votes is not legally mandated, they represent another important source of potentially hidden voting power. Voting rights that have been exercised are publicly accessible at local company registers. There are several obstacles to assessing the true voting power of a bank: (1) exercised votes need not represent all voting rights available to the bank; (2) no centralized register or electronic access to the data exists; and (3) in many cases it takes months until documents are accessible, because the local registers are severely understaffed. Most importantly, proxy by mail is not allowed in Germany. The natural consequences include low attendance rates at AGMs and a substantial increase in the effective voting power of block-holders and banks.

3.4. *Identity of ultimate block-holders*

Iber (1985) identifies foreign shareholders, the German government, and families as the most important German shareholders. His analysis is based on cash-flow ownership, because for his sample periods (1963, 1973, and 1983) no voting data was available. Boehmer (1999) analyses firms reporting voting rights in excess of 5 per cent, which is mandatory since new legislation (WpHG) became effective in 1995. He shows that compared to other developed economies, the German stock market is dominated by large shareholders. Large block-holders control 77 per cent of the median firm's voting rights, corresponding to 47 per cent of the market value of all firms listed in Germany's official markets. Banks, industrial firms, holdings, and insurance companies control about two-thirds of this amount. Most importantly for outside investors, due to current legislation it is unclear for neither group who exerts ultimate control over the shareholding firm itself. For the remaining block-holders, only blocks controlled by voting pools and individuals can be traced back to the highest level of ownership. Taken together, both groups control only 5.6 per cent of all reported blocks. The German government controls 8 per cent, and it is not clear who ultimately is responsible for the consequences of decisions. Without knowing whose interests are represented using those voting rights, it is very difficult for outside investors to assess the incentives of large shareholders in the same firm to act in the interest of all shareholders.

Additional opaqueness results from 'control alliances' among the largest shareholders. For example, Boehmer (1999) finds that the top five banks and the top three insurance companies are closely related through direct ownership and voting control. Jointly, these eight firms report control over 14 per cent of all listed firms, or a market value of DM 147b. considering only reported voting blocks. He argues that this figure substantially underestimates the true value under control of these block-holders. The reason is that large ownership links exist between the large shareholders that do not trigger legal reporting requirements. Consequently, joint majority control by business groups cannot be inferred from published data.

3.5. *Share ownership and control by financial institutions*

Baums and Fraune (1995) analyse AGM participation and voting for those 24 out of the top 100 listed firms that have more than 50 per cent of their shares widely held. In 1992, about 58 per cent of outstanding voting rights are present at the AGM. Out of the attending votes, banks control 13 per cent due to own shareholdings, 10 per cent due to dependent investment funds, and 61 per cent due to proxy votes. Thus, Baums and Fraune find that banks control 84 per cent of all attending votes while owning only about 7 per cent of equity. The five largest banks alone control about 45 per cent of attending votes, and additionally a majority in each other's AGMs. They further show that the resulting voting power is typically used to support management; while legally mandated items on the AGM agenda are approved with an average of about 99.8 per cent of attending votes, only between 0.35 and 7.74 per cent support items are opposed by management.

Supervisory-board composition has an additional influence on control leverage. Schroeder and Schrader (1998) find that in 1995, financial institutions held 19 per cent of the seats of shareholder representatives on the boards of the top 100 German corporations. Even excluding mandates held by managers of other bank-controlled firms, this figure is about twice the percentage of equity owned by these institutions. Gorton and Schmid (1998*b*) find that bank representation on supervisory boards increases with their direct equity stake, but also with the fraction of proxy votes. Thus, due to proxy votes and board membership, bank control over German corporations is substantially larger than it would be in a 'one-share-one-vote' situation. See also Albach and Kless (1982), who analyse personnel interlockings among the 75 largest German firms for the years 1964 and 1978.

3.6. *Transparency of ownership and control*

Becht and Boehmer (1999) analyse legal provisions relating to corporate transparency in Germany. Using disclosed ownership information, they show that despite the new securities trading law (WpHG) of 1995 the practical efficacy of disclosure regulation is very low. In several cases, ultimate ownership cannot be inferred from published filings. On the one hand, the formation of business groups involving less regulated legal forms as intermediate layers can systematically reduce transparency. On the other hand, the implementation of the law is not practical and not very effective. The paper illustrates the importance of additional reporting requirements for proxy voting by banks, voting control by investment funds, by firms not listed in an official market, and by business groups whose members jointly control a majority in each other. So far, neither needs to be reported to the public or, in the case of proxy votes, is not readily available.

4. LIMITATIONS ON THE MONITORING OF MANAGEMENT

In the following sections, I discuss potential mechanisms for disciplining management. Given the high concentration of ownership in Germany, block-holders and especially banks can potentially exert control over management, while the role of small shareholders is negligible. Analysing the turnover of managing and supervisory boards, Franks and Mayer (1996), however, find no evidence that either banks or other block-holders act on behalf of other shareholders. While they document an active market in large blocks, they conclude that it cannot substitute for a market for corporate control as in the USA or the UK.

4.1. *The market for corporate control*

Due to the concentrated ownership of shares, hostile takeovers are not possible without support by incumbent block-holders. While management can be bypassed (making an offer hostile), large shareholders and/or banks must generally be courted to support the bid for it to succeed. Since there are no immediate publication requirements for such negotiations, little is known about the consequences for the target firm. Some individual cases are illustrated by Peltzer (1989), Franks and Mayer (1996), and Jenkinson and Ljungqvist (1997). The latter paper in particular documents well the hostile character of several transactions, challenging the belief that hostile takeovers do not exist in Germany. On the other hand, outright hostile tender offers are difficult to achieve. The recent hostile attempts against Thyssen AG and Mannesmann AG involve two of only four officially listed firms that have no large block-holders (see Boehmer, 1999). It seems unlikely that hostile offers against other firms can proceed without the support of banks or block-holders.

4.2. *Managerial remuneration*

Empirical analysis of the pay–performance relationship is difficult in Germany because only aggregate, not individual compensation is disclosed. §285 IX HGB requires that the aggregate compensation of board members and management, respectively, is included in the annual report. Companies are exempt from this rule if publishing this information allows the public to identify compensation paid to a specific individual (§ 286 IV AktG).

Furthermore, it is very common for managers of the parent firm to hold a seat on the supervisory boards of one or more subsidiaries. Since their compensation includes fractions of several aggregates, it is nearly impossible to calculate the total remuneration of the most important managers. Despite these difficulties, Schwalbach and Graßhoff (1997) analyse the relationship between managerial pay and performance and find little evidence of a positive sensitivity. Schmid (1996b) obtains a marginally significant positive relationship, and Knoll, Knoesel, and Probst (1997) find no sensitivity for the remuneration of supervisory board members. Thus, different samples and methodologies yield diverging estimates. Unfortunately, due to the data problems mentioned above, neither result can ultimately answer the question of how remuneration depends on performance. In a related study, Kaplan (1994) finds no significant relationship between bank control and board turnover for German corporations.

4.3. *Block-holders*

Large block-holders have incentives to maximize the value of their shares. Whether this involves maximizing firm value depends on the degree to which they can (or cannot) extract transfers from small shareholders. First, the typical German group includes several firms with outside equity and several without. Thus, it may be rational for large shareholders to transfer resources from subsidiaries with outside equity to other group units. Second, German law effectively allows sizeable transfers to block-holders once a coalition owns at least 75 per cent of the votes. Specifically, a 75 per cent majority may factually make a binding tender offer to minority shareholders below market value.[8] The 75 per cent majority need not even be held by one party, since two or more large block-holders may collude. Wenger, Hecker, and Knoesel (1996) analyse such offers to minority shareholders and find that in 39 of 53 cases, the offer is below the market value on the day before, and in 32 cases below the market value three months earlier. For the former 39 cases, the market value on average exceeds the compensation to minority shareholders by 74 per cent. Additionally, block-holders may use cross-holdings and pyramidal groups to transfer resources from subsidiaries with outside shareholders to units without. Therefore, a priori it is not clear that it is easier for block-holders to increase the value of their stake by acting on behalf of all shareholders, an issue clearly deserving future research efforts.

4.4. *Institutional investors*

The German pension system currently does not involve public funds, but rather leaves pension contributions under the control of either the government or the employer. Therefore, institutional investors consist primarily of banks, insurance firms, dependent investment funds, and foreign funds. Of these, banks play the most important role. They can exert control over corporations in several ways. The most obvious are direct ownership of shares, the provision of loans, by being represented on supervisory boards, and other business relations. Perhaps most importantly, a further channel of substantial influence comes via proxy votes that small shareholders delegate to the banks administrating their stock portfolios. For discussions of the German proxy-voting mechanism, see, for example, Köndgen (1994), Baums and Randow (1995) and Baums (1996*b*). For a comparison of different mechanisms in the EU member countries, see Baums (1997). None of these channels taken individually constitutes an issue that would draw public attention in the way that 'the power of banks' has in recent years. Rather, the combination of power from the various sources is what deserves critical and thorough attention.

The capital representatives on German supervisory boards are legally required to represent shareholders, voice their concerns at annual general meetings (AGMs), and guard shareholders against value-decreasing actions by management. From this perspective, the important issue is how many board seats are filled by bank representatives and how many votes are controlled by banks, relative to the shares directly owned by banks. Edwards and Fischer (1994) and Gerum, Steinmann, and Fees (1988) show that banks hold more seats than warranted by their shareholdings, and, in addition, the correlation between the number of bank seats and direct bank stakes is low. Since banks also control most votes of small shareholders via the proxy system, the important question is whether the interests of banks coincide with those of shareholders.

Due to their information advantage, banks are potentially very effective monitors but will generally have little incentive to act on behalf of other shareholders. First, due to proxy votes and board membership their control rights substantially exceed their interest in equity cash flow. Second, for the typical firm, the amount of debt held by banks exceeds the amount of equity held in the same firm by a factor greater than ten and much likely substantially larger.[9] A third reason is additional fee-generating activity involving these firms. It is widely known that decisions maximizing the value of loans often reduce the market value of equity. The same argument holds for fee-maximizing decisions. Therefore, the objective of the banks should be to balance decisions increasing the value of debt versus those increasing the value of equity. Given the substantially larger size of the debt portfolio, it is rational, legal, and fully ethical for banks to act as debtors in all respects.[10] The legally and politically sensitive issue is that board seats that do not mirror share ownership and proxy votes supposed to exclusively represent shareholders are used to achieve that goal. While this practice is legal and widespread, it would be in the interest of shareholders to prevent it and thereby increase firm value by assuring that voting rights are exercised in their own interests.

In this sense, the voting process is an essential element towards shareholder-oriented AGMs and supervisory boards.[11] It represents the major source of the potential mismatch between banks' cash-flow risk and voting power and several proposals have been made to modify it. Köndgen (1994) suggests professionalizing the proxy agents, and discusses incentive problems of various alternatives. Baums (1996*b*) and Latham (1999) explicitly suggest different procedures for electing voting agents. Baums proposes new regulation that lets shareholders elect one or more representatives who exercise their voting rights. Latham, in contrast, proposes a market solution where professional firms compete for shareholders' voting rights.

Furthermore, if maximizing the value of debt is the common goal of banks, disagreement across banks on the firm's optimal course of action is very unlikely. Therefore, the number of different banks casting votes at the AGM does not appear to matter. The results in Baums and Fraune (1995) support this, because banks virtually always vote in favour of management proposals, independent of the number of banks involved.[12]

These arguments illustrate the importance of bank influence for affected firms. If banks can indeed exert influence over firms by voting at AGMs and by being represented on supervisory boards, their decisions are likely to affect firm value. If banks use their power to maximize debt value, their decisions will have a negative effect on the value of equity. Thus, the effectiveness of banks as actively monitoring shareholder representatives is ultimately an empirical question and is discussed below.

5. OWNERSHIP STRUCTURE, BANK CONTROL, AND FIRM PERFORMANCE

From the previous discussion, block-holders and banks are the main candidates for efficient and effective monitoring of management. Thus, the question is whether they use their power to act on behalf of other shareholders or whether they act in their own interest (transferring resources from other shareholders or maximizing the value of other financial interests in the firm). Due to the important public policy implications, most empirical studies analyse the relationship between bank control and firm performance.

Before I report this evidence, two papers analyse the effect of ownership concentration from a different angle. Weigand and Lehmann (1998) find a positive relationship between ownership concentration and performance (ROA) if a family is the block-holder. Herrmann and Franke (1996) compare the performance of foundation-owned firms to that of other corporations. Although foundation-owned firms should exhibit the greatest agency problem, they find no significant differences in performance. They document some evidence, however, that foundation-owned firms act more in the interest of employees as opposed to equity holders.

Most studies on the effects of bank control take ownership structure as exogenous and model selected performance measures as a function of bank control, other ownership characteristics, and various control variables. Unfortunately, the results are inconsistent with each other, and extremely sensitive to the sample, the period, and the methodology.

Specifically, only Cable (1985) and Gorton and Schmid (1998b) obtain evidence of a positive relationship between bank control and performance. Cable (1985) finds a positive relationship between a concentration measure of bank votes, bank representation on the supervisory board, and the ratio of bank loans to total debt on average performance between 1968 and 1972. (Cable (1985) gives little indication of his sampling period. He uses proxy-voting data from 1974, thus implying a relationship to past performance.) The small sample of only 48 firms diminishes the explanatory power of the study. More problematic is using the ratio of equity income to total assets as a performance measure. As Chirinko and Elston (1996) point out, equity income is negatively related to leverage. They find that bank-influenced firms have lower leverage and conclude that Cable's performance measure is biased upwards.

Gorton and Schmid (1998b) find that bank ownership significantly increases the return on equity while proxy votes have no effect. When performance is measured by the market-to-book ratio of equity, the result is less pronounced. Their estimations are based on two sets of firms each in 1975 and 1986, both years with below-average GNP growth. Chirinko and Elston (1996) therefore suspect that the results may not be representative. Supporting this claim, Schmid (1996a) uses the same basic methodology as in Gorton and Schmid (1998b) but a sample from 1990. The author documents a U-shaped relationship between direct bank ownership and return on equity. The fraction of bank ownership representing the minimum varies with concentration measures of all shareholders and banks, respectively. Schmid estimates that bank equity ownership has a negative relationship to performance up to blocks between 15 and 45 per cent depending on the concentration measures. Since this appears to apply to most firms in his sample, his results are at odds with those from Gorton and Schmid (1998b).

Seger (1997) obtains some evidence of a positive relationship between direct bank ownership and several performance measures, but its significance depends strongly on the specification of the ownership variable. He obtains stronger result for firms where a banker chairs the supervisory board and the fraction of bank loans is high, both of which are negatively related to performance.

Chirinko and Elston (1996) find no discernible effect of equity held by banks and insurance companies on the cost of capital and on the average return on assets between 1965 and 1990. Perlitz and Seger (1994) find that firms under strong bank influence are less profitable (performance is measured using alternative ratios based on accounting profits and cash flows averaged from 1990 to 1993). However, when financially distressed firms are excluded from the sample, the negative relationship between bank influence and profitability is no longer significant. The primary shortcoming of this study is that only a univariate two-sample comparison is used. Chirinko and Elston (1996) replicated the analysis in a multivariate regression framework and, using the same period did not obtain significant estimates. Nibler (1995) uses similar performance measures and a similar regression framework as did Cable (1985). For more recent data the author finds a positive relation between direct bank ownership and average performance between 1988 and 1992, but a negative effect of bank proxy votes and the ratio of bank loans to total debt. Using the same data, Edwards and Nibler (1999), however, conclude that banks play no empirically discernible role in governing German corporations. They do find a positive effect of the shares controlled by the two largest block-holders on profitability, but provide no evidence on the sensitivity of this result on their specific concentration measure. Finally, Edwards and Weichenrieder (1999) estimate that the harmful effects of concentrated ownership are more than outweighed by the associated beneficial effects.

Except for Gorton and Schmid (1998b) and Edwards and Weichenrieder (1999), who employed market-to-book ratios in addition to other variables, all previous studies have used performance measures based on book values. While market returns should be a superior measure, their forward-looking nature leads to ambiguous inferences in such studies. For example, Wenger and Kaserer (1997) find a negative relationship between holding-period market returns from 1973 to 1995 and bank ownership. While their interpretation is that bank ownership has caused lower returns, the causal relationship could as well go the other way (and alter the conclusions substantially). For example, if banks tend to invest primarily in struggling firms that have lost market value over a couple of years, the estimated relationship between bank involvement and market returns would be negative. Contrary to their conclusions, however, such a causal relationship would support a monitoring function performed by banks. A second problem with market returns is that, in efficient markets, returns should be affected only at the time of a change in bank influence, but not afterwards. Therefore, it is not clear what the negative relationship estimated by Wenger and Kaserer (1997) means.

Using a different approach to analysing market returns, Boehmer (2000) analyses the effect of bank influence on the net present value of major investment decisions, namely corporate acquisitions, instead of estimating a cross-sectional regression. He finds that bank control does not imply better monitoring, and that majority control by banks is detrimental to shareholders. However, large block-holders controlling less than 50 per cent appear to play an important monitoring role, especially if banks are involved. Specifically, bidders where banks potentially control a large fraction of the voting power via proxy votes clearly benefit from minority block-holders. Bank involvement is beneficial if financial institutions control the second or third largest stake, but not if they control the largest stake. Therefore, it seems that only if there is a force independent of the bank that decision quality is going to be improved (in the sense of increasing shareholder wealth). This result is consistent with evidence obtained by Edwards and Weichenrieder (1999), who find that increases in the second-largest shareholder's voting rights increases the market-to-book ratio.

Finally, Boehmer (2000) documents that bidders whose groups include firms that are majority-controlled by financial institutions complete the most value-reducing takeovers. This result is not consistent with the presumption that German banks provide an efficient monitoring function to corporations and is robust with respect to various specifications of the test. Even if these acquisitions are part of an efficiency-enhancing restructuring programme, bidder shareholders will lose wealth as a result.

6. CONCLUSIONS AND OPEN QUESTIONS

In Germany, large block-holders and banks control a substantial portion of exchange-listed firms. Block-holders naturally have incentives to act on behalf of shareholders. On the other hand, they are sufficiently powerful to divert resources from other shareholders to their own portfolio. To date, there is some evidence that implies such transfers and little evidence that block-holders positively affect firm value. Studies of this kind are scant because at least until 1995 there was little information published on the identity, activity, and transactions of block-holders. Future research on the incentives and behaviour of large shareholders would clearly be beneficial.

Following the transposition of the EU Large Holdings Directive effective in 1995, AGs listed in an official German stock market must disclose parties controlling more than 5 per cent of the voting rights. Since creditor protection is deeply rooted in German commercial law, the practical efficacy of disclosure regulation is still very low; the formation of groups involving less regulated legal forms as intermediate layers can substantially reduce transparency. Similarly, investment funds and banks face even less restrictive disclosure requirements. Voting rights deriving from proxy votes or fund ownership are generally exempt from the 5 per cent filings mandatory for other firms.

Due to proxy votes and board memberships, banks control a substantially higher fraction of voting rights than cash-flow claims. Moreover, banks extend more loan money to the typical firm than they hold as equity. Therefore, it is an empirical question whether the resulting voting power is used rationally to act as creditors or idealistically on behalf of shareholders. Previous empirical studies have produced conflicting evidence and many suffer from shortcomings relating to data and methodological issues.

6.1. *Concentration and transparency of control in Germany*

Compared to other developed economies, the German stock market is dominated by large shareholders. However, even after introducing the WpHG in 1995, the ultimately controlling parties are often not disclosed. This has important consequences for outside shareholders. First, an investor in a typical German corporation faces a majority of voting rights controlled by large shareholders. To the extent that expropriation in the form of wealth transfers to larger shareholders (when a block-holder has control) or to creditors (when proxy votes give majority control to banks) is possible, he will discount the value of shares to reflect his weak bargaining position. Put differently, an uninformed investor is likely to increase his required rate of return with increasing uncertainty about the incentives of large shareholders in the same firm. Therefore, the low transparency of control is likely to increase the cost of capital to affected German corporations relative to their international competitors listed in markets that are more transparent. Full disclosure of control would probably reduce uncertainty with respect to expropriation and increase the value of affected firms. To determine the cross-sectional value of transparency, in national or international settings, is an important question for future research.

6.2. *The relationship between ownership structure and firm performance*

Several previous and concurrent studies analyse the relationship between ownership structure (in particular focusing on bank control) and performance in Germany. The results depend strongly on sample, period, and methodology used. In sum, both highly concentrated ownership and substantial bank control per se apparently have only a modest cross-sectional effect on German corporations. A deeper analysis of these issues that incorporates more specific variables about the firms' industries would help to understand the real consequences of concentration and bank control.

In addition, most empirical efforts are rather ambiguous on the date of the employed ownership and bank-control data. Although it would be essential for a cross-sectional study, none of these rationalizes when and for how long bank control should affect performance. All implicitly assume that current performance depends on bank control in a close-by period, either before or after the period over which performance is measured (under the questionable assumption that control does not change over time).

For example, probably due to the extremely high cost of reliable data, no study tests restrictions on the lead–lag relationship between performance and bank control. Such tests could illuminate the actual efficacy of powerful banks and large shareholders and represent another fruitful area for future research.

6.3. *Policy implications and future research*

Empirical studies on German corporate governance raise intriguing questions for future research and have important political implications. First, current German transparency legislation (WpHG) is not sufficient to achieve the objective of transparency as stated by the European Commission and the German parliament. Proxy voting by banks, voting control by investment funds or by firms not listed in an official market, and voting by business groups whose members jointly control a majority in each other, do not need to be reported to the public (or, in the case of proxy votes, is not readily available).

Second, the involvement of financial institutions in the corporate sector has ambiguous effects on the affected companies' performance. Given that on average banks extend substantially more debt than equity to listed firms, they clearly have incentives to maximize the value of debt, as opposed to that of equity. At least since Jensen and Meckling's (1976) analysis of agency problems, it is basic knowledge in financial economics that creditors and shareholders have distinctly different interests. Therefore, banks represent a priori poor candidates for representing shareholders at annual general meetings, especially when their voting rights come from proxy votes and not from direct shareholdings.

Empirically, bank involvement appears to have a very limited effect on performance. Since it has no discernible positive effect on listed firms empirically, it is hard to support the claim that the interests of small shareholders are well represented via the proxy-voting mechanism. The absence of an effect, however, is likely to mask important differences across different types of bank involvement. For example, a bank with a substantial equity stake and no outstanding loan to the same company is likely to act in the interest of shareholders. On the other hand, if a bank without equity ownership, but with substantial loan interests, controls a majority of (proxy) votes, it is unlikely that it acts irrationally and does not maximize the value of the firm's debt. Additionally, since the interest in debt maximization is common to most banks, they are likely to act in concert even without explicit agreements to this end. Due to the latent threat that shareholders' voting rights are used against them in this way, it is mandatory for legislators and the BAWe to assure that the type of bank control is publicly revealed. In particular, legal provisions should ensure that direct share ownership by banks (which tends to increase the alignment of their interests with that of shareholders) and control via other means, such as supervisory board representation, proxy votes, and especially amount and type of lending, are treated separately and fully disclosed if listed companies are affected.

To a similar extent, the argument above also applies to block-holders not affiliated with financial institutions. Without knowing who ultimately controls a corporation and without being able to infer his incentives to act in the interest of all shareholders, outside investors will require a higher rate of return. To alleviate their fear of expropriation, transparency is necessary to let uninformed investors make educated decisions about where to invest and to whom to give authority over their voting rights.

Future research should address the relationship between ownership structure and performance in more detail. For example, it is still not clear what the causal relationship between bank control and performance is. Do block-holders and banks pick their control targets based on their performance and remain passive afterwards, or do they choose deliberately and then actively steer the firm? Both strategies would cause an empirical correlation between the control structure and performance in most previous studies. To disentangle the two, it is necessary to distinguish between past, concurrent, and subsequent ownership-induced performance changes.

Another intriguing question is why Germany has failed to implement full transparency with the WpHG, given the clear intentions to that end at the outset of discussions at the EU level. It is possible that true transparency is not beneficial to the German economic sector, as it has developed over the centuries. It is also possible that it has the potential to significantly reduce the cost of capital of German corporations, and consequently improve their competitive position in world markets. In my opinion, these issues have not received sufficient attention in the way of positive empirical research. One potential explanation for the current state of transparency legislation is that legislators have expected unreasonably high costs for firms affected by the legislation. In that case empirical research, for example comparative analyses of German firms and those in more transparent markets, could corroborate or alleviate those concerns. Another potential explanation is that benefactors of less transparency (i.e. creditors represented by financial institutions and large shareholders able to divert wealth from small shareholders) have had a sufficiently powerful lobby to prevent substantial deviations from the status quo. Also in the latter case, empirical research of a comparative nature could convince legislators to take measures that promote German capital markets and reduce the cost of capital to firms listed there, independent of potentially one-sided interest in either direction.

Notes

1. Heisenberg Fellow and University of Georgia. I thank the German Science Foundation (DFG) for substantial financial support. The European Corporate Governance Network supported parts of this study. Theodor Baums, Marco Becht, Klaus Gugler, and Beatrice Kuehn were very helpful in discussing and commenting on various parts of this study. In addition, participants at the 1996 DFG Colloquium, the 1997 Workshop on Banking in Münster, the 1997 and 1998 ECGN Conferences in Milan, and the finance department of the University of Amsterdam provided helpful comments.
2. Compare OECD Internal Documents SG/CG (98) 6 and SG/CG (98) 9 providing guidelines for corporate governance standards in member states, the EC Large Holdings Directive, the 1995 Gutachten to the Monopolkommission by Professor Adam, Baums, and Wenger. The German legislators' involvement is evidenced, for example, by the second and third *Finanzmarktförderungsgesetz* and the KonTraG.

3. Monks and Minow (1995) provide a comprehensive introduction and description of corporate governance. See Kojima (1995) or Shleifer and Vishny (1997) for general surveys. Baums (1996a) and Charny (1999), for example, provide a discussion of potential convergence of the different systems. Zingales (1998) analyses corporate governance in an environment of incomplete contracting. Mayer (1997) points out that differences in the various approaches to governance are mostly rooted in the varying structure of ownership and control across countries.

4. See Becht and Boehmer (1999) for an extensive review and analysis of Germany's implementation of the Large Holdings Directive. We document several shortcomings of the implementation and show that several control relations are not revealed by current reporting procedures. Nevertheless, the required filings provide valuable data on voting control over officially listed corporations.

5. See also Figure 3.1 for 1994.

6. Ekkehart Wenger is a tenured professor of business administration at the University of Würzburg and a well-known shareholder activist.

7. For empirical analyses of cross-shareholdings, see Prowse (1995) and Wenger and Kaserer (1997). For an analysis of personal interlockings, see Pfannschmidt (1995).

8. §§ 304, 320b AktG. See also Hecker and Wenger (1995) for a detailed discussion of potential transfers between large and small shareholders and Adams (1994) for the implications of cross-shareholdings in this regard. Bebchuk and Kahan (1999) model and discuss the problems arising in determining an appropriate consideration in such transactions.

9. No publicly available figures provide information on the precise composition of banks interests in equity and debt to German listed corporations. A back-of-the-envelope calculation proceeds as follows. In 1996, the DAI reports that the equity-to-capital ratio of listed corporations is 39 per cent (DAI Fact Book 1996). Own calculations reveal that banks own about 8 per cent of these firms' equity. Since German firms very rarely use public bonds, it is safe to assume that most long-term debt consists of bank loans. Thus, the portfolio of a typical bank can be described as a function of the ratio of bank loans to total corporate liabilities. For example, if all corporate debt were from banks, the banks finance 8%*39% = 3.12 per cent of listed firms' total assets in the form of equity shares, and 61 per cent in the form of loans. Using the cautious assumption that only one-third of corporate liabilities consist of bank loans, banks still finance about 20 per cent of the corporations' total assets using loans. Therefore, for the typical bank the value of its loan portfolio to a typical listed corporation exceeds the equity interest in the same firm by a factor of between 7 and 20. Economy-wide, Edwards and Fischer (1994) estimate that bank-supplied equity to non-banks is about 3 per cent of bank-supplied loans to the same firms.

10. For the USA, Payne, Millar, and Glezen (1996) document evidence consistent with the view that banks use their voting rights in the interest of management (as opposed to that of shareholders) when banks have debt or fee-related income associated with the firm.

11. Böhm (1992) obtains similar conclusions and suggests a voting procedure where the voting rights of absent small shareholders are granted to small shareholders present at the AGM (p. 211). See also Köndgen (1994) and Baums (1996b) for critical discussions.

12. While proponents of the current system claim that banks do represent shareholders, Köndgen (1994) points out an interesting inconsistency in this regard. When the German corporate code (AktG) was revised in 1965, legislators discussed a proposal that would prevent banks from proxy voting shares at their own AGMs. According to Zöllner (1973), it was rejected on the ground that then banks' AGMs would be dominated by their competitors. Therefore, legislators could not have been convinced that proxy votes represent shareholder interests and should have modified the proxy system in the first place.

References for Chapter 9

Adams, M. (1994), 'Die Usurpation von Aktionärsbefugnissen mittels Ringverflechtung in der "Deutschland AG" ', *Die Aktiengesellschaft*, 39: 148–58.

Albach, H. and H.-P. Kless (1982), 'Personelle Verflechtungen bei deutschen Industrieaktiengesellschaften', *Zeitschrift für Betriebswirtschaft*, 52: 959–77.

Baums, T. (1993), 'Corporate Governance in Germany: System and Recent Developments', in M. Isaksson, and R. Skog (eds.), *Aspects of Corporate Governance*, Stockholm: Juristförlaget, 31–54.

—— and C. Fraune (1995), 'Institutionelle Anleger und Publikumsgesellschaft: Eine empirische Untersuchung', *Die Aktiengesellschaft* 40: 97–112.

—— and P. v. Randow (1995), 'Der Markt für Stimmrechtsvertreter', *Die Aktiengesellschaft*, 40: 145–63.

—— (1996*a*), 'Corporate Governance Systems in Europe: Differences and Tendencies Toward Convergence', Working paper, University of Osnabrück.

—— (1996*b*), 'Vollmachtstimmrecht der Banken-Ja oder Nein?', *Die Aktiengesellschaft* 41: 11–26.

—— (1997), 'Shareholder Representation and Proxy Voting in the European Union: A Comparative Study', Working paper, University of Osnabrück.

—— (1999), 'Corporate Governance in Germany: System and Current Developments', Working paper, University of Osnabrück.

Bebchuk, L. A. and M. Kahan (1999), 'The "Lemons Effect" in Corporate Freeze-outs', Discussion paper no. 248, Harvard Law School.

Becht, M. and E. Boehmer (1999), 'Transparency of Ownership and Control in Germany', Preliminary Report to the European Commission (1997), and Working paper, University of Georgia.

Boehmer, E. (2000), 'Who Controls Germany? An Exploratory Analysis', Working paper, University of Georgia.

—— (forthcoming), 'Business Groups, Large Shareholders, and Bank Control: An Analysis of German Takeovers', *Journal of Financial Intermediation*.

Böhm, J. (1992), 'Der Einfluss der Banken auf Grossunternehmen', Duisburger volkswirtschaftliche Schriften 13, Hamburg: W & W Verlag.

Cable, J. (1985), 'Capital Market Information and Industrial Performance: The Role of West German Banks', *Economic Journal*, 95: 118–32.

Charny, D. (1999), 'The German Corporate Governance System', Working paper, Harvard Law School.

Chirinko, R. S. and J. A. Elston (1996), 'Finance, Control, and Profitability: An Evaluation of German Bank Influence', Working paper, WZB Berlin.

Edwards, J. and K. Fischer (1994), *Banks, Finance, and Investment in Germany*, Cambridge: Cambridge University Press.

—— and M. Nibler (1999), 'Corporate Governance in Germany: The Influence of Banks and Large Equity Holders', Working paper, University of Cambridge.

—— and A. J. Weichenrieder (1999), 'Ownership Concentration and Share Valuation', Working paper, CES, University of Munich.

Franks, J. and C. Mayer (1996), 'Ownership, Control, and the Performance of German Corporations', Working paper, London Business School.

Franks, J. R. and C. Mayer (1997), 'Corporate Ownership and Control in the U.K., Germany, and France', in D. H. Chew (ed.), *Studies in International Corporate Finance and Governance Systems*, Oxford: Oxford University Press, 281–96.

Gerum, E., H. Steinmann, and W. Fees (1988), *Der mitbestimmte Aufsichtsrat: Eine empirische Untersuchung*, Stuttgart: C. E. Poeschel Verlag.

Gorton, G. and F. A. Schmid (1998*a*), 'Corporate Finance, Control Rights, and Firm Performance: A Study of German Co-determination', Working paper, University of Pennsylvania.

—— —— (1998*b*), 'Universal Banking and the Performance of German Firms', Working paper, University of Pennsylvania.

Hecker, R. and E. Wenger (1995), 'Der Schutz von Minderheiten im Vertragskonzern: Ein Betriebsunfall des Aktienrechts', *Zeitschrift für Bankrecht und Bankwirtschaft*, 7: 321–424.

Herrmann, M. and G. Franke (1996), 'The Performance of Foundation-owned Firms in Germany', Working paper, University of Constance.

Hopt, K. J. (1998), 'The German Two-Tier Board: Experience, Theories, Reforms', in K. J. Hopt, H. Kanda, M. J. Roe, E. Wymeersch, and S. Prigge (eds.), *Comparative Corporate Governance: The State of the Art and Emerging Research*, Oxford: Clarendon Press.

Iber, B. (1985), 'Zur Entwicklung der Aktionärsstruktur in der Bundesrepublik Deutschland (1963–1983)', *Zeitschrift für Betriebswirtschaft*, 55: 1101–19.

Jenkinson, T. and A. Ljungqvist (1997), 'Hostile Stakes and the Role of Banks in German Corporate Governance', Working paper, University of Oxford.

Jensen, M. and W. Meckling (1976), 'Theory of the Firm: Managerial Behavior, Agency Costs and Ownership Structure', *Journal of Financial Economics*, 3: 305–60.

Kaplan, S. (1994), 'Top Executives, Turnover, and Firm Performance in Germany', *Journal of Law, Economics, and Organization*, 10: 142–59.

Knoll, L., J. Knoesel, and U. Probst (1997), 'Aufsichtsratsvergütungen in Deutschland: Empirische Befunde', *Zeitschrift für betriebswirtschaftliche Forschung*, 49: 236–53.

Kojima, K. (1995), 'Corporate Governance: An International Comparison', Working paper, Kobe University.

Köndgen, J. (1994), 'Duties of Banks in Voting Their Clients' Stock', in T. Baums, R. M. Buxbaum, and K. J. Hopt (eds.), *Institutional Investors and Corporate Governance*, Berlin, New York: de Gruyter, 531–54.

Korn/Ferry International (1996), 'Board Meeting in Session', European Boards of Directors Study, London.

Latham, M. (forthcoming), 'The Corporate Monitoring Firm', *Corporate Governance: International Review*, 7.

Mayer, C. (1997), 'Financial Systems and Corporate Governance: A Review of the International Evidence', Working paper, University of Oxford.

Mella, F. and R. Jähnke (1996), 'Wem gehören die deutschen Aktiengesellschaften?', *Börsen-Zeitung*, 12 (Jan.), 6.

Monks, R. and N. Minow (1995), *Corporate Governance*, Cambridge, Mass.: Blackwell.

Nibler, M. (1995), 'Bank Control and Corporate Performance in Germany: The Evidence', Working paper, University of Cambridge.

Payne, T. H., J. A. Millar, and G. W. Glezen (1996), 'Fiduciary Responsibility and Bank–Firm Relationships: An Analysis of Shareholder Voting by Banks', *Journal of Corporate Finance*, 3: 75–87.

Peltzer, M. (1989), 'Hostile Takeovers in der Bundesrepublik Deutschland?', *Zeitschrift für Wirtschaftsrecht*, 10: 69–79.

Perlitz, M. and F. Seger (1994), 'The Role of Universal Banks in German Corporate Governance', *Business and the Contemporary World*, 6: 49–67.

Pfannschmidt, A. (1995), 'Mehrfachmandate in deutschen Unternehmen', *Zeitschrift für Betriebswirtschaft*, 65: 177–203.

Prowse, S. (1995), *Corporate Governance in an International Perspective: A Survey of Corporate Control Mechanisms Among Firms in the U. S., UK, Japan, and Germany*, NYU Salomon Center 4, Cambridge, Mass.: Blackwell.

Schiffels, E. (1981), *Der Aufsichtsrat als Instrument der Unternehmenskooperation*, Frankfurt/Main.

Schmid, F. A. (1996*a*), 'Beteiligungen deutscher Geschäftsbanken und corporate performance', *Zeitschrift für Wirtschafts und Sozialwissenschaften*, 116: 273–310.

—— (1996*b*), 'Vorstandsbezüge, Aufsichtsratsvergütung und Aktionärsstruktur', *Zeitschrift für Betriebswirtschaft*, 67: 69–83.

Schneider, U. (1995), 'Mitteilungs und Veröffentlichungspflichten bei Veränderungen des Stimmrechtsanteils an börsennotierten Gesellschaften', in: H.-D. Assmann and U. Schneider (eds.), *Wertpapierhandelsgesetz: Kommentar*, Cologne: Verlag Dr. Otto Schmidt KG.

Schroeder, U. and A. Schrader (1998), 'The Changing Role of Banks and Corporate Governance in Germany: Evolution Towards the Market?', in S. W. Black, and M. Moersch (eds.), *Competition and Convergence in Financial Markets*, Amsterdam: Elsevier, 17–34.

Schwalbach, J. and U. Graßhoff (1997), 'Managervergütung und Unternehmenserfolg', *Zeitschrift für Betriebswirtschaft*, 67: 203–17.

Seger, F. (1997), *Banken, Erfolg und Finanzierung*, Wiesbaden: Gabler Verlag.

Shleifer, A. und Robert Vishny (1997), 'A Survey of Corporate Governance', *Journal of Finance*, 52: 737–83.

Weigand, J. and E. Lehmann (1998), 'Does the Governed Corporation Perform Better?', Working paper, University of Erlangen-Nürnberg.

Wenger, E. and C. Kaserer (1997), 'German Banks and Corporate Governance: A Critical View', Working paper, University of Würzburg.

—— R. Hecker, and J. Knoesel (1996), 'Abfindungsregeln und Minderheitenschutz bei börsennotierten Kapitalgesellschaften', Working paper, University of Würzburg.

Zingales, L. (1998), 'Corporate Governance', in *The New Palgrave Dictionary of Economics and the Law*, London: Macmillan.

Zöllner, W. (1973), 'Kölner Kommentar zum Aktiengesetz', Köln.

10

France

ELIZABETH KREMP AND PATRICK SEVESTRE

The French situation appears to be unique in that it is the only one to offer the opportunity of choosing either a unique board (*Conseil d'Administration*) or a dual structure (*Conseil de Surveillance* and *Directoire*) for any corporate firm, even when listed.

Viénot Report (1999)

1. INTRODUCTION

Almost 70 years ago, Berle and Means (1932) raised in their seminal book the question of the relationship between firms' corporate governance systems and their performances. However, in France, the interest of economists, managers, and economic decision-makers in corporate governance issues has been noticeable only in the last few years. Indeed, 90 per cent of the empirical studies devoted to this question have been published in the last five years and, following the Cadbury Report, the French Employers' Syndicates Organization (MEDEF—Mouvement des Entreprises de France, formerly the CNPF, Conseil National du Patronat Français), asked for two successive reports about corporate governance in France (Viénot 1995, 1999).

This quite recent interest in corporate governance is one of the reasons explaining the rather limited number of empirical studies available in France, the other one being the non-availability of the necessary statistical information. For example, due to the lack of data about top managers' compensation (Alcouffe and Alcouffe 1997) and the fact that hostile takeovers have been very rare in France for a long time (Mayer 1988), it is difficult to have an idea about their possible impact on managers' behaviour. This also explains why most of the French empirical literature about corporate governance focuses on the influence of ownership type and/or structure on economic performance, i.e. most studies look at whether family-owned firms perform better than others, or whether concentrated ownership is favourable.

The structure of the survey is as follows. We first consider the question of the relationship between the structure of ownership and corporate performance. Then we summarize the very few available studies focusing on manager-disciplining devices such as the existence of a supervisory board, the takeover threats, or the managers' compensation structure.

2. THE STRUCTURE OF OWNERSHIP AND CORPORATE PERFORMANCE

2.1. *What do we know about the structure of ownership in France?*

A common way of characterizing the corporate governance system in a country is to consider the degree of ownership concentration and the ownership structure. Bloch and Kremp (2001), using a dataset with more than 280,000 firms, provide a very detailed analysis of these two issues. They show that the concentration of ownership is very high both in non-listed and listed companies. On average, the largest shareholder of a non-listed company owns 66 per cent of the capital. This degree of ownership concentration increases with firm size; the largest shareholder owns 63 per cent of the equity in firms with less than 20 employees, but more than 88 per cent in firms with more than 500 employees. For listed companies (680 in the sample), the degree of ownership concentration is lower but still substantial (the largest shareholder holds, on average, more than 50 per cent of the equity). However, for the 40 listed firms belonging to the CAC40, the share of the largest identified stake is around 29 per cent (see also Table 2.1).

Considering non-listed firms' capital as a whole, Bloch and Kremp (2000) show that individuals (or 'families') represent the main category of owners; they hold, on average, half of this capital. Non-financial firms and holdings are the second most important category of owners, with more than 30 per cent of the capital. Financial firms (banks and insurance companies) and foreign firms each own almost 3 per cent of the capital, while the State is unimportant as a shareholder. However, when financial firms, holdings or the State are effectively owners, they hold more than the majority of the capital. The type of ownership of listed firms appears to be more equally distributed among the five categories of owners, holdings, non-financial firms, public, banks, and families than that of unlisted firms.

Several studies look specifically at non-resident ownership of firms located in France (Bloch and Kremp 2001; Chocron and Marchand 1998; Chocron 1998; Maréchal 1998; and Dietsch 2000). Although these studies obtain estimates of different magnitudes, due to different statistical methods and sample coverage, they all agree that shareholdings by non-residents in French firms is increasing, especially in listed firms. For example, Maréchal (1998), using a survey covering the largest 40 listed firms in France, finds that non-residents hold on average 25 per cent of the equity. Most foreign owners hold more than 10 per cent of the capital, and nine more than 40 per cent. Dietsch (2000), using the Global Equity ownership database, shows that non-residents hold 22 per cent of listed firms in France. Bloch and Kremp (2001) find that although, on average, foreign firms hold only 3–4 per cent of listed firms' capital as a whole, when they are effective owners, their holding rises to almost 30 per cent. For non-listed firms, these figures are respectively 3 and 79 percent. Therefore, concentration of foreign ownership is very high in France.

2.2. *What do we know about ownership structure and economic performance in France?*

2.2.1. *Ownership structure, concentration, and performance: an unclear relationship*

Several tests of the relationship between firms' performance and their ownership structure are provided by Charreaux (1997), based on a sample of about 80 French firms observed over the period 1974–9. Different performance measures are related to one of the following variables: the capital percentage owned by known shareholders, the capital percentage represented by administrators (in order to account for the separation of ownership and control), the capital percentage represented by managers (to account for the separation of decision and ownership), as well as a size variable (total assets) and a measure for risk. Whatever the performance measure and the explanatory variables used, no significant link between performance and ownership structure appears to exist. In a second set of regressions, the influence of ownership concentration on performance is tested. Following the criticism of Demsetz and Lehn (1985) by Morck, Shleifer, and Vishny (1988), the non-linear relationship between ownership structure and performance is taken into account by specifying threshold variables. Again, the results show no really significant relationship.

In a multinational comparative study, Gedajlovic and Shapiro (1998) examined the relationship between firms' ownership concentration and their profitability. They consider five countries: USA, UK, Canada, France, and Germany. For France, the sample covers around 80 medium to large publicly traded firms, observed over the 1986–91 period. Ownership concentration is measured by the percentage of shares held by the largest shareholder, and performance by the ratio of net income to total assets (ROA). The authors control for different effects (industrial diversification, foreign diversification, firm size, sales growth), and they allow for a non-linear relationship between performance and ownership concentration. They do not find any ownership effect for France either.

Another multinational study by Thomsen and Pedersen (2000) examines the same relationship using data on 435 firms from 12 European countries, including France, over the period 1990–5. However, the authors do not split up the sample according to the nationality of the firms. They find a non-linear and significantly positive relationship between two measures of performance (market-to-book value of equity and return on assets) and ownership concentration.

Using a very large dataset comprising more than 80,000 firms observed in 1996, Kremp and Sevestre (2000) find a significant, though not very strong, impact of ownership concentration on several performance ratios: return on fixed assets, return on own funds, a dividends/own funds ratio, and an operating income/value-added ratio. This positive link appears to be heterogeneous, depending on the nature of the ultimate owner (large or small family groups, large or small corporate groups, individuals). Another study by Romieu and Sassenou (1996), based on a sample of 80 heads of a group (among the 250 largest listed firms) observed over the period 1990–4, also finds a positive relationship between ownership concentration (defined as the percentage of capital owned by the manager) and firm performance (measured as the amount of paid dividends).

On the contrary, Paquerot (1997) finds a negative influence of ownership concentration on performance (measured as the Sharpe ratio), using a sample of 170 firms observed in 1993.

2.2.2. *Owners' identity and performance: conflicting results*

Jacquemin and de Ghellinck (1980) look at a sample of 100 firms among the largest 200 French companies for which they compute yearly rates of return (ratio of cash flow over owners' capital book value) averaged over the period 1970–4. They do not find a significant difference between majority-controlled and minority-controlled firms neither between family- and non-family controlled firms. Charreaux (1997) also provides a set of tests in which the type of ownership (family-controlled, group-controlled (subsidiary), or manager-controlled firms) is taken into account. Although the author emphasizes that family-owned firms have a different governance organization, no clear-cut conclusions can be drawn about the impact of this form of organization on the performance of firms. The above-mentioned study by Kremp and Sevestre (2000) does not lead to clear-cut conclusions on the impact of the nature of ultimate ownership (individuals, families, small firms, large firms) on performance, either. Indeed, this impact is sometimes significant but its sign is highly dependent on the performance ratio considered.

Belin-Munier (1997) specifically looks at the relative performance of firms belonging to a holding structure. She studies 400 listed firms and differentiates them according to the existence of a link with a holding, but does not find a significant difference in performance.

These results conflict with those presented by Beau (1990) based on a sample of 1,600 firms over the 1984–6 period. The author compares the average financial return of 800 independent firms with that of 800 subsidiaries and heads of groups. The return measure is higher for the former group than for the latter. This last result is in agreement with that of Romieu and Sassenou (1996), who find that family-owned and managed firms (i.e. independent firms) have higher returns (both on equity and on total assets), as well as a higher Tobin's Q than others. However, Mulkay (1997), using a random sample of 2,600 French firms' unconsolidated balance sheets over the 1978–93 period, finds that heads of groups have a higher ratio of net profit to total assets than other firms (either independent or subsidiaries of a group).

Romieu and Sassenou (1996) also show that non-financial firm participations do not have a significant impact on firm performance. The main aim of this kind of equity holdings seems to rely mainly on industrial strategy considerations. The owners do not appear to exert any influence on investment, indebtedness, or growth policy. The same conclusion applies to the impact of institutional investors' holdings.

In their multi-country study, Thomsen and Pedersen (2000) underline the importance of the owner identity. Compared to the other owners financial investors' ownership is found to be associated with higher shareholder value and profitability, but lower sales growth. The effect of ownership concentration is also found to depend on owner identity, as in Kremp and Sevestre (2000).

3. WHAT DO WE KNOW ABOUT CORPORATE GOVERNANCE STRUCTURE, TAKEOVERS AND MANAGERS' COMPENSATION IN FRANCE?

3.1. *The corporate governance system in France*

The 1966 French Business Law allows two different corporate governance systems by corporate companies (*Sociétés Anonymes*) in France. (1) A one-board system, relying on a Board of Directors (*Conseil d'Administration*), elected by the General Meeting of Shareholders. The Board of Directors appoints a Chairman/CEO (*Président Directeur Général*) of the company in charge of the day-to-day running of the company. At least in theory, the Chairman/CEO has to own shares in the company. (2) A two-board system relying on a Supervisory Board (*Conseil de Surveillance*) and a Management Board (*Directoire*). As in the one-board system, the members of the Supervisory Board are shareholders appointed by the Shareholders General Meeting. This Supervisory Board then appoints the members of the Management Board as well as its Chairman. The Management Board, whose members do not necessarily own shares in the company, is in charge of the day-to-day running of the company but has stricter reporting obligations than the Chairman/CEO in the one-board system.

Among the CAC40 listed companies, 75 per cent have a one-board system and 25 per cent have a two-board structure. The two-board system is chosen by only 2–3 per cent of all corporate firms (Viénot, 1999). An example of each system is given in Table 10.1.

The second Viénot Report on Corporate Governance in France (1999) notices that the two-board system is costly and not necessarily very efficient. Because the definition of independent administrators is not very precise, the composition of the Supervisory Board does not always ensure its full independence from the Management Board and the most important shareholders (Frontezak 1999). Indeed, the report advocates a change in the French law, which would allow listed firms with a one-board system to have the opportunity to separate the functions of Chairman and CEO. For the evidence on board structure and performance, see section 3.4 below.

3.2. *Takeovers*

There have been only a few hostile takeovers in the past. Therefore, the possible link between takeovers and managers' behaviour has not been studied. Nevertheless, Artus (1998), looking at the likelihood of takeovers in France, points out several factors which are favourable to takeovers: the very high percentage of capital held by non-residents, the relatively small size of listed firms, and their increased return on equity.

3.3. *Managers' compensation*

Information on top executives' compensation is limited in France. The only available data is about the total amount of compensation of all directors, without any individual information. Articles 168-4 of the 1966 French Business Law state that any shareholder can obtain information on 'the global amount, as certified by the statutory auditors, of

Table 10.1a. *Two examples of corporate governance structures of firms belonging to the CAC40 (France)*

LVMH (30 June 1999)	ACCOR (31 March 1999)
One-board system	Two-board system
Board of directors:	*Supervisory board*:
One chairman/CEO; six shareholder representatives; six independents	Two co-chairmen (co-founders of the group); five shareholder representatives; five independents
	Management board:
	One chairman and CEO; three members
Council of advisors:	
Five members (shareholders)	
Executive committee:	
One chairman; one CEO; 11 members	
Audit committee: 3 members (2 independents)	Audit committee: 5 members (2 independents)
Compensation committee: 3 members (2 independents)	Compensation committee: 4 members (2 independents)
Nominating committee: 3 members (2 independents)[a]	

[a] All members of the various committees are members of the board of directors or of the council of advisors, however no member of the executive committee can be also a member of the audit committee.

Table 10.1b. *Breakdown of share capital and voting rights*

LVMH (30 June 1999)	Share capital %	Voting rights %	ACCOR (31 March 1999)	Share capital %	Voting rights %
Financière Jean Goujon[a]	40.7	57.5	Caisse des Dépôts et Consignations	5.5	9.6
Public	59.3	42.5	Founders (P. Dubrule and G. Pélisson)	3.5	4.5
			Société Générale	1.8	1.7
			Worms & Cie (IFIL)	1.3	2.4
			BNP	0.7	1.3
			Supervisory board total	12.8	19.5
			International institutional investors	47	
			French institutional investors	30	80.5
			Private individuals	10.2	

[a] At June 30, 1999, groupe Arnault held directly and indirectly 47.1% of LVMH's share capital, including the 40.7% held by financière Jean Goujon.

Sources: Annual reports, available on the respective websites.

the compensation of the best-paid persons in the company, their number being either ten or five, depending on whether the total number of employees is larger or smaller than two hundred people'. Moreover, when they set up a registration statement for the French Stock Exchange Commission (COB), listed companies must indicate the total amount of direct and indirect compensation received, from all firms controlled by the group, by the Board of Directors' members as a whole.

As explained by Alcouffe and Alcouffe (1997), the relationship between executive pay, corporate control, and performance has become a major issue in France following the publication of the first Viénot report in 1995. They stress that ownership, control, and structure of large firms have been extensively affected by shifts in state policy during the last three decades. French corporate groups qualified as 'technocracy-controlled' used to exhibit particular features. For example,

the presence of a large number of shareholders in the parent company, each holding less than 10 per cent of the stock, but a certain number of whom may be assumed to have a direct interest in the control of the company, without necessarily having sole control; a board of directors without any direct link to the shareholders. ... co-opted from the upper ranks of civil servants; and a system of shareholdings through which the parent exercises minority control of most of the subsidiaries of the group.

Alcouffe and Alcouffe (1997) describe very precisely the different aspects of compensation in large French groups and conclude that one should focus not only on the total amount of compensation paid to the top managers, but also on other aspects of the remuneration package that are more important in motivating managers as, for example, recruitment and salary review methods, initial setting of compensation levels, and duration of contracts. The complexity of these issues may explain, besides the lack of data, why there are so few empirical studies on the link between managerial compensation and performance. However, the second Viénot report (1999) does not recommend providing information on top managers' individual compensation.

3.4. *What do we know about the impact of board structure on economic performance?*

The existing literature concerning the impact of supervisory boards on economic performance does not point to a clear relationship. Indeed, as suggested by Weisbach (1993) and Hanke and Walterr (1994), firms employing supervisory boards should perform worse, because they reduce the probability of takeover bids and impede the direct contacts between managers and stockholders. Rosentein and Wyatt (1990), on the other hand, find a positive relationship between the appointment of outside directors and share value.

To evaluate the impact of the two-board system on French firms' performances, Shyy and Vijayraghavan (1996) use a sample of 83 firms with a one-board system (Board of Directors) and 20 firms with a two-board system (Supervisory Board and Management Board). They regress the price/book ratio (averaged over the five-year period 1989–94) on the return on equity, total assets, and leverage (debt over total assets), and a dummy variable accounting for the board system. They do not find any statistically significant impact of the corporate governance system on the price/book ratio. On the other hand, Charreaux (1997) finds a positive relationship between the percentage of independent administrators and the performance of large corporate companies.

4. CONCLUSION

This survey does not give support to the hypothesis that type and concentration of ownership are strongly related to corporate performance. Many other aspects of the corporate governance–firm performance relationship still have to be looked at. For example, no study was found in the French economic literature about the impact of bank–firm relationships on corporate performance. This can be due to the fact that bank ownership is still very low in France despite the recent privatizations and the development of cross participations. Likewise, no empirical study seems to be available on the impact of takeovers or managerial compensation structure on performance in France, which may be explained by data non-availability.

References for Chapter 10

Alcouffe, Alain and Christiane Alcouffe (1997), 'Control and Executive Compensation in Large French Companies', *Journal of Law and Society*, 24/1 (March): 85–103.

Artus, Patrick (1998), 'Pourquoi les entreprises françaises sont-elles opa-bles?', *CDC Marché, Flash*, 23 Feb.

Berle, A. A and C. G. Means (1932), *The Modern Corporation and Private Properties*, New York: Commerce Clearing House.

Beau, Denis (1990), 'Les influences de l'appartenance à un groupe sur les structures et les résultats des entreprises françaises et industrielles', *Cahiers Economiques et Monétaires*, Banque de France: 105–40.

Belin-Munier, Christine (1997), 'Les holdings comme outils de gouvernement des entreprises', in G. Charreaux (ed.), *Le Gouvernement des Entreprises*, 87–103.

Bloch, Laurence and Elizabeth Kremp (2001), 'Ownership and Control in France', in F. Barca and M. Becht (eds.), *The Control of Corporate Europe*, Oxford: Oxford University Press.

Charreaux, Gérard (1997), 'Structure de propriété, relation d'agence, et performance financière', in Gérard Charreaux, 'Le Gouvernement des Entreprises: Corporate Governance, Théorie et Faits, Paris: MEDEF, 55–85.

Chocron, Monique (1998), 'La détention des actions françaises cotées et de titres d'OPCVM en France de décembre 1996 à Septembre 1997', mimeo, Conseil National du Crédit et du Titre, Paris.

—— and Lydie Marchand (1998), 'La Clienèle des principaux établissements dépositaires de titres en France au troisième trimestre 1997', Bulletin de la Banque de France, (Jan.) 49: 175–79.

Demsetz, H. and K. Lehn (1985), 'The Structure of Corporate Ownership: Causes and Consequences', *Journal of Political Economy*, 93: 1155–177.

Dietsch, Michel (2000), 'La part des non-résidents dans le capital des sociétés en Europe', Working paper, Institut d'Études Politiques de Strasbourg (Sept.).

Frontezak, Sylvie (1999), 'Gouvernement d'entreprise: Evolutions récentes en France et à l'étranger', *Bulletin de la COB*, 338 (Sept.): 1–24.

Gedajlovic, Eric and Daniel Shapiro (1998), 'Management and Ownership Effects: Evidence from Five Countries', *Strategic Management Journal*, 19: 533–53.

Hanke, Steve and Alan Walterr (1994), 'Governance', *Forbes*, April 11.

Jacquemin, Alexis and Elizabeth de Ghellinck (1980), 'Familial Control, Size and Performance in the Largest French Firms', *European Economic Review*, 13: 81–91.

Kremp, Elizabeth and Patrick Sevestre (2000), 'Ownership Concentration and Corporate Performance : Some New Evidence for France', *Research in International Business and Finance*, special issue (June).

Mayer, Colin (1988), 'New Issues in Corporate Finance', *European Economic Review*, 32: 1167–189.

Maréchal, Anne (1998), 'Les critères d'investissement des grands gestionnaires de fonds internationaux dans les entreprises françaises', *Bulletin de la COB*, 322 (March).

Morck, R., A. Shleifer, and R. W. Vishny (1988), 'Management Ownership and Market Evaluation: An Empirical Analysis', *Journal of Financial Economics*, 20: 293–315.

Mulkay, Benoît (1997), 'To be Independent or to be Within a Group: What are the Effects on Investment of Firms', Paper presented at the 7th International Conference on Panel Data, June 19–20.

Paquerot, Mathieu (1997), 'Stratégie d'enracinement des dirigeants, performance de la firme et structure de contrôle', in Gérard Charreaux (ed.) *Le Gouvernement des Entreprises: Corporate Governance, Théorie et Faits*, Economica, 105–38.

Romieu, Nathalie and Najib Sassenou (1996), 'Quels liens établir entre la structure de l'actionnariat de la firme et ses performances économiques et financières?', *CDC Marché, Flash*, 5 Jan.

Rosentein, Stuart and Jeffrey Wyatt (1990), 'Outside Directors, Board Independence and Shareholders Wealth', *Journal of Financial Economics*, 26: 175–91.

Shyy, Gang and Vijayraghavan Vasumathi (1996), 'Is a Supervisory Board Valuable? The French Evidence', Paper presented at the Conference 'Which Way Ahead for European Financial Markets?', American Institute for Contemporary German Studies, June 10–11.

Thomsen, S. and T. Pedersen (2000), 'Ownership Structure and Economic Performance in the Largest European Companies', *Strategic Management Journal*, 21: 689–705.

Viénot, Marc (1995), *Le conseil d'Administration des sociétés cotées*, Paris: CNPF.

—— (1999), *Rapport du comité sur le gouvernement d'entreprise*, Paris: AFEP, MEDEF.

Weisbach, Michael (1993), 'Corporate Governance and Hostile Takeovers', *Journal of Accounting and Economics*, 16: 199–208.

11

Italy

MAGDA BIANCO

1. CORPORATE GOVERNANCE IN ITALY

The Italian corporate governance system has a number of peculiarities compared with the better known Anglo-Saxon or Continental systems. As opposed to the Anglo-Saxon countries, public companies are still rare and the separation between ownership and control is limited. Contrary to the Continental systems, banks and financial companies have played a limited role in ownership structures. Instead, ownership is extremely concentrated, as in most other European countries. In 1999 the largest shareholder in listed companies owned on average 44 per cent of voting rights (weighted by market capitalization); the three largest shareholders owned 50 per cent. In a representative sample of manufacturing companies (mainly non-listed) the largest shareholder owned (in 1999) 64 per cent (73 per cent if weighted by employees, see Bianchi, Bianco, and Enriques 1998). The stock market was until recently relatively small, but has recently experienced a rapid growth. At the end of 1999, market capitalization represented 65 per cent of Italian GDP.

The limited amount of separation observed has been achieved mainly through instruments different both from those prevailing in the UK and the USA, and from those observed in Germany and Japan. Pyramidal structures have been one of the most common modes of achieving separation, especially for groups including listed companies. Approximately 45 per cent of manufacturing companies with more than 50 employees and almost all large firms (more than 1,000 employees) are organized in groups. If we consider those which include one listed company, the average degree of separation (measured by the amount of capital 'under control' for each unit of capital 'owned') was approximately two in 1996 (see Bianchi, Bianco, and Enriques 1998).

An important agent in Italian corporate governance is the state. In 1996 the voting rights share of the state represented approximately 30 per cent of the Italian stock market capitalization. However, the effects of the privatization programme, started in 1993, are now becoming evident. At the end of 1999 the share of the state was 19 per cent. In Italy, contrary to some Continental countries, banks have played a limited role until recently, since they were forbidden from owning shares in non-financial companies.

I would like to thank Marcello Bianchi for having provided some of the data and for extremely useful discussions.

However they have played a more informal role, for example through interlocking directorates (see Ferri and Trento 1997; Bianco and Pagnoni 1997). Since 1992 they have been allowed to invest in non-financial companies, but they have not exploited this opportunity to any great extent.

These aspects may be exemplified by a description of the corporate governance structure of some large companies. In what follows I briefly describe the cases of Telecom Italia, Fiat, and Pirelli. However, it should be remembered that more than 90 per cent of Italian employees work in firms with less than ten employees, and hence the importance of large companies should not be overvalued in the Italian context.

One important set of companies is represented by the recently privatized corporations: on the one hand they are among the largest ones; on the other hand, at least soon after their privatization, they represented the first examples of large public companies in Italy. In some instances, however, this corporate governance structure did not survive for long on the market.

Telecom Italia is the largest Italian listed company. At the end of 1999 it represented 10 per cent of the total market capitalization. Until the liberalization of the telecommunications market Telecom was the national, state-owned telecommunications company. It was privatized in 1997, with the creation of a *noyeaux dur*, which owned approximately 6 per cent. In 1999 the company was taken over by Olivetti, which is controlled, through a complex chain of control, by a group of Italian entrepreneurs. Hence, the control chain over Telecom currently includes Tecnost (55 per cent of Telecom), Olivetti (70 per cent of Tecnost), Bell SA (25 per cent of Olivetti), which is a foreign company controlled (with approximately 50 per cent of voting rights) by a group of companies, owned in turn by some Italian entrepreneurs. The degree of separation between ownership and control is extremely high (approximately 20 units of capital controlled for each unit of capital owned) and is achieved by means of a complex pyramidal structure.

Fiat spa is the largest Italian manufacturing company and one of the world's largest car producers. It is the fourteenth largest listed company as measured by market capitalization. It is controlled by the Agnelli family (linked, through a shareholder agreement, with Assicurazioni Generali and Deutsche Bank, each with approximately 2 per cent of voting capital) through a chain of control which includes Giovanni Agnelli & c. Sapa (a private company), IFI (controlled by Giovanni Agnelli & c. Sapa with 50 per cent of the voting rights), which owns 15 per cent of Fiat, IFIL (controlled by IFI, with both a direct share and through a controlled company), which owns 5 per cent of Fiat. The degree of separation between ownership and control is relatively large (almost ten). This is probably the best-known example of a family-controlled Italian company where control is exercised through a pyramidal group structure.

Finally Pirelli, a tyre and cable producer, is the twenty-ninth largest Italian listed company. It is controlled by a group of financial and holding companies (the most relevant are Camfin, owned by M. Tronchetti Provera, CEO of Pirelli; Mediobanca, Assicurazioni Generali, HPI, Edizione Holding, SAI Assicurazioni) linked by a shareholders' agreement, again through a chain of control which includes Pirelli & c. Sapa (controlled by the agreement with approximately 60 per cent) and Pirelli International

SA (controlled by Pirelli & c. Sapa, with 100 per cent), which in turn has 27 per cent of Pirelli. These examples highlight the role of pyramidal structures and, in various cases, shareholders' agreements in large Italian companies.

The institutional framework plays a large role in explaining the observed structure. Even if, on the one hand, disclosure requirements are extremely tight in Italy (tighter than in most European countries, see Bianchi, Bianco, Enriques 2000), rules for minority shareholders protection have still been considered poor until recently. For example, derivative suits were not possible for minority shareholders and proxy voting was basically forbidden. This implied that within pyramidal groups the defences against minority shareholders' expropriation were limited.

The recent corporate governance reform (Testo Unico in materia di intermediazione finanziaria, decreto legislativo 24 febbraio 1998, n. 58.) has introduced some of these instruments to the Italian system too (for a brief discussion, see Bianchi and Enriques 1999) and might have an impact on the performance of companies.

Given this structure, the survey on the relationship between corporate governance and performance will concentrate more on the evidence on rent extraction than on the effects of the separation between ownership and control. In what follows, the evidence is based mostly on data until 1996–7. Hence the effects of the privatization programme and of the listed company law reform are not yet apparent. In particular it would be interesting to address the emergence (and in various cases the rapid disappearance) of public companies, and the reasons for and effects of recent takeovers.

2. EFFECTS OF BLOCK-HOLDER CONTROL

In Italy the most common control device is block-holder control, which means that a comparison between this type of control and management control is not really significant (even if, recently, with the privatization of public utilities and of some large Italian state-owned companies, the situation is slowly changing). Therefore I report here mainly on the analyses of the effects of shareholders' concentration and control type on performance and on the evidence regarding rent extraction.

Bianco and Signorini (1996), for a representative sample of manufacturing companies, compare profitability and productivity levels (measured by balance sheet data) for different 'control models' (absolute control, family control, coalition control, group control, 'pseudo-public company') without finding significant differences. Some control models perform marginally significantly better in some sectors, i.e. family control in traditional sectors and group control in scale or high-tech sectors.

For a representative sample of manufacturing firms with more than 50 employees, Bianco and Casavola (1999) find that, after controlling for market concentration, productivity, growth opportunities, balance sheet profitability measures (ROI, ROE, ROS, since most of the companies are not listed, stock market returns cannot be used) are related to ownership concentration in a non-linear fashion. The lowest profitability level is achieved where the largest shareholder owns more than two-thirds of the voting capital, whereas the largest profits are attained at an intermediate level, where the largest shareholder holds between 50 and 66 per cent of the equity. A possible interpretation is linked to the fact that a two-thirds majority allows the controlling shareholder full rights of decision (and hence possibly expropriation of minority shareholders), since two-thirds is the majority required for decisions in extraordinary shareholder meetings. At the intermediate level there is a larger coincidence between the interests of majority and minority shareholders, and the latter are able to intervene to oppose the former in the extraordinary shareholders' meetings.

Other studies test more directly for the possibility of rent extraction. Zingales (1994), by looking at data on Italian listed companies over the period 1987–90, finds that the value of control estimated as the premium of voting shares over non-voting shares is extremely high in Italy (nearly 100 per cent). Most of it is due to private benefits of control. He estimates that in Italy 'private benefits of control represent between 16 per cent and 37 per cent of the value of the underlying asset'. Private benefits of control increase the more contestable is control (where the contestability is measured either by the concentration of ownership or by a Shapley value). This extremely high value as compared internationally is likely to be due to the poor shareholder protection in Italy.

Caprio and Floreani (1996) investigate 33 controlling block transfers in the period 1980–91 (one-third of all transfers that occurred) and find evidence of large control premia. The median ex-post global premium (measured as premium per share times the number of shares in the controlling block) is approximately 18 per cent of the value of the equity of the corporation. After the transfer of the block, excess returns disappear.

Nicodano and Sembenelli (1996), for a sample of 121 block transactions of 78 listed companies in the period 1987–92, relate estimates of the private benefits of control to the 'power' of the blocks as measured by the Shapley value. They estimate private benefits to be of an order between 20 and 35 per cent of the market price of voting shares.

Bianco, Casavola, and Ferrando (1997), for a sample of firms belonging to pyramidal groups which include at least one listed company, for the year 1993, find that the amount of external finance that controlling shareholders are able to raise is positively related to the guarantees for minority shareholders and negatively related to the opportunities for expropriation. Expropriation is proxied, among other things, by the degree of vertical integration of the group which facilitates intragroup resource transfers.

This evidence suggests that the existence of block-holders in Italy may have induced mainly rent extraction rather than aligned incentives of majority shareholders with minority ones.

3. TAKEOVERS

Two questions are usually considered when evaluating whether takeovers are an efficient corporate governance mechanism. (1) What induces them, i.e. which companies are more subject to changes in control? (2) What are the effects of takeovers?

In Italy control transfers are not extremely frequent and are rarely hostile. Among manufacturing companies (mainly non-listed) over the period 1992–7, approximately 2 per cent every year have been subject to a control transfer (excluding those occurring within the same group). Among listed companies the percentage is approximately 3.5 per cent per year, which is lower than in France and the UK.

Guelpa (1992) suggests that horizontal takeovers in Italy in the period 1983–7 were not driven by the need to correct agency problems. For a sample of 117 acquired companies there are no significant differences between these and a matching sample of companies where control was not transferred for profitability, growth, technology, and financial structure. However, takeovers improve the financial structure and labour productivity of the acquired company. These results appear more consistent with the search for economies of scale and scope (and possibly for market power) than with the correction of managerial inefficiencies.

Bianco and Signorini (1996), for a representative sample of manufacturing companies for the years 1984–92, do not find significant differences between companies that are going to be taken over and others, with respect to productivity, sales growth, and employment growth. There are also no significant differences between companies that were taken over and companies that were not taken over, except for employment growth, which is lower for the former, controlling for size, sector, and geographical area differences.

Caprio and Floreani (1996) analyse the effects of control transfers on stock market prices. Changes in control are not beneficial for minority shareholders, since the event appears to have a neutral average impact on the stock market prices. However, Bianco and Casavola (1999) find that firms with lower performance or with greater financial problems have a slightly greater probability of changing ownership. Takeovers are more frequent if the company is less profitable, more credit constrained, and if the company uses less capacity.

In general, takeovers in Italy have not represented until recently an instrument to solve agency problems or to guarantee that inefficient controlling agents are substituted. Rather, as a survey on small and medium manufacturing companies has shown (see Barca *et al.* 1994), they are induced by liquidity problems (33 per cent of the sample), death or ageing of the controlling agent (4 per cent), conflicts within the control structure (10 per cent), or, when they occur by the free will of the controlling agent, by 'industrial' factors.

4. BOARD STRUCTURE, MANAGERIAL COMPENSATION AND TURNOVER

Very limited evidence is available in Italy on management compensation and its relationship to company performance. Even for listed companies data have not been available until recently for board members separately. Only aggregated data for the board as a whole had to be communicated to the stock exchange supervision authority.

Brunello, Graziani, and Parigi (1999b), based on a dataset of 1,522 managerial positions in 74 firms, find that managerial pay is sensitive to firm performance, and that there is evidence of relative performance evaluation. The pay–performance relationship is affected by standard measures of risk. They also find that the pay of managers who work for foreign-owned firms or for firms affiliated to a multinational group is more sensitive to the current performance of these firms than the pay of managers who work for domestically owned firms. Italian capitalism does not appear to be prone to use pay–performance schemes.

Regarding the relationship between board of directors' turnover and performance, Brunello, Graziani, and Parigi (1999*a*), for a sample of listed companies over the period 1988–96, find that firms with a worse performance experience a higher CEO turnover rate. This relationship depends on the ownership characteristic of the firm. In family-controlled firms turnover is lower; however, it is more sensitive to performance. Moreover the authors find evidence of a monitoring role of the second largest share-holder, i.e. the larger his/her share is, the more sensitive turnover is to performance. This suggests limited entrenchment options for the CEO. The result of no significant relationship between performance and turnover of the entire board might be evidence of entrenchment for the board as a whole.

5. IDENTITY OF OWNERS

5.1. *Bank–firm relationships*

In Italy banks were not allowed to own shares in non-financial companies until 1992. Hence only links based on close and stable credit relationships have been possible, and even those to a limited extent. The impact of these relationships has been extensively analysed with different datasets and methodologies. Most empirical studies are based on the matching of balance-sheet data with credit register data and agree that, consistent with the theory, a close and stable credit relationship with a bank reduces credit rationing and liquidity constraints (see Angelini and Guiso 1996; Bianco 1997; and Bianco, Ferri, and Finaldi Russo 1998). The tests are either based on a measure of credit rationing derived from a survey or on estimates of the Euler equation for investment including a proxy for liquidity constraints. The cost paid by the firms increases with the concentration of credit, measured either by the share of the main bank of the firm or by a Herfindahl concentration index (see D'Auria and Foglia 1997; Conegliani, Ferri, and Generale 1997; Sapienza 1997; and Bianco, Ferri, and Finaldi Russo 1998). On the other hand, a close relationship appears to partially insure against the effects of monetary restrictions, i.e. smaller firms with more stable and closer relationships with banks are less penalized by increased interest rates when there are restrictions in monetary policy (see Conegliani, Ferri, and Generale 1997; and Bianco, Ferri, and Finaldi Russo 1998).

Still limited, however, is the role of direct share participation of banks in non-financial firms. At the end of 1996 total share participation were approximately 2.2b. lira, mostly linked to debt restructuring. A role in firms' corporate governance of non-financial companies might have been played by banks through interlocking direc-torates (see Ferri and Trento 1997; and Bianco and Pagnoni 1997).

As already noticed, in Italy the Continental model based on bank supervision was not common. The survey by Barca *et al.* (1994) on small and medium companies shows that banks and financial intermediaries play only a limited role in favouring control transfers and in financing them.

5.2. *Institutional investors*

In Italy institutional investors still play an extremely limited role in corporate governance. First their shares in listed companies are not large. In 1996, open-end funds owned approximately 5 per cent of listed companies' capital, in 1998 this share increased to 7.5 per cent (see Bianchi and Enriques 1999). Second, until recently some institutional investors were controlled by industrial companies and this might have introduced conflicts of interests and discouraged activism. Finally, rules regarding in particular proxy voting have not favoured an active role in shareholder meetings. In 1995 and 1996 various episodes of opposition during shareholders' meetings have occurred, and the open-end fund association has pushed for greater transparency of listed companies. As a whole, however, institutional investors are basically passive (see Rubino and Verna 1996).

Bianchi and Enriques (1999) discuss how likely institutional investor activism is in Italy, based on institutional investor shareholdings, investment strategies, ownership structure, and corporate governance of listed companies. Moreover, they evaluate whether the 1998 company law reform has made activism more likely. The concentration of shareholdings is consistent with a potentially active role, however, the ownership structure (institutional investors currently mostly owned by banks) as well as the ownership structure of listed companies (mostly controlled by a single shareholder) is not. The 1998 reform introduced the possibility of soliciting proxies and made the legal environment more favourable to institutional investors' activism. However, according to the authors, the reform has not significantly changed the rules for shareholders' meetings which make it costly and difficult for institutions to exercise their vote.

6. CONCLUSIONS

In Italy, control models are different from those common in the Anglo-Saxon system. This implies that the links between governance and performance have a different nature from those traditionally analysed in the literature. Takeovers are extremely infrequent, rarely hostile, and do not appear to be used to replace inefficient controlling agents. Management compensation is not a common mechanism to reduce agency problems. Institutional supervision is still rare.

The main conflict of interest has developed between block-holders and minority shareholders (see Becht 1997; and Gugler 1998) especially in pyramidal groups. However, since these have frequently represented an instrument to grow and achieve some degree of separation, it is often difficult to disentangle these effects.

References for Chapter 11

Angelini, P. and L. Guiso (1996), 'Razionamento del credito: Cause, diffusione e persistenza', Banca d'Italia, mimeo.
Barca, F. (1996), 'On Corporate Governance in Italy: Issues, Facts and Agenda', Fondazione Eni Enrico Mattei, Working paper no.10/96.

Barca, F., M. Bianco, L. Cannari, R. Cesari, C. Gola, G. Manitta, G. Salvo, and L. F. Signorini (1994), *Assetti proprietari e mercato delle imprese*, i, Bologna: Il Mulino.

Becht, M. (1997), 'Strong Block-holders, Weak Owners and the Need for European Mandatory Disclosure', mimeo.

Bianchi, M. and P. Casavola (1996), Piercing the Corporate Veil: Truth and Appearance in Italian Listed Pyramidal Groups, Fondazione Eni Enrico Mattei, Working paper no. 6/96.

—— and L. Enriques (1999), 'Corporate Governance in Italy after the 1998 Reform: What Role for Institutional Investors?', mimeo.

—— M. Bianco, and L. Enriques (2001), 'Ownership, Pyramidal Groups and Separation between Ownership and Control in Italy', in Barca, F. and M. Becht (eds.), *The Control of Corporate Europe*, Oxford: Oxford University Press.

Bianco, M. (1997), 'Vincoli finanziari e scelte reali delle imprese italiane: gli effetti di una relazione stabile con una banca', in I. Angeloni *et al.* (ed.), *Le banche e il finanziamento delle imprese*, Bologna: Il Mulino.

—— and P. Casavola (1999), 'Italian Corporate Governance: Effects on Financial Structure and Performance', *European Economic Review*, 43/4–6 (April): 1057–69.

—— and E. Pagnoni (1997), Interlocking Directorates across Listed Companies in Italy: The Case of Banks', *Banca Nazionale del Lavoro Quarterly Review*, Special Issue (March).

—— and L. F. Signorini (1996), 'Modelli di controllo, riallocazione e performance: alcune evidenze per l'Italia', in S. Beretta and P. Bianchi (eds.), 'Cambiamento delle istituzioni economiche e nuovo sviluppo in Italia e in Europa', Bologna: Il Mulino.

—— P. Casavola, and A. Ferrando (1997), 'Pyramidal Groups and External Finance: An Empirical Investigation', Fondazione Eni Enrico Mattei, Working paper no. 61/97.

—— G. Ferri, and P. Finaldi Russo (1998), 'Condizioni di accesso al credito bancario e nuove esigenze per il finanziamento delle piccole e medie imprese', mimeo.

—— C. Gola, and L. F. Signorini (1996), 'Dealing with Separation between Ownership and Control: State, Family, Coalitions and Pyramidal Groups in Italian Corporate Governance', Fondazione Eni Enrico Mattei, Working paper no. 5/96.

Brunello, G., C. Graziani, and B. Parigi (1999*a*) 'Ownership or Performance: What Determines Board of Directors' Turnover in Italy?', Fondazione Eui Enrico Mattei Working paper no. 30/99.

—— —— —— (forthcoming *b*)'Executive Compensation and Firm Performance in Italy', *International Journal of Industrial Organization*.

Caprio, L., and A. Floreani (1996), 'Transfer of Control of Listed Companies in Italy: An Empirical Analysis', Fondazione Eni Enrico Mattei, Working paper no. 8/96.

Congliani, C., G. Ferri, and A. Generale (1997), 'The Impact of Bank-firm Relations on the Propagation of Monetary Policy Squeezes: An Empirical Assessment for Italy', *Banca Nazionale del Lavoro Quarterly Review*, 202.

D'Auria, C., and A. Foglia (1997), 'Le determinanti del tasso di interesse sui crediti alle imprese', in Angeloni *et al.* (ed.), *Le banche e il finanziamento delle imprese*.

Ferri, G., and S. Trento (1997), 'La dirigenza delle grandi banche e delle grnadi imprese: ricambio e legami', in F. Barca (ed.), *Storia del capitalismo italiano dal dopoguerra a oggi*, Roma: Donzelli.

Guelpa, F. (1992), *Crescita esterna e performance competitive*, Roma: Nuova Italia Scientifica.

Gugler, K. (1998), 'Corporate Governance and Economic Perfomance', mimeo.

La Porta, R., F. Lopez de Silanes, A. Shleifer, R. Vishny (1998), 'Law and Finance', *Journal of Political Economy*, 106: 1113–55.

Nicodano, G., and A. Sembenelli (1996), 'Block Transaction and Partial Private Benefits: An Empirical Investigation', Working paper no. 112, Centro di economia monetaria e finanziaria 'Paolo Baffi'.

Rubino, E. and A. Verna (1996), 'Tendenze recenti in tema di corporate governance: l'esperienza italiana e quella estera a confronto', in IRS (ed.), *Rapporto IRS sul mercato azionario 1996*, Milano: Il Sole 24 Ore Libri.

Sapienza, P. (1997), 'Le scelte di finanziamento delle imprese italiane', in Angeloni *et al.* (ed.), *Le banche e il finanziamento delle imprese.*

Volpin, P. F. (1998), 'Entrenchment in Pyramidal Groups: Evidence from Top Executives' Turnover in Italy', mimeo, Harvard University.

Zingales, L. (1994), 'The Value of Voting Right: A Study of the Milan Stock Exchange Experience', *Review of Financial Studies*, 7: 125–48.

12

Japan

KYOKO SAKUMA

1. INTRODUCTION

This survey highlights the relationship between firm ownership structure and corporate performance in Japan. It also examines the board structure and managerial compensation. While there are many studies looking at differences in performance between *keiretsu*-affiliated firms (i.e. business groups centred around a large commercial bank) and non-*keiretsu* firms, there are few studies focusing on different types of dominant owners (banks, insurance companies, institutional investors, families, etc.).

One reason for the low attention paid to the relationship between ownership structure and corporate performance is that Japanese firms, regardless of their ownership structure and size, have generally low profit and low return on equity (ROE) compared to firms in other OECD countries. Despite the concern for rapid corporate reform, in order to regain competitiveness in today's economic slump, there is still the widely held view in Japan that a firm exists for the sake of its employees and all other stakeholders including shareholders. Value or profit maximization remains a secondary objective.[1] Given that financial institutions and private firms are dominant shareholders in Japan, the main interests of shareholders will probably not be high profits, but rather a stable long-term relationship with the management of the firm. To understand the relation between ownership structure and corporate performance, it is essential, therefore, to explore Japan's unique mechanism of 'contingent governance'. It is important to note, however, that among large companies a new Japanese management style is emerging, giving weight to shareholder value.

Furthermore, the insider-oriented board composition of Japanese companies, and the seniority-based remuneration system for managers, are essential elements of the contingent governance. Again, among a few large companies, a shift towards outsiders on the board and performance-based payment is observed. These large firms are viewed as driving the new Japanese corporate governance model, based on a new balance between employees, shareholders and creditors.

The survey is organized as follows. Section 2 describes the ownership structure of Japanese firms and gives some historical explanation for its present form. Then 'contingent governance' is explained. Section 3 describes the board structure of Japanese companies as well as its role. Section 4 reviews the seniority-based compensation pattern for managers and discusses some recent cases of merit-based compensation including stock options. Section 5 reviews some empirical studies that test the relationship between ownership structure and performance. Section 6 describes the market for corporate control in Japan. Section 7 discusses the growing role of institutional investors as cross-holdings dissolve, and their possible influence on corporate performance. The last section suggests future areas of research in light of the emergence of a new role of foreign and institutional investors, as well as outside board members, in Japanese corporate governance.

2. OWNERSHIP STRUCTURE OF THE JAPANESE COMPANY SYSTEM

2.1. *Dominance of financial institutions*

More than one-third of shares are in the hands of financial institutions, namely, banks and insurance companies (see Table 12.1). As a result of the dismantling of business cliques (*zaibatsu*) under the US Occupation in 1947, most of the corporate shares (70 per cent) were transferred to individuals (mainly to employees and inhabitants of the areas where the businesses were founded). These shares, however, were soon transferred to the corporate sector due to two factors. Firstly, a huge fall in stock prices on the Tokyo Stock Exchange in the late 1940s forced individual shareholders to sell shares. Secondly, both remaining *zaibatsu*-origin companies and non-*zaibatsu* companies gradually increased cross-shareholding ratios to alleviate takeover pressures from overseas. Such cross-holding further accelerated in the 1960s and the 1970s (Miyajima 1995).[2]

Share holdings of individuals continued to decline and stood at 24 per cent of the total shares in 1996. Thus, the concentration of shares in the hands of financial institutions is the result of the last three decades.[3] The percentage of shares owned by financial institutions (after the peak in 1988, 42.5 per cent) remained at around 40 per cent until recent years. Since 1987, commercial law (Art. 11) has stated that a bank is allowed

Table 12.1. *Share distribution by ownership type in Japan* (%)

Ownership type	1949	1988	1990	1993	1994	1995	1996
Financial institutions	9.9	42.5	41.6	40.8	40.9	39.3	39.3
Private companies	5.6	24.9	25.2	23.9	23.8	23.6	23.8
Individuals	69.1	22.4	23.1	23.7	23.5	23.6	23.6
Foreigners	n.a.	4.0	4.2	6.7	7.4	9.4	9.8
Investment trust	n.a.	3.1	3.6	3.0	2.6	2.1	2.0
Securities companies	12.6	2.5	1.7	1.3	1.1	1.4	1.1
Government	2.8	0.6	0.6	0.6	0.7	0.6	0.5

Source: Study on Share distribution (*kabushiki bunnpu jyoukyou chosa*), 1991 & 1996 by the Association of Stock Exchanges in Japan.

to hold a maximum of 5 per cent in a single non-financial institution (previously 10 per cent). There is, however, no restriction on total share holding.

The Japanese corporate system can be characterized by (1) a main bank system, (2) the *keiretsu* system, and (3) life-time employment.[4] These three characteriztics imply that Japanese firms have enjoyed less pressure from the capital market, due to intermediate finance via banks, and stable shareholding among a group of firms (Miyajima 1998c). The cross-share holding has been an instrument for protecting against hostile takeovers (see also section 6).

Due to recent mergers among large banks, today there are only four financial *keiretsu* left (see section 2.3). These four largest financial groups are Mitsubishi-Tokyo Financial Group, Sumitomo-Mitsui Banking Corporation, Mizuho Financial Group, and the United Financial of Japan. Previously there were six financial groups, Mitsubishi, Mitsui, Sumitomo, Fuyo, Daiichikangin, and Sanwa, headed by Tokyo-Mitsubishi Bank, Sakura Bank, Sumitomo Bank, Fuji Bank, DKB, and Sanwa Bank, respectively.

The most recent data by Nikkei indicate a significant increase in foreign ownership in Japanese non-financial companies, particularly in the automobile sector and the financial services sectors.[5] Their ownership increase is largely driven by stock split.[6]

Besides, 'Organizational control' (Horiuchi 1995) exists, where the management aims to maximize the predetermined weighted interests of both employees and shareholders (Aoki 1994; Aoki and Okuno 1997; and Fukao 1997).

2.2. *Contingent governance*

Aoki (1988) uses the term 'Bipartite control' (*Sotaiteki* control) to describe a system where the management is subject to control by shareholders on the one hand and employees on the other hand. The weight of control rights pertaining to management decisions is predetermined and shifts between the two parties, depending on the financial condition of a firm (Aoki, 1994). Under this 'Contingent governance', potential moral hazard by employees is eliminated by installing an incentive system for employees to improve their efforts. Such incentives for employees are long-term employment (if not lifetime, Aoki and Okuno 1997) and Employee Stock Ownership Programmes (ESOPs, Nakatani, 1987; and Jones and Kato 1995). Thus, investment in firm-specific assets is relatively large. Using panel data, Jones and Kato found that ESOPs increase productivity by 4–5 per cent with a lag of three to four years. Productivity gains by bonus systems are further enhanced by ESOPs.

Contingent governance has a 'monitor' who checks the financial conditions and executes the transfer of control rights. The monitor must not be an insider of the firm, and in Japan it is always a main bank. The main bank has incentives to replace the management of a low-performing firm, since it is often one of the largest shareholders, and it wants to maintain a stable and long-term customer relationship with the firm.

There are, however, insufficient incentives for other shareholders to monitor under the contingent governance system. Shareholders only receive the predetermined level of dividends even when the firm is performing fairly well. In contrast, employees receive extra income as the firm's performance soars. When performance is bad, employees receive the minimum agreed income, while the shareholders continue to receive the predetermined level of dividends.[7]

Contingent governance has developed on the premise that the private sector should provide a safety net. The Japanese public sector does not provide sufficient security nor an insurance system to support individuals who are out of work. Contingent governance is only compatible with a system where long-term employment protects firm-specific investments. It does not work in an environment where the market for corporate control is highly developed and the labour market is highly flexible (Aoki 1995*b*); and Aoki and Okuno 1997).

2.3. *New trend*

The recent financial turmoil and subsequent collapse of some large financial institutions changed the banks' role and the tightly held affiliated companies. Many large companies are questioning the importance of stable share holding as the value of mutually held shares deteriorated severely during the recent crisis.

A recent survey by the Ministry of Finance (2000) reveals, however, that main banks will remain a vital source of finance for the majority of companies. Among 1,433 respondents, 71 per cent said that the main benefits of main banks are that they provide a source of finance in unexpected incidents, and that they provide relevant information services for new investments. Other reasons for maintaining a main bank relationship are the expectation of being bailed out when in financial distress (particularly for the largest size category with capital of more than ¥30bn., and the companies with capital of ¥1bn.–¥3bn.). For the companies in the smallest size category (capital less than ¥1bn.), the reason is not being bailed out, but relatively cheap and easily obtainable finance.

The question is how contingent governance can adapt to the recent crisis. At least three legal changes point to a new balance among shareholders, employees, financial institutions, and management. Firstly, since 1997, holding companies have been allowed. Second, stock options were introduced in 1997 (see section 4). Third, the most important factor is the comprehensive reform of Japan's stock corporation system under the commercial laws, which is planned for 2002. The planned reform will strengthen general shareholders' meetings, giving more power and responsibility to boards of directors, publishing their remuneration basis, strengthening the role of auditors, and redefining the system of shareholder litigation. The reform will also provide a legal framework for accountability requirements.[8]

Furthermore, the implementation of new merit-based remuneration systems and of a new corporate pension scheme based on defined contribution (see section 7) by large companies might give an impetus to changing the work organization in Japan. The new supplementary corporate pension scheme, the so-called Japanese 401 k pension, obliges individuals to be responsible for investment plans and thus for the final benefits received at the time of retirement or exit from the company.

3. BOARD STRUCTURE AND ITS ROLE

3.1. *Board composition*

The Japanese board is larger than in Western countries. The average number of board members of top 100 firms was 30.7 in 1990 with a mode of 37 and a range from 8 to 56. The size of the board has diminished in some large companies but it appears to remain too large. There are very few outside directors. According to a survey conducted by Yomiuri Journal in 1997, 17 out of 40 large companies had outside directors. The total number of outside directors for the 17 firms was 32 including 13 main bank officials or *keiretsu* members.

The current board structure is based on the revised Commercial Code of 1951, which stipulates that the board members should not be owners of a company but representatives of the interests of the firm, i.e. employees. Persons eligible to be board members are senior employees who have been in the company for many years. The revision of 1951 practically abolished the distinction between decision-making function and management oversight function (Baum and Schaede 1994; and Ballon and Matsuzaki 2000). This means that most directors are executive managers. This 'management forum' in the boardroom is further reinforced by having very few outside directors, and by the typical role of board chairman in Japan. The chairman of the board is expected to be a guardian of the president, is typically the ex-president, and has the power to select the top management of the company.[9]

As a result of the concentration of power and control among executive managers, Japanese companies do not have a built-in check and control device. The disadvantage of a single decision centre within a company has become clear in recent years, as a main bank will no longer bail out a company as easily as before the 'bubble economy'.

3.2. *New trend*

Among some large companies, there is a move towards a reduced number of directors and towards more outside directors on the board, driven partly by the 1998 consultation paper 'OECD Principles (Benchmark) on Corporate Governance'. Sony, for example, reduced its directors to one-third (from 38 to 10) and introduced 3 outside directors whose respective backgrounds were banking, consultancy, and academia. Among the company's 41 executive officers only 5 insiders were retained. Sony set up a nominating and compensation committee, composed of outside directors (*Nikkei Weekly*, March 1998, and 'Notice to Shareholders on the Results of the Shareholders' Meeting', 29 June 1999, reported in Ballon and Matsuzaki 2000: 39).

The issue of outside directors has a profound bearing on the work organization in Japan. It remains unclear, however, whether the so-called Anglo-Saxon board structure will be successful in the Japanese corporate culture. As a matter of fact, the NASDAQ Japan, a new stock market created by the National Association of Stocks and Derivatives (NASD), Soft Bank and Osaka Stock Exchange, is currently examining the adoption of the US NASDAQ listing criteria of a minimum of 2 outside directors and half of the auditing committee members being outsiders.

As an example, Figure 12.1 presents the board structure of Nissan before and after the tie-up with Renault in 1999. The board structure of Nissan represented the typical governance of large Japanese companies until the company tied up with Renault. The board was composed of 37 directors, who all participated in the board meetings irrespective of subject areas. These directors were composed of one chairman, one president, six vice-presidents, thirteen *jomu* (executives), sixteen directors (*torishimariyaku*), and five auditors.

The management team from Renault, which came into Nissan in 1999, overhauled this practice, to gain efficiency in decision-making. First of all, the size of the board was reduced to nine members: a chairman (Chief Executive Officer), a president (Chief Operating Officer), and seven vice-presidents (one of whom is Chief Financial Officer). Executive directorship was introduced, so that 22 *jomu* as well as four auditors are no longer board members. *Jomu* participate in the Executive Committee only when their expertise is required. Auditors, despite their position as board members prior to 1999, were considered to be outside of the chain of command and decision-making of the chairman and CEO. Auditors are completely outside the decision-making process today. The new structure clarifies the responsibilities of the CEO and COO as well as their line of command. The vice-chairman assumes a role of external contact and negotiation and is no longer a board member.

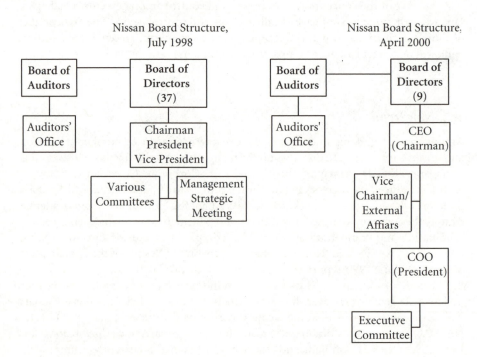

Figure 12.1. *Nissan board structure before and after tie-up with Renault (Japan)*

4. MANAGERIAL COMPENSATION

Compared to other developed countries, the remuneration of top managers in Japanese companies is low. The data by Towers Perrin show that the average total pay for chief executives in Japan was USD 0.49m., compared to USD 1.35m. in the USA, USD 0.67m. in the UK and Canada, and USD 0.53m. in Germany in 1999 (*The Economist*, 27 November 1999). The share of incentive-related benefits is also low. Only one-third of the total pay is non-basic pay in Japan, while more than half of the total pay is remunerated as incentive-based pay in the USA.

The small share of merit- and incentive-related payment for Japanese executives reflects the long-standing system of seniority-based payment, and the way in which board members are selected. The pay level is predominantly determined by 'rank', and incentives are created for the employees to achieve higher ranks.[10] Three-quarters of the basic pay is usually determined by the job title, and the remaining quarter is determined by age (Koike 1998). The pay level of board members is not disclosed and does not require the shareholders' agreement.

A growing number of companies are considering a move towards merit/result-based pay. In 1998, 74 per cent of the surveyed companies had already introduced annual pay contracts for management posts, based on the previous year's performance.[11] Furthermore, some large companies introduced stock options for managers as an incentive scheme. Stock options were introduced in Japan in 1997 with a considerable tax advantage. Income from options below 10 million yen is exempt from income tax under certain conditions. When the share is sold, the holder is subject to a 26 per cent income tax. Stock options are expected not only to increase the pay level of Japanese managers, but also to shift management style to be more shareholder-value oriented.

5. OWNERSHIP CONCENTRATION AND PROFITABILITY: *KEIRETSU* FIRMS VS. NON-*KEIRETSU* FIRMS

There is no empirical evidence that concentrated ownership has a positive influence on profitability in Japan. Nakatani (1984) finds that member companies of *keiretsu* are less profitable than non-affiliated companies, but show more stable sales growth and profit rates. Nakatani (1984) attributes the low profitability of *keiretsu* firms to the 'implicit insurance mechanism' of the main bank system for which these firms are obliged to pay. Weinstein and Yafeh (1998) confirm low profitability of companies with close ties to banks, and suggest that close ties with financial institutions do not foster faster growth or higher profit, as banks extract rents via higher interest rates in the absence of alternative financial funds. The study by Hoshi and Ito (1991) further supports this by showing that average stability of performance is greater for firms in a more coherent *keiretsu* group.

Prowse (1992) reveals, however, that for *keiretsu* and for independent firms, ownership concentration (based on financial institutions ranked among the top five shareholders) is positively but insignificantly related to profitability in 1984. Prowse suggests that shareholdings are less effective in monitoring management than other control means, such as direct monitoring by banks through credit records when compared to US firms. Prowse (1992) also tests the relationship between ownership concentration and profit volatility, to see if there is an insurance mechanism that stabilizes a member company's performance (see also Nakatani 1984). The result, however, is that the concentration of ownership among *keiretsu* firms has a negative relationship to profit volatility, thus no such insurance mechanism seems to be at work.

Concentrated share- and debt-holdings by a bank appear to provide effective incentives for rescue operations when a firm becomes financially distressed (Fuji 1993; Fukao 1997). Likewise, these are effective tools for banks, enabling them to restructure the financially distressed firm's liabilities without having to rely on bankruptcy courts (Suzuki and Wright 1985). Member companies of *keiretsu* are more resistant to financial distress and less affected by liquidity problems (Hoshi, Kashyap, and Sharfstein 1991; Asako, Kunanori, Inoue, and Murase 1991; and Okazaki and Horiuchi 1992). Hoshi, Kashyap, and Sharfstein (1991) find that the companies in a *keitretsu* structure invest and sell more than non-*keiretsu* companies in the years following financial distress.

The contingent governance system has been considered to be a social norm.[12] Fukao (1997), however, suggests that weakening cross-holding commitments on both sides, i.e. companies and banks, and increasing share ownership by foreigners and institutional investors, may result in increased pressures on the management to achieve higher returns on investment and to raise dividend payout ratios in the future. The recent empirical study conducted by Miyajima and Arikawa (1999) on the effect of expected return on debt choice (bond issue or bank borrowing) indeed indicates that a management with high return expectations tends to select bond financing, i.e. borrowing without potential rescue operation by banks. This relation holds more clearly in the early 1990s than in the late 1980s, and it is more pronounced for firms with close main bank ties than those with weaker ties.

Furthermore, the bargaining position of employees will decrease, as the newly active shareholders will press for more lay-offs. Fukao predicts that the profitability of a formerly cross-held firm will increase as institutional shareholders gain more control. However, there is some evidence to suggest that contingent governance in Japan is unlikely to falter even with increasing shareholder control. One reason is that the Japanese labour market has remained fairly inflexible due to long-term employment and due to lengthy legal processes for lay-offs. Based on the Post-War Labour Court cases in Japan, employers are obliged to follow the administrative steps stipulated by the Court if they want to lay off people. They must prove the need for rationalizations, try to find solutions other than redundancy (replacement etc.), and establish objective criteria for employees to be laid off. When a labour union exists, the employer must negotiate with it. It is, therefore, extremely difficult for Japanese employers to lay off employees (Fukao 1997).[13]

6. TAKEOVERS AND MANAGEMENT TURNOVER

6.1. *Takeover*

The market for corporate control is not highly developed or viewed as a good control device in Japan. Under contingent governance, takeovers have been fairly difficult to pursue in Japan. As explained previously, Japanese banks, particularly large commercial banks, take control over important management decisions in times of financial distress. The control rights, however, return to the incumbent management once the firm recovers from distress and starts making profits again (Aoki 1997).

The shareholding structure has served as an effective takeover defence device, too. It is nearly impossible for outside investors to obtain enough voting shares to proceed with takeover bids. The first takeover case among Japanese companies indicates such underlying difficulties. MAC's (an M&A company) bid for Shoei ended up with a purchase of 6.52 per cent of the equity, since Canon and Fuji Bank (Fuyo Keiretsu) blocked two-thirds of the total equity. Absence of disclosure requirements on a consolidated account basis is also an obstacle to investors as financial performance of subsidiaries is unknown.

Furthermore, Japanese regulations on takeovers are designed to protect the existing shareholders and management. A bidder, once a bid is made, is not permitted to purchase shares in the target firm other than via the takeover bid. The restrictions extend to the bidder's family members, the company officials and any company or person that has a controlling stake in the bidding company. The bidder is not allowed to withdraw the bid and is obliged to purchase all shares of the target company. In contrast, shareholders are allowed to change their decision and to withdraw from the acceptance of a bid within ten days.

Foreign companies as shareholders are an effective tool for management reform or business reorganization. The bid by Beringer-Ingelheim Japan (a subsidiary of German BI) for 33.4 per cent of the shares of SS (a pharmaceutical company) marks a start in restructuring the Japanese pharmaceutical industry. SS's president states that the injection of foreign capital and the replacement of board members is positive, as the incumbent management can be refreshed.

The new bankruptcy law, Corporate Restructuring Law, which took effect in April 2000, plays a particular role in encouraging a distressed company to sell shares to foreign partners. The law will diminish the collateral right of lending banks and almost obliges them to co-operate with the restructuring company.

It is important to note, however, that there are still uneasy feelings towards takeover bids. The president of Canon, for instance, expressed his concern that it is hardly possible to combine the Anglo-Saxon style takeover bids with the company's responsibility towards employees' job security in Japan. Canon opposed MAC's offer principally because MAC had no specific proposal for dealing with employees in Shoei's subsidiaries.

6.2 *Management turnover*

Kaplan and Minton (1993) observe that top executives of Japanese firms are replaced by outside directors when the stock performance is poor. Such appointment of outsiders is more frequent among companies with stronger bank ties and with more concentrated shareholdings than companies with weaker bank ties and a dispersed shareholding structure. Kaplan and Minton measure the intensity of bank ties by the amount of borrowing from banks. Furthermore, stock performance in the year after outside-director appointment improves modestly, and the company's performance stabilizes. This supports the view that main banks and corporate groups play an important role in correcting managerial failure.

Miyajima (1998*a*) analyses a special kind of management turnover besides ordinary managerial turnover under Japanese contingent governance, namely the temporary appointment of outsiders while the incumbent president remains or is replaced by another insider. Miyajima observes that before the oil shocks of the 1970s the turnover rate was low and most of the turnover was replacement by outsiders. This changed after the oil shocks, when turnover rates increased dramatically and the presidents of badly performing firms were increasingly replaced by other insiders. At the same time, appointments of outsiders to decision-making posts have increased. Furthermore, Miyajima found that the correlation between management turnover and performance has weakened gradually since the oil shocks.

Usually, a leaving president becomes the chairman of the same company in Japan. However, there exists 'non-standard turnover' or 'non-routine turnover' (Kaplan 1994; Kang and Shivsadani 1995; and Miyajima 1998*a*) where the leaving president does not become the chairman. Non-standard turnover is understood as correcting managerial failure. However, the incidence of non-standard turnover declined dramatically from 45 per cent of total turnover in the late 1960s to 17 per cent in the mid 1990s.

7. OBSTACLES TO INSTITUTIONAL INVESTORS AND THE ABSENCE OF PROFIT-MAXIMIZING INCENTIVES

Institutional investors such as insurance companies, pension funds, and investment trusts owned 20 per cent of the corporate shares in 1996. Despite the global recognition that institutional shareholders may entail efficiency gains, several institutional arrangements and regulations have kept Japanese institutional investors from playing a prominent role in the governance of corporations.

There are at least three institutional factors which limit the control rights of institutional investors in Japan (see Fukao 1997). First, as most of the board members are insiders, institutional investors have very limited access to management decision-making. The sole shareholders who have occasional access to management decision-making are banks, with the level of involvement contingent on the financial condition of the firm. In fact, in 1993 an overwhelming majority of firms still expected their main banks to rescue them (including a transfer of bank officials to the board) in case of financial distress.[14]

Second, as the bankruptcy law in Japan favours creditors, shareholders with no credit relations have little to say concerning management turnover. In financial distress, shareholding creditors such as main banks assume absolute control over the fate of management (Packer and Ryser 1992).[15]

Third, the base for dividend payments is confined to a firm's profit in Japan. Paying back the paid-in capital to shareholders in the form of dividends is prohibited in Japan. Since the paid-in capital remains under the control of management, shareholders have less discretion and power—compared to the USA—over the firm's capital (Fukao1997). The 'pecking order' in terms of right of claims on the firm's capital is, according to Aoki (1995*b*): creditors > core employees > management > shareholders > employees with contracts. Fukao (1997) suggests that the ranking of shareholders with respect to claims on firm assets remains the same in the future, although the increasing ownership of foreign and institutional investors will deprive management of full discretion over unrealized values of shares.

In addition to the obstacles mentioned above, the way in which the general shareholders' meetings are set up by the management decreases the motivation of shareholders to perform their monitoring function well. Most shareholders' meetings in Japan take place on the *same* day (Ramseyer and Nakazato 1998). Ballon and Matsuzaki (2000) report that 1,807 companies (94 per cent of the sample) held their general meetings on 27 June in 1997, while in 1998 2,325 companies on 26 June (originally reported in *Nihon Keizai Shinbun*, 26 and 27 June 1998.) In 2000, 29 June was a peak day with 2,161 companies holding the shareholders' meeting (*Nihon Keizai Shinbun*, 30 June 2000). Three-quarters of general meetings last for less than thirty minutes (*Shoji Homu*, Special Issue, November 1997: 108–9, as reported in Ballon and Matsuzaki 2000). Some reform-oriented and/or foreign-owned companies are reported to hold meetings that last longer than thirty minutes. Among them, Nissan Motor recorded the longest meeting (four hours) in 2000, in the first shareholders' meeting after the tie-up with Renault of France.

There are also some legal obstacles to playing an important role for institutional investors. Concerning investment trusts, their subordinate status to securities houses makes it impossible to attract individual investors. Japanese securities houses may dismantle the investment trust whose period is over, and switch to a new fund. This practice undermines the individual investor's confidence (Ueda 1994). Furthermore, the current tax system is disadvantageous for investments in stocks via investment trusts.[16]

Corporate pension funds have not developed as important investors in Japan, either, mainly due to tax disadvantages. Another hurdle for corporate pension funds was a regulation on asset management, the so-called 5–3–3–2 rules. The funds had to maintain an investment portfolio which consists of (at least) 50 per cent in safe assets such as national bonds, corporate bonds with collateral, or corporate bonds with minimum A rating. Moreover, investment was restricted to less than 30 per cent in company shares, as well as in assets denominated in foreign currencies, and less than 20 per cent in real estate. Compared to US pension funds whose portfolios consist of up to 60 per cent of company stocks and 12 per cent of national bonds, Japanese portfolios look the reverse (Saito 1997). The 5–3–3–2 rule was gradually lifted from 1996 onwards, and finally abolished in April 1999. However, the statistics of the Ministry of Health and Welfare shows that 40 per cent of pension assets continued to be allocated to safe bonds, and only 36 per cent in equities, in 1997.

There is some progress in both legal instruments and procedural developments for the exercise of shareholder rights. The 1993 Amendment of the Commercial Code facilitates the filing of a lawsuit by shareholders. The amendment clarifies the responsibilities of directors by providing the safeguard that they can be sued for their wrong-doing for a ten-year period after retirement from the board position (Ballon and Matsuzaki 2000).

Whether institutional investors become a driving force for profitability in Japan in the future is certainly dependent on reform in the above-mentioned areas.

8. CONCLUSION—NEW JAPANESE CORPORATE GOVERNANCE MODEL?

The system of management control in Japan is best described by a contingent governance system. In this system, control is shifted to the main bank if financial conditions of a firm deteriorate. This system of control demonstrates quite different relationships among stakeholders than, for example, the Anglo-Saxon or the Continental European systems.

Japanese firms are today undergoing tremendous change in the way they view stable ownership, main banks and life-long employment. Watanabe and Yamamoto (1992) and Hirota and Ikeo (1994), for instance, argue that the lack of disciplinary mechanisms of management in the Japanese contingent governance was the direct cause of inefficient management and excess investment. Dismantling cross-shareholdings of *keiretsu* firms, fading relationships with main banks which can no longer afford rescuing all the failing member firms due to their own financial problems, and increasing corporate bankruptcies and unprecedented lay-offs of employees will all have an impact on the future Japanese corporate governance system.

Stock options, as well as merit-based remuneration systems, are expected to have a major impact on the Japanese contingent governance. Each employee will have different incentives according to what is remunerated on the basis of his/her performance. Thus it is probably difficult to determine the minimum predetermined or agreed benefits when a company falls into financial distress.

An increase in mergers and acquisitions or takeover bids by foreign companies will pose challenges to the Japanese management system, too. With increasing foreign participation, Japanese managers are pressed to be accountable, raise capital more efficiently, cut costs by laying off employees, and increase shareholder value.

The debate on a new model of corporate governance centres around strengthening the role of the board of directors. Separating management from supervision is recognized as an important control mechanism in Japanese corporate governance. Associated accountability of management to supervisors and investors is viewed as an indispensable condition particularly for large companies.

The Corporate Governance Forum of Japan (1997) has been discussing the new model of Japanese corporate governance since 1996. It put forward that the supervisory function of outside auditors should be strengthened to establish an accountable control system of management.[17] Fukao calls for an equal weight of power of outside auditors by granting them the same voting rights as the other board members. Introducing an outside auditor into the current board structure is, however, far from enough to ensure more than one command line (top executive and supervisor).[18] Multiple decision centres to integrate an internal check and control mechanism have long been recognized, for example in the Cadbury Report in the UK.

What remains to be answered is whether outside board members or auditors are able to serve as an effective supervisory agent in the Japanese management, and how the larger accountability of the management influences the way in which employees, shareholders, and main banks will interact under the contingent governance system.

Notes

1. Mr Yotaro Kobayashi, Chairman of the Board of Fuji Xerox, explains that the reason for this management view originated in the fact that Japanese corporations have long substituted for the government by providing a social safety net, such as life-long security. Japanese companies are under pressure to raise productivity to regain competitiveness and wish to remove their function as a social institution by laying off people. However, tight labour laws and the absence of an established safety net make it impossible to reorganize work. In the financial sector, a good example is the restructuring of two banks which went bankrupt in 1998. After nationalizing them as the Deposit Insurance Corporation at the expense of taxpayers, the government did not manage to bring down the costs per person and to reform the work organization and payment systems at the Long-Term Credit Bank and the Nippon Credit Bank.
2. For a historical overview of Japanese corporate governance (pre-war and post-war comparison), see also Okazaki (1998).
3. Miyajima (1998c) observed that in the period 1965 to 1972 cross-shareholdings among the financial sector and the automobile sector grew substantially. Miyajima also argues that the main-bank system in Japan matured in this period. For a detailed analysis of the evolution of Japanese corporate governance, see Miyajima (1998c).
4. The most accepted definition (Fuji Research Institute) for a main bank is: (1) largest creditor; (2) large shareholder; (3) chief trustee for corporate bond issues. (Banks basically approve bond with collateral, although issuance of non-collateral bond was liberalized in 1989 in Japan.) See for example, Fukao (1997), Aoki and Okuno (1997), and Miyajima (1998c).
5. In the automobile sector, Renault purchased 33.4 per cent of Nissan Motor and 22.5 per cent of Nissan Diesel, Daimler Chrysler purchased 33.4 per cent of Mitsubishi Motor, GM also raised its stake in Isuzu to 49 per cent. In the financial services sector, GE Capital, Ripplewood Holdings, and other insurance and investment companies bought entirely or partly the Japanese companies to penetrate mainly in the M&A and pension markets.
6. According to a recent survey conducted by the Japanese Stock Exchange Association (Nihon Shoken Torihiki Kyokai) in 1999, the decline in share ownership by financial institutions and by non-financial companies compared to the previous year (−3.2 per cent and −0.4 per cent respectively) was gained by foreign owners (+2.4 per cent) and individuals (+1 per cent). Among companies that exercised stock split into more than double numbers, Fujitsu Support and Services raised its individual shareholders from 200 to 6,579 (*Nihon Keizai Shinbun*, 26 June 2000).
7. Aoki and Okuno (1997) explain the mechanism as follows: when a firm is performing above the predetermined target level, the extra profit (after the predetermined sum paid out to outside investors) is to be distributed to employees. When performance is below target but above the lowest acceptable level (predetermined by the main bank), the main bank allows payment of the minimum agreed salaries to employees and the predetermined sum to the outside investors, and covers a potential deficit. When the firm's performance falls below the lowest acceptable level, the main bank replaces or lays off employees, after providing them with the minimum agreed salaries. The main bank also pays to the outside investors, although less than the predetermined sum. In the last case, thus, the main bank must cover a substantial deficit.

8. A fourth factor would be the possible revision of the 5 per cent ownership rule for banks. The revised plan for the Three-year deregulation package (1998–2000), drafted by the Regulation Reform Committee of the Administrative Reform Promotion Body headed by last Prime Minister Obuchi, calls for an increase of the bank ownership upper limit in view of cushioning an imminent pressure for merged banks to reduce their shareholding, thus preventing the share price of the companies held by these banks from declining radically.

9. The role of the 'president' in Japan is worth explaining. The president of a company is a top management position, however not subject to control by the board of directors. The president enjoys autonomy and in most of the cases is a symbolic figure and assumes little responsibility. See more discussion in Baum and Schaede (1994).

10. Itoh (1998) explains that the seniority system and slow promotion are designed to prolong the incentive effects for non-performing employees. He also points out that the rotation system among several posts in local offices within a company is designed to remove potential conflict/competition among employees entering in the same year.

11. Japan Labour Research Institutes Survey on 1,604 managers of 104 companies, extracted from *Nikkei Journal*, 3 Feb. 2000.

12. Miyajima and Arikawa (1999), Aoki and Patrick (1994), Sheard (1994), Berglof and Perotti (1994), Kaplan (1994), Kang and Shivdasani (1995), Miyajima (1998*a*).

13. Companies are shifting their recruitment policy to part-time workers for reasons of cost (no retirement/pension or health benefits) and flexibility reasons (easy to lay off). According to the recent survey appeared in *Nihon Keizai Shinbun*, 27 June 2000, one out of five employees in Japan is a part-time worker.

14. 89 per cent of surveyed firms (1,088) in 1993 responded that they expect a rescue operation by bank(s) when they are in financial distress. This percentage is even higher among the listed firms on the Tokyo Stock Exchange (more than 90 per cent) than for unlisted firms (85 per cent).

15. Avoiding the high administrative costs of legal bankruptcy procedures, banks usually resort to private solutions such as suspension of transactions or private liquidation. For a detailed analysis of non-legal bankruptcy procedures, see Packer and Ryser (1992).

16. When an individual investor directly invests in stocks, he/she is subject to the tax on investment securities and a 20 per cent tax on the return. When investing through the trust, however, the tax is not based on the individual stake, but on the average of the entire trust fund. Therefore, an investor may be taxed even when his investment makes no profit if other investors of the fund had capital gains.

17. See the debates on the new model of corporate governance, in annual reports of CGRJ, available from Professor Kawauchi, Department of Business, Yokohama City University, 22-2 Seto, Kanazawa-ku, Yokohama-shi, Kanagawa Prefecture 236, Japan. Tel/Fax: 0081-45-787-2117.

18. Fukao (1997) also points out the low budget spent on auditing in Japanese companies compared to US companies. For banks auditing budgets are less than one-tenth of what is spent in the USA.

References for Chapter 12

Aoki, Masahiko (1988), *Information, Incentives, and Bargaining in the Japanese Economy*, Cambridge: Cambridge University Press.

—— (1994), 'The Contingent Governance of Teams: Analysis of Institutional Complementarity', *International Economic Review*, 35/3 (August): 657–76.

—— (1995*a*), *Evolution and Multi-functionality of Economic Systems: Analysis of Comparative Systems* (Keizai shisutemu no shinka to toayasei : Hikaku seido bunseki josetsu), Tokyo: Toyo Keizai.

—— (1995*b*), 'Controlling the Insider Control', in M. Aoki and H. Kim (eds.), *Corporate Governance in Transitional Economies: Insider Control and The Role of Banks*, EDI Developmental Studies, Washington: World Bank.

—— and Hugh Patrick (eds.) (1994), *The Japanese Main Bank System: Its Relevancy for Developing and Transforming Economics*, Oxford: Oxford University Press.

—— and M. Okuno (1997), *Comparative Institutional Analysis* (Keizai Sisutemu no Hikaku Seido Bunseki), Tokyo: Tokyo University Press.

Asako, K., M. Kunanori, T. Inoue, and H. Murase (1991), 'Fixed Investment Financing' (Setsubitoshi to shikinchotatsu), *Economics Today* 11/4, Japan Development Bank's Research Institute of Fixed Investment.

Ballon, Robert J. and Makoto Matsuzaki (in cooperation with Tohmatsu Research Centre) (2000), *Japanese Business and Financial Disclosure*, Nikkei Custom Publishing Services, INC.

Baum, Harald and Ulrike Shaede (1994), 'Institutional Investors and Corporate Governance in Japan', in T. Baums, R. M. Buxbaum, and K. J. Hopt (eds.), *Institutional Investors and Corporate Governance*, Berlin, New York, deGruyter, 609–64.

Berglof, Eric and Enrico Perotti (1994), 'The Governance Structure of Japanese Financial Keiretsu', *Journal of Financial Economics* 36: 259–84.

Corporate Governance Forum of Japan (1997) *Annual Report*, 2/1, Seibundo.

Fuji Research Institute Corporation (1993), 'A Study of Main Bank System and Cross-Shareholding' (Meinbanku Sisutemu oyobi Kabushiki Michiai ni tsuiteno Chousa), Ministry of International Trade and Industry.

Fukao, Mitsuhiro (1997), 'The Japanese Financial System and the Prospect for Structure of Corporate Governance' (Nihon no Kinnyu Sisutemu to Corporate Governance Kouzou no Tennbou), Report submitted to the Third Research Group of the Institute of International Trade and Industry, MITI.

—— (2000), 'Information Disclosure and Corporate Governance', *Nikkei Journal*, 13 March.

—— and Yasuko Morita (1994), 'Main Arguments of Corporate Governance and International Comparisons' (Koporeto gabanansu ni kansuru rontenseiri to kokusai hikaku), *Kinyukenkyu*, Bank of Japan, 13–23.

Hirota, Shinichi and Ikeo Kazuhito (1996), 'Corporate Finance and Management Efficiency', in H. Itoh (ed.), *Company System in Japan*, Tokyo: Tokyo University Press.

Horiuchi, Akiyoshi (1995), 'Financial Structure and Managerial Discretion in the Japanese Firm: An Implication of the Surge of Equity-Related Band', in M. Okabe (ed.), *The Structure of the Japanese Economy*, London: Macmillan.

Hoshi, Takeo and Itoh Takatoshi (1991), 'Measuring Coherence of Japanese Enterprise Groups', Paper prepared for TCER Finance Conference, 21–22 March.

—— A. Kashyap, and D. Sharfstein (1991), 'The Role of Banks in Reducing the Costs of Financial Distress in Japan', *Journal of Financial Economics*, 27: 67–88.

Itoh, Hidefumi (1998), 'Human Resource Management of Japanese Companies from Perspective of Incentive Theory' (Insentibu riron no kenchi kara mita nihonkigyo no jinntekishigen no manejimento), in M. Aoki and R. Dore (eds.), *Japanese Firm as a System* (Shisutemu to shite no nihonkigyo), Tokyo: NTT Publisher.

Jones, C. Derek and T. Kato (1995), 'The Productivity Effects of Employee Stock-Ownership Plans and Bonuses: Evidence from Japanese Panel Data', *American Economic Review*, 85/3: 391–414.

Kang, J. and A. Shivdasani (1995), 'Firm Performance, Corporate Governance, and Top Executive Turnover in Japan', *Journal of Financial Economics* 38: 29–58.

Kaplan, Steven (1994), 'Top Executive Rewards and Firm Performance: A Comparison of Japan and the United States', *Journal of Political Economy*, 102/3: 510–46.

—— and Bernadette Minton (1993), 'Outside Activity in Japanese Companies: Determinants and Managerial Implications', Working Paper, Graduate School of Business, Chicago University.

Koike, Kazuo (1998), 'Formation Methods of Technical Skills and Remuneration Methods' (Ginou keisei no houshiki to houshu no houshiki), in Aoki and Dore (eds.) *Japanese Firm as a System*, Ch. 2.

Ministry of Finance, Japan (2000), 'A Survey Result on Corporate Finance and Corporate Governance in Japan', (Wagakigyo no financsu sistemu to coporeto gabanansu ni kansuru ankehto chosa kekkakentokai), Report prepared for the Discussion Group.

Miyajima, Hideki (1995), 'Regulatory Framework, Government Intervention and Investment in Post-war Japan: The Structural Dynamics of J-type Firm-Government Interaction', first draft, prepared for 23rd Fuji Conference, Jan. 1996.

—— (1998*a*), 'Management Turnover and Performance for Large Companies in Post-war Japan' (Sengo Nihon Daikigyo ni Okeru Keieisha no Koutai to Kigyo Performance), *Economic Journal of Hitotsubashi* (Hitotubashi Keizai Kenkyu).

—— (1998*b*), 'The Impact of Deregulation on Corporate Governance and Finance', in L. E. Carlile and M. C. Tilton (eds.), *Regulation and Regulatory Reform in Japan: Are Things Changing?*, Washington: Brookings Institution.

—— (1998*c*), *Structural Change in Corporate Finance and Evolution in Corporate Governance* (Kigyokinyu no kozo henka to gabanansu no henyo), GFRS Issues Series no.5, Global Foundation for Research and Scholarship.

—— and Yasuhiro Akikawa (1999), 'Relational Banking, Less Active Market for Corporate Control, and Debt Choice: Evidence from the Liberalization in Japan', Working paper series no. 9905, Institute for Research in Contemporary Political and Economic Affairs, Waseda University.

Nakatani, Iwao (1984), 'The Economic Role of Financial Corporate Grouping', in M. Aoki (ed.), *The Economic Analysis of the Japanese Firm*, Amsterdam: North-Holland.

Nakatani, Iwao, 1987, *Japanese Companies in Transition*, Osaka University.

OECD (1999), 'Overview of the Corporate Pension Scheme in Japan (Note by the Delegation from Japan)', Working party on Private Pensions, Directorate for Financial, Fiscal and Enterprise Affairs Insurance Committee, 9 Dec.

Okazaki, Tetsuji (1998), 'Evolution of Corporate Governance in Japan: Historical Perspective' (Nihon ni kokeru coporeto gabanansu no hatten —rekishiteki pasupekutibu), in Aoki and Dore (eds.), *Japanese Firm as a System*.

—— and A. Horiuchi (1992), 'Corporate Fixed Investment and Main Bank Relationships' (Kigyo no setsubioshi to mainbanku kankei), *Finance Today*, 11, Bank of Japan's Research Institute of Finance.

Packer, Frank and Marc Ryser (1992), 'The Governance of Failure: An Anatomy of Corporate Bankruptcy in Japan', Working paper no. 62, Center on Japanese Economy and Business, Columbia Graduate School of Business, Columbia University.

Prowse, Stephan D. (1992), 'The Structure of Corporate Ownership in Japan', *Journal of Finance*, 47: 1121–40.

Ramseyer, J. Mark and Minoru Nakazato (1998), *Japanese Law: An Economic Approach*, Chicago: University of Chicago Press.

Saito, Takenori (1997), 'Restructuring of Corporate Pension System', *Economics of Organisation and Human Resource* (Soshiki to Jinteki Shigen no Keizaigaku), Association of Tax and Accounting (Zeimu Keiri Kyoukai), Ch. 7.

Sheard, Paul (1994), 'Main Banks and the Governance of Financial Distress', in Aoki Patrick (eds.), *The Japanese Main Bank System*.

Suzuki, Sadahiko and Richard Wright (1985), 'Financial Structure and Bankruptcy Risk in Japanese Companies', *Journal of International Business Studies*, 97–110.

Ueda, Akihiro (1994), *Investment Trust: What are the Problems?* (Tohshi Shintaku: Nani ga Mondai ka?), Tokyo: Toyo Keizai.

Watanabe, Shigeru and I. Yamamoto (1992), 'Corporate Governance of Japanese Firms: From the Lowest ROE in Post-War (Nihon kigyo no coporeto gabanansu-senngo saitei no ROE kara)', *Zaikai Kansoku*, September 1992.

Weinstein, David, and Yishay Yafeh (1998), 'On the Costs of a Bank-Centered Financial System: Evidence From the Changing Main Bank Relations in Japan', *Journal of Finance*, 53/2: 635–72.

13

The Netherlands

ABE DE JONG

1. INTRODUCTION

Corporate governance structures determine the relationships between management and financiers. As in any other country, in the Netherlands a set of instruments exists that motivates managers, disciplines managers, and allows managers to hide from disciplining forces. In the Netherlands several studies in Dutch and international journals and the public debate have paid attention to specific governance devices that prevail. In this overview I discuss these devices and their impact on corporate performance.

In the Netherlands, for years, corporate governance has been mainly associated with technical takeover defences. Firms' managers justified these defences as a protection against (foreign) hostile takeovers, while (groups of) shareholders were complaining about a lack of influence on the management. The market for corporate control was virtually absent. Nowadays, academic research and public debate in the Netherlands increasingly recognize the versality of governance structures. Discussions deal with the ownership structure, the board structure, managerial compensation, and takeover defences. The empirical studies which are reviewed describe the governance structures and investigate the impact of these factors on firms' performance, investment, and capital structure.

The choice of the topics in the literature that is reviewed is largely driven by specific elements of the Dutch institutional setting and the availability of data. In section 2, I discuss the role of the ownership structure, i.e. the presence of large shareholders and the identity of shareholders. In section 3 the board structure is discussed. In the Netherlands the literature on corporate governance and performance focuses mainly on the technical takeover defences. Section 4 deals with the impact of these takeover defences. The disciplining role of leverage and the role of financial institutions are discussed in section 5. For illustrative purposes, I describe the governance structure of a major Dutch firm in section 6. In 1996, a committee, the 'Peters' Committee' was installed to provide recommendations on potential improvements of corporate governance in the Netherlands. In section 7 I describe the public debate on governance in the Netherlands and the conclusions of this Dutch committee for corporate governance. In section 8 the conclusions are presented.

2. OWNERSHIP STRUCTURE

Van Kampen and Van de Kraats (1995) investigate the relationship between the presence of large shareholders and stock-price performance. The authors study a cross-section of firms listed on the Amsterdam Stock Exchange per 31 December 1992. The data set contains 159 firms. Besides, two subsamples are constructed, of 54 industrial firms and 51 firms in the financial and non-financial services sector. The analysis consists of regressions in which the annual stock return is explained by variables that represent risk, growth, sales, and variables for large shareholders. In order to measure the presence of large shareholders two dummy variables are introduced. The first dummy is one if a shareholder owning more than 25 per cent of the shares is present, and zero otherwise. With this 25 per cent threshold no significant result is found for the full sample. For the subsample of industrial firms a positive relationship is found at the 5 per cent significance level, which is explained by successful monitoring by large shareholders. For the services industry no significant results are found. The authors explain this finding by the influence of government regulation in the financial services sector and therefore a reduced need for monitoring of shareholders. An alternative definition of the dummy variable is based on a threshold of 50 per cent. For this threshold a significantly negative relationship is found (at the 5 per cent significance level). The authors interpret this result as large shareholders allowing private gains at the expense of smaller shareholders.

Van der Goot (1997, ch. 8) studies 74 initial public offerings at the Amsterdam Stock Exchange between 1983 and 1992. The stakes of managers, institutional block-holders, mutual funds, and the sum of these stakes are compared with the price–earnings ratio. Managerial shareholdings are significantly (at the 10 per cent level) related to the price–earnings ratio. As hypothesized, this relation is positive. The presence of other shareholders does not have a significant relationship with the price–earnings ratio. The role of managerial shareholdings is further investigated by dividing the sample into a subsample where the management owns more than 50 per cent and a subsample with stakes below 50 per cent. Only for shareholdings below 50 per cent the positive relationship is found to be significant (at the 5 per cent level). The conclusion is that managerial shareholdings are positively related to performance and this relationship especially holds for shareholdings below 50 per cent.

Vente and Cantrijn (1997) specifically investigate the role of institutional shareholders. The authors received questionnaires from 36 Dutch institutional investors. The main finding is that the investors perceive liquidity of their investments to be more important than exercising control. For example, the authors ask whether it is a task of the institutions to supervise the firm's remuneration policy. Of the respondents, 56 per cent do not consider this to be a task (33 per cent consider this as a task and 11 per cent have no opinion). Similarly, 58 per cent of the respondents would not interfere with the firms' investment policies (20 per cent would interfere and 22 per cent have no opinion). Although the investors tend to abstain from controlling the firm, they do prefer to have the opportunity to control the management. For example, 88 per cent of the respondents would control the firm in order to ensure that the managers are not able to entrench themselves with technical takeover defences (6 per cent would not control these firms and 6 per cent have no opinion). These findings indicate that Dutch institutional investors consider liquidity to be important. Direct control is not viewed as the task of the institutional investors, although they want to have the opportunity to exercise control.

3. BOARD STRUCTURE

The board structures of listed firms in the Netherlands are characterized by two-tier boards. A Dutch company operates under a two-tier management structure consisting of a supervisory board (*Raad van Commissarissen*) and a managerial board (*Raad van Bestuur*).

The supervisory board is independent of the company and its members are responsible for the supervision of management policy and the company's general course of affairs. The Dutch company law requires that the board members serve the firm's interest. The Dutch supervisory board provides some form of co-determination for all stakeholders, because the supervisory board members have to serve the interests of all the firms' stakeholders. Labour is not allowed to have a representative on the supervisory board. However, the legally installed work council has a right to relevant information and a right to advise on major issues (e.g. transfers of ownership, plant closings, and major investments). Its permission is only required for changes in social arrangements (e.g. pensions, working hours, wages, safety rules) and if the council disagrees, the employer must obtain the decision of a local judge to go ahead.

Van Manen and Hooghiemstra (1999) discuss the results of questionnaires filled out by 43 supervisory board members of 22 top-25 firms in the Netherlands. The board members undoubtedly acknowledge that their task is the supervision of managers and that they tend to leave operational decisions to managers. They also agree that conflicts of interests arise in the case of supervisory board members acting as banker, customer, or supplier of related firms. However, shareholdings and membership of the supervisory board are not considered conflicting.

The managerial board is the firm's management team. The managerial board reports to the supervisory board and is responsible for attaining the company's objectives, its strategy and policy, and the firm's performance. An important aspect of the Dutch board structure is the structured regime (*structuurregime*). The structured regime has two variations, i.e. the full and the mitigated structured regime.

The most prevalent is the full structured regime, which is legally required for Dutch companies with more than 100 employees, a legally installed work council and book value of shareholders' equity in excess of NLG 25m. (about USD 12.5m.). The full structured regime requires a supervisory board that takes over the following powers from shareholders: establishing of the annual accounts, the election of the managerial board and the election of the supervisory board itself (called co-optation). The supervisory board also has expanded authority over major decisions made by the managerial board.[1]

Next to the full structured regime, firms may adopt the mitigated structured regime. The mitigated structured regime requires a supervisory board along with a system of co-optation. However, the approval of the annual accounts rests in the hands of shareholders and it prohibits the supervisory board from hiring and/or firing the managerial board members. The mitigated structured regime is required if a foreign company holds more than 50 per cent of a Dutch subsidiary's shares.

In 1997, 39 per cent of Dutch listed firms had not adopted the structured regime. Of the remaining 61 per cent of firms, which adopted the structured regime, 26 per cent adopted the full regime voluntarily, 6 per cent adopted the mitigated regime, and 68 per cent were obliged to adopt the full regime (see Monitoring Commissie Corporate Governance 1998). A further description of the Dutch board is De Jong and Moerland (1999), who study 135 non-financial firms over the 1992–6 period. The average size of the supervisory board is 5.2 members and the average size of the managerial board is 2.9 persons. The managerial board members hold on average 4.5 per cent of the firm's shares, while supervisory board members hold 2.2 per cent of the shares (only shareholdings above 5 per cent are included).

De Jong, Moerland, and Nijman (2000) describe the influence of the presence of the structured regime on firm performance.[2] The data set consists of 50 firms over the 1993–7 period, in which firms with the structured regime are matched, based on industry and size, with non-structured regime firms. Firm performance is measured by stock returns, accounting returns on equity, or Tobin's Q. The results show that the structured regime has a negative impact on performance (this finding is significant at the 5 per cent level for accounting returns and not significant for the other measures). Besides, board size has a negative influence on performance, which is significant for each of the three measures. Other interesting results are found for stock returns. The presence of large shareholders and certificates (see section four) have a significantly negative impact.

Van Oijen and Bouwman (1999) investigate the relationship between management turnover and firm performance. For 156 Dutch listed firms in the 1992–6 period, the turnover of the chairman and members of the managerial board is measured. After correcting for turnover due to illness, death, or (early) retirement, the non-natural turnover is 8 per cent for the members (scaled by board size) and 9 per cent for the chairman. Logit regressions which explain turnover by firm performance show that lower stock returns, decreases of profitability, losses, and lower sales growth induce turnover of both ordinary members and chairmen. The strongest effects are found in cases where performance is measured in the year of the turnover or in the preceding year.

Van Melle (1997) investigates stock-option plans of the 50 largest Dutch listed firms. In 1996, 88 per cent of the firms had option plans for their top management. Over 50 per cent of the options are exercised within two years. The author concludes that the structure and use of option plans are mainly driven by tax advantages over other forms of compensation. After Van Melle's research the tax-treatment of stock options has changed in order to decrease the fiscal benefits of this type of compensation. More recently, Duffhues, Kabir, and Mertens (1999) discuss stock-option plans in the Netherlands. The authors conclude that the maximum expiration date is two to eight years after issuance, the options expire when managers leave, options cannot be exercised in the first three years, and that the options are normally issued at-the-money.

4. TAKEOVER DEFENCES AND LIMITATIONS TO SHAREHOLDER INFLUENCE

The corporate governance structures in the Netherlands are characterized by the presence of technical takeover defences. These defences have two consequences. First, they limit the influence of shareholders. Shareholders may have no or limited voting power and specific shareholders may have exclusive rights to vote on specific decisions. Consequently, managers are protected from disciplining by the current shareholders. The second consequence is that managers are shielded from disciplining because the disciplining power of the market for corporate control is mitigated. A Coopers & Lybrand report (1990) concludes that firms in the Netherlands have the most severe technical takeover defences in the European Community. The effectiveness of these takeover defences is illustrated by the finding that since 1960 only one hostile takeover has taken place.[3]

The technical takeover defences that prevail in the Netherlands are listed in the first column of Table 13.1. Priority shares are a small number of shares that carry superior voting rights, e.g. with regard to takeover attempts. Preferred shares serve as a takeover defence device in case firms that have preferred shares have an arrangement which allows an issue of preferred shares without further approval of shareholders and for which only 25 per cent of the nominal value has to be paid up. In case of a takeover attempt, the firm can place these shares with a befriended party and pay for the shares using debt. The dilution creates an effective takeover defence. For firms with certificates (depository receipts) the shareholders own receipts which only carry the cash flow rights. The voting rights remain with a trust that owns the shares and issued the certificates. Under the structured regime, voting rights have been delegated to the supervisory board members (see section three). Shareholders can also have limited voting power, which is normally 1 per cent. This implies that shareholders can have a maximum of 1 per cent of all votes, irrespective of the number of shares they possess. Binding appointment is a construction for owners of priority shares that allows them to appoint board members. In case of the structured regime binding appointments have less power, because they are no longer binding (see Slagter 1996: 209 and 231). In case of a joint-ownership (*gemeenschappelijk bezit*) arrangement, the firm's shares are held by a holding company and the shareholders of the holding company can only influence the policies of the holding company and these may not include the policies of the underlying firm. The result of this construction is similar to certificates. The Pandora arrangement covers a group of defences, that (1) change the firm into a non-attractive target (for example, the crown-jewel construction, poison pills, and golden parachutes); or (2) disable a takeover through share transactions (for example, the white knight construction, the pac-man construction, buy-outs, and cross-holdings). Table 13.1 indicates that priority shares, preferred shares, certificates, and the structured regime occur often in the Dutch firms. De Jong and Moerland (1999)

Table 13.1. *Takeover defences in the Netherlands (percentages)*

	Voogd (1989)	Van der Hoeven (1995)	Kabir *et al.* (1997)	De Jong and Moerland (1999)
Priority shares	53	41	45	40
Preferred shares	51	61	59	65
Certificates	32	[n.a.]	40	38
Structured regime	44	65	[n.a.]	[n.a.]
Limited voting power	6	[n.a.]	4	10
Binding appointment	49	[n.a.]	36	[n.a.]
Joint-ownership	[n.a.]	8	[n.a.]	[n.a.]
Pandora constructions	[n.a.]	2	[n.a.]	[n.a.]
Period	1988	1992 or 1993	1992	1992–6
Observations	237	135	177	610

Note: n.a.=not available; these defences have not been investigated in the study.

report that on average firms have 1.5 defences and that the median firm has two defences out of the four defences mentioned in the fifth column of Table 13.1.

Bosveld and Goedbloed (1996) study 178 announcements of takeover defence measures by listed firms from 1960 until 1992. The authors aim to test the managerial entrenchment hypothesis, which leads to the hypothesis that announcement effects of takeover defences are negative. Standard event-study methodology based on the market model for normal returns is used. For the announcements an insignificantly negative average abnormal return is found. For a subsample of 43 firms the authors find a threat of a takeover to be present. The definition of a threat is that an offer was made on the firm's shares, attention to a potential takeover was paid in the Dutch financial daily (*Het Financieele Dagblad*), or a notification that a third party bought shares of the firm had been released. For this subsample a significantly negative average abnormal return is found. These results support the managerial entrenchment hypothesis.

Van Frederikslust and Van Veldhuizen (1996) study the relationship between takeover defences and ownership structure. The data set contains takeover defences and ownership concentration for 162 listed firms on 30 September 1995. The authors mention that 60.5 per cent of the firms have preferred shares, 40.1 per cent have priority shares, and 37.7 per cent of the firms have depository receipts. Firms without takeover defences have larger shareholders and the number of takeover defences is negatively related to the presence of block-holders. The authors also investigate the relationship between average price–earnings ratios over 1990–4 and the number of takeover defences. No consistent relationship is found. However, no statistics are presented in the article. It is mentioned that firms with two takeover defences have a significantly higher price–earnings ratio in comparison with firms with one defence measure. These two groups represent 81 per cent of the sample. In addition, the authors describe the results of a questionnaire, based on 96 returned questionnaires. The results confirm the trade-off between the presence of large shareholders and takeover defences.

Van der Goot and Van het Kaar (1997) describe the impact of takeover defence measures for initial public offerings. From 1983 until 1992, 74 offerings installed 146 defence measures. These measures can be divided into five categories: priority shares (50 per cent), preferred shares (49 per cent), depository receipts (42 per cent), structured regime (42 per cent) and limited voting rights (15 per cent). For each takeover defence measure the price–earnings ratios are compared between firms that adopted this measure and other firms. Firms with a structured regime have lower price–earnings ratios, at the 1 per cent significance level. At the 10 per cent significance level, firms with priority shares have higher price–earnings ratios. For the other measures no significant differences are found. The authors also consider abnormal returns from the market-adjusted model for one, three, six, or twelve months after the initial public offering. These abnormal returns decrease with the number of takeover defences. This result is stronger for firms with the structured regime and for three and six months.[4]

Kabir, Cantrijn, and Jeunink (1997) study takeover defences of listed firms. First an overview is provided of the use of the following defences: priority shares (45 per cent of the firms), preferred shares (59 per cent), depository receipts (40 per cent), limited voting power (4 per cent), and binding appointment (36 per cent). In 1992, only 9.1 per cent of the 177 firms had no takeover defences. Data is also collected concerning the ownership structure of the firms, i.e. the concentration of block-holders in 1992. A negative relationship is found between ownership concentration and the number of takeover defences.[5] Finally, preferred share issues are further investigated using event-study methodology. For a sample of 44 announcements during 1984–90, the two-day abnormal return is −1.18 per cent, which is significant at the 10 per cent level. Separate abnormal returns are calculated for the creation of the possibility to issue preferred shares (n=17), the grant of this option (n=10) and the actual issue (n=17). The two-day abnormal returns for the announcements are 1.23 per cent (significant at the 10 per cent level), −0.41 per cent and −4.09 per cent (significant at the 5 per cent level), respectively. Managerial entrenchment occurs by the creation of the takeover defence (possibility to issue preferred shares and the grant of the option), however, these effects do not appear to affect firm value negatively. While the negative effect of actual issue may be the result from preferred shares as a takeover defence, the actual issue may also be a capital structure decision and the negative wealth effects are not necessarily driven by managerial entrenchment behaviour.

5. THE DISCIPLINING ROLE OF LEVERAGE AND THE ROLE OF BANKS

Kemna, Kloek, and Pieterse (1994) study determinants of leverage of 158 listed non-financial firms for the years 1984–90. The authors test Jensen's (1986) free cash flow theory, which predicts that firms with free cash flow and low growth tend to overinvest. This overinvestment behaviour is reduced by the disciplining role of debt. Firms with higher free cash flow and lower growth are expected to have more debt. Regression analysis is performed in order to test the impact of several determinants of leverage. Leverage is defined as long-term debt over book or market value of equity. Free cash flow, defined as a percentage of total assets, is positively related to debt at the 1 per cent significance level. Growth, measured as the annual change in market value of assets, is significantly negatively related to the market value measure of leverage at the 1 per cent level. The relationship is significantly positive for the book-value measure. Except for the latter finding, the results confirm the free cash flow hypothesis.

Van Dijk and De Jong (1998) also test Jensen's free cash flow theory. A questionnaire is used to measure several variables that are related to overinvestment, including the presence of an overinvestment problem. The questions concern simple firm character-istics, which are known by the firms' financial managers. The analysis is based on 102 re-turned questionnaires and the response rate is 61 per cent. Confirmatory factor analysis is used to improve the measurement of the variables. Then, a structural equations model is estimated to test the influence of the determinants of leverage (including the presence of an overinvestment problem) and to test the determinants of the overinvestment problem. It is found that overinvestment does not lead to higher debt levels. Overinvest-ment is related to free cash flow (positive at the 5 per cent significance level), managerial shareholdings (negative, 5 per cent), takeover barriers (positive, 10 per cent), takeover threat (negative, 5 per cent) and block-holdings (positive, 5 per cent). Growth opportu-nities, performance-based income, managerial option plans, bank relationships, and a proxy for asymmetric information are not significantly related to overinvestment. These results confirm the free cash flow hypothesis. Overinvestment is caused by excess cash and takeover defences, and is mitigated by managerial shareholdings.

Studies concerning the impact of liquidity on investment decisions provide evi-dence on the relationships between firms and financiers. Van Ees and Garretsen (1994) study determinants of investments in fixed assets of Dutch listed firms in the period 1984–90. An equation is estimated in which the gross investment of a firm is explained by Tobin's Q, cash flow and liquid assets. The two latter variables, that explain the abil-ity to finance investments through internal financing, are found to be more important than the investment opportunities (Tobin's Q). This finding is explained as a liquidity constraint due to imperfections on the Dutch market for investment funds. In an ad-ditional analysis the total sample is divided into firms with a board member who is also a board member with a bank and other firms. For firms with ties to banks, the rela-tionship between cash flow and investment is weaker. The authors explain this finding as the ability of firm–bank relationships to relieve liquidity constraints.

The next section presents the governance structure of Koninklijke Ahold NV.

6. GOVERNANCE STRUCTURE OF KONINKLIJKE AHOLD NV[6]

Koninklijke Ahold NV operates retail grocery stores in 17 countries in Europe, the United States, South America, and Asia. The book value of total assets per 31 December 1997 is NLG 18,839m. and the sales over 1997 were NLG 50,568m. On average, in 1997 142,020 people were employed (full-time equivalents).

The shares of Ahold are quoted at the Amsterdam Exchanges and Swiss Exchange. Besides, ADR's are traded on the New York Stock Exchange. The annual report mentions the following notifications in accordance with the Dutch Law on Disclosure of Ownership (*WMZ*): AMEV/VSB NV 7.95 per cent; ING Groep NV 7.42 per cent; Coöperatie Achmea UA 7.2 per cent; AEGON NV 6.11 per cent; and Algemeen Burgerlijk Pensioenfonds 5.42 per cent. The block-holders of Ahold are all Dutch financial institutions. The firm has the option to sell preferred shares to the Foundation Ahold Continuity (*Stichting Ahold Continuïteit*) up to a total par value that is equal to the total par value of all other issued and outstanding shares. The foundation has three voting members, who are not board members of the firm and two non-voting members, i.e. the chairmen of the managerial and supervisory boards.

The two-tier board consists of six managerial board members and seven supervisory board members. The firm is under the structured regime and this is voluntarily, because more than 50 per cent of the workers are employed abroad. The supervisory board members have 28 positions on other boards, which implies that on average each member serves on seven other boards. The average age of the supervisory board members is 64.3 years. On average, they have served 8.3 years on Ahold's supervisory board. No shareholdings have been reported in accordance with *WMZ*, which implies that none of the managerial and supervisory board members owns more than 5 per cent of the shares. The current and former managerial board members received in 1997 in total NLG 15,017,000, while the supervisory board members received NLG 547,000. Options for common shares have been issued to a limited number of managers. The rights for Dutch managers are valid for a term of 5 years and can be exercised after a two-year period. Of all outstanding options for employees, 9.8 per cent is owned by managerial board members (per 31 December 1997).

7. THE PUBLIC DEBATE

Initially the public debate on corporate governance focused on takeover defences. In the annual report for 1985, the stock exchange authorities (*Vereniging voor de Effectenhandel, VEH*), pleaded for a discussion in order to reduce the accumulation of technical takeover defences. In 1986 the Van Grinten Committee was installed in order to investigate the advantages and disadvantages of takeover defences. In 1987 the majority of the committee advised to maintain the existing possibilities to prevent hostile takeovers. However, the VEH disagrees with the committee and intends to reduce takeover defences. As a countervailing power, the association of listed companies (*Vereniging Effecten Uitgevende Ondernemingen, VEUO*) was founded. In 1992, the parties decided on a temporary agreement, *Bijlage X*, which limits future takeover defences. In 1995 a takeover panel was proposed. This panel can suspend takeover defences in case of an attempted takeover. If a shareholder has a substantial majority (70 per cent) for at least twelve months, the *Ondernemingskamer* in Amsterdam can be addressed. As a result of this agreement between VEH and VEUO, in 1996 the Corporate Governance Committee was installed. The committee, known as the Peters' Committee, was appointed jointly by VEH and VEUO and consists of persons that serve the interests of both parties and external experts.

In 1997 the report 'Corporate Governance in the Netherlands: The Forty Recommendations' was published (see Commissie Corporate Governance 1997; and Moerland 1997). Generally, the report proposes to increase the control of shareholders. Firms are invited to consider improvements and report their governance situation as compared to the recommendations in the 1997 annual reports. The management is invited to explain whether they follow, or plan to follow, the 40 recommendations (in case of disagreement a motivation is asked for). The emphasis of the report is on the improvement of control for shareholders through self-regulation by the firms.

In 1998 the Monitoring Committee Corporate Governance reported on the reactions to the 40 recommendations of the firms in the 1997 annual reports (see Monitoring Commissie Corporate Governance 1998). Besides, the report provides a detailed overview of the limitations of shareholders' influence. The general conclusions are that most firms did not change their governance structures, while some firms chose to adopt minor changes. In total 14 out of 159 firms included in the study changed their governance structures. Only 13 (out of 159) firms have no protections against shareholder influence (See *Het Financieele Dagblad* of 12 December 1998).

In 2000, the Centre for Applied Research reported to the Ministry of Finance on the impact of the structured regime and takeover defences on financial performance. The report states that the structured regime and certificates negatively influence performance (see also section three). Currently, the debate on corporate governance in the Netherlands focuses on the choice between continued self-regulation versus new legislation by the Ministry of Finance.

8. CONCLUSIONS

The literature on the relationship between corporate governance and performance in the Netherlands does not lead to unequivocal results concerning the relationship between the presence of large shareholders and performance (see Van Kampen and Van de Kraats 1995 and Van Dijk and De Jong 1998). Managerial shareholdings are found to be related to higher performance (see Van der Goot 1997; and Van Dijk and De Jong 1998). Institutional investors tend to abstain from active monitoring (Vente and Cantrijn 1997). Board structures are characterized by the two-tier boards and the structured regime. The structured regime appears to have a negative influence on performance (De Jong, Moerland, and Nijman 2000). However, the turnover of managerial board members is related to performance which indicates that managers of poorly performing firms must leave their firms. Takeover defences reduce firm performance (see Bosveld and Goedbloed 1996, Kabir, Cantrijn and Jeunink 1997 and Van der Goot and Van het Kaar 1997). Takeover defences are negatively related to ownership concentration (see Van Frederikslust and Van Veldhuizen 1996, and Kabir, Cantrijn, and Jeunink 1997). Jensen's free cash flow hypothesis is relevant for Dutch firms (see Kemna, Kloek and Pieterse 1994; and Van Dijk and De Jong 1998). Bank–firm relationships are important determinants of the firms' liquidity–investment relationships (see Van Ees and Garretsen 1995).

The articles in this review provide interesting information on the relationship between corporate governance and performance in the Netherlands. However, many aspects of corporate governance remain underexposed. Examples are managerial remuneration, the impact of the identity of large shareholders, the role of creditors, and the multiple roles of banks. It should also be noted that in most studies the disciplining forces, or the absence of these forces, are studied independently or bilaterally, while the combination of all forces is expected to determine the effect on firm performance. These aspects provide interesting directions for further research.

Notes

1. There are exceptions to the legal requirements for the full structured regime. Dutch multinationals with more than 50 per cent of their employees outside the Netherlands are exempt. For the Dutch subsidiary of a Dutch multinational, the full structured regime is not required if the parent adopts the structured regime and owns more than 50 per cent of the subsidiary. Otherwise, the subsidiary is required to have the mitigated structured regime. It should be noted that a Dutch company may voluntarily adopt the structured regime even though it is not legally required to do so due to the exceptions mentioned above. See Slagter (1996) for legal details of the stuctured regime.
2. The authors summarize the results of a report by the Centre for Applied Research (2000) to the Dutch Ministry of Finance. The report studies the influence on performance of ownership structure, takeover defences and board structures in the Netherlands, Belgium, and the United Kingdom.
3. In 1979, Lantana Beheer took over Tilburgse Waterleiding Maatschappij (see Bosveld and Goedbloed, 1996).
4. Further discussions of the results of Van der Goot and Van het Kaar (1997) are Pape, Van Triest, and Weimer (1998) and Van Oijen (1998). In both comments, it is argued that the empirical results show that firms with the structured regime have higher returns in comparison with firms without the structured regime.
5. This finding is similar to Van Frederikslust and Van Veldhuizen (1996). Moreover, De Jong and Moerland (1999) show that the negative relationship is confirmed for four individual defence measures. These authors also provide anecdotal evidence which explains this trade-off. In 1997, Smit Internationale announced that two block-holders, who each owned 40 per cent of the shares, indicated that they intend to sell part of their shares. According to the Dutch financial daily (*Het Financieele Dagblad*, 28 May 1997), in the following annual shareholders' meeting the intention is referred to as 'the loss of a takeover defence' which requires a change of the statutes allowing, in case of the threat of a takeover, the issuance of preferred shares. Apparently, block-holdings serve as a takeover defence in Dutch firms.
6. Sources: the Annual report of Koninklijke Ahold NV of 1997 and Monitoring Commissie Corporate Governance (1998). On 31 December 1997 NLG 1 equals about USD 0.49.

References for Chapter 13

Bosveld, R. and A. M. Goedbloed (1996), 'Effecten van beschermingsconstructies op aandelenkoersen', *Maandblad voor Accountancy en Bedrijfseconomie*, 70 (May): 261–70.

Centre for Applied Research (2000), 'Zeggenschapsverhoudingen en financiële prestaties van beursvennootschappen', Report to the Ministry of Finance by the Centre for Applied Research, Tilburg University, 20 March.

Commissie Corporate Governance (1997), 'Corporate goverance in the Netherlands: Forty Recommendations', 25 June.

Coopers & Lybrand (1990), 'Effects of "Bangemann Proposals" on Barriers to Takeovers in the European Community'.

De Jong, A. and P. W. Moerland (1999), 'Beheersingsmechanismen in Nederland: Substituut of complement?', *Maandblad voor Accountancy en Bedrijfseconomie*, 73 (October), 499–512.

—— —— and T. E. Nijman (2000), 'Zeggenschapsverhoudingen en financiële prestaties', *Economisch Statistische Berichten* (5 May), 368–71.

Duffhues, P., M. Kabir and G. Mertens (1999), 'Personeelsoptieregelingen in Nederland: Theorie en praktijk', Report to ABP and PGGM by Centre for Applied Research, Tilburg University, 28 June.

Jensen, M. C. (1986), 'Agency Costs of Free Cash Flow, Coporate Finance, and Takeovers', *American Economic Review*, 76: 323–29.

Kabir, R., D. Cantrijn and A. Jeunink (1997), 'Takeover Defences, Ownership Structure and Stock Returns in the Netherlands: An Empirical Analysis', *Strategic Management Journal*, 18/2: 97–109.

Kemna, A., T. Kloek, and A. Pieterse (1994), 'Een empirische verklaring voor de vermogensstructuur van Nederlandse ondernemingen', *Maandblad voor Accountancy en Bedrijfseconomie*, 68 (Dec.): 737–51.

Moerland, P. W. (1997), 'Corporate Governance: Theorie en praktijk in internationaal perspectief', *Financiële & Monetaire Studies*, Groningen: Wolters-Noordhoff.

Monitoring Commissie Corporate Governance (1998), *Monitoring Corporate Governance in Nederland*, Deventer: Kluwer.

Pape, J. C., S. P. van Triest, and J. Weimer (1998), 'Beschermingsconstructies, structuurregime en ondernemingswaarde: Een reactie (2)', *Maandblad voor Accountancy en Bedrijfseconomie*, 72 (April): 213–16.

Slagter, W. J. (1996), *Compendium van het ondernemingsrecht*, Deventer: Kluwer, 7th edn.

Van Dijk, R. and A. de Jong (1998), 'Determinanten van de vermogensstructuur van Nederlandse beursfondsen', *Maandblad voor Accountancy en Bedrijfseconomie*, 72 (July/Aug.): 383–97.

Van Ees, H. and H. Garretsen (1994), 'Liquidity and Business Investment: Evidence from Dutch Panel Data', *Journal of Macroeconomics*, 16/4: 613–27.

Van Frederikslust, R. and A. van Veldhuizen (1996), 'Bescherming van Nederlandse beursfondsen in Europees perspectief', *Holland/Belgium Management Review*, 48: 80–6.

Van der Goot, L. R. T. (1997), *Valuing New Issues*, academic diss., Amsterdam.

—— and R. H. van het Kaar (1997), 'Beschermingsconstructies, structuurregime en ondernemingswaarde', *Maandblad voor Accountancy en Bedrijfseconomie*, 71 (Oct.), 497–507.

Van der Hoeven, B. (1995), 'Beschermingsconstructies Nederlandse beursfondsen: Een burcht met vele verdedigingswallen', *F&O Monitor*, 1/2: 23–31.

Van Kampen, M. W. J. M and B. P. J. van de Kraats (1995), 'Grootaandeelhouderschap en aandelenrendement', *Economisch Statistische Berichten*, (7 June), 534–7.

Van Manen, J. A. and R. B. H. Hooghiemstra, (1999), 'Normen voor commissarissen: Een verwachtingskloof?', *Maandblad voor Accountancy en Bedrijfseconomie*, 73 (Oct.): 513–24.

Van Melle, H. (1997), 'Optieplannen en corporate governance: Relatie tussen inspanningen van het management en de marktwaarde van de onderneming', Research report, Dutch Corporate Governance Services, Part 3.

Van Oijen, P. (1998), 'Beschermingsconstructies, structuurregime en ondernemingswaarde: Een reactie (1)', *Maandblad voor Accountancy en Bedrijfseconomie*, 72 (April), 209–12.

—— and C. H. S. Bouwman (1999), 'Managementverloop en bedrijfsprestaties: Nederland in internationaal perspectief', *Maandblad voor Accountancy en Bedrijfseconomie*, 73 (July/Aug.), 384–92.

Vente, J. and D. Cantrijn (1997), 'Institutionele beleggers en corporate governance in Nederland', *Bedrijfskunde*, 69/4: 51–60.

Voogd, R. P. (1989), *Statutaire beschermingsmiddelen bij beursvennootschappen*, academic diss., Deventer.

14

Spain

RAFEL CRESPÍ-CLADERA

1. INTRODUCTION

This review focuses on the recent developments of corporate governance issues in Spain. The environment of this research is a thin, though in importance increasing, equity capital market. There were around 600 listed companies in Spain in 1997, half of which operated in the financial sector. Effective market turnover is highly concentrated: nearly 70 per cent of effective market turnover is attributed to ten companies on the Electronic Market. The emphasis of this research lies on the agency relationships in large corporations where ownership and decision rights are separated.

This report uses a quite common classification: external versus internal control mechanisms of agency problems. In terms of external or market mechanisms, I will consider the takeover market focusing on the consequences for shareholder wealth. There are mechanisms in place that distort takeover activity. Recent research about governance of Spanish companies has focused on internal mechanisms of control due to better data availability from the CNMV, the Spanish securities commission. The role of the ownership structure, the board of directors, its size, composition, turnover, and compensation are related to company performance. Recommendations in terms of board characteristics are derived.

As a first step, I portray one of the largest Spanish companies, Telefonica, which has interesting features of both internal and external control devices.

2. THE MOST RELEVANT SPANISH CORPORATE GOVERNANCE CASE: TELEFONICA

Telefonica is a telecommunications company owned by the state until 1997. This former monopoly in telecommunications is currently involved in a liberalization process of the industry, a common trend in all member states of the European Union. Actually it is the second largest Spanish company with sales turnover of ESP 2,906,021m. (EUA 17,468m.) and 103,662 workers at the end of 1998.

The market capitalization of Telefonica represents a share of 22.67 per cent of the 1999 total Spanish market capitalization and accounts for 37.31 per cent of the total transactions on the Spanish Options Markets during 1999. Telefonica represents 25.83 per cent of IBEX35, an index representative of the 35 most liquid companies on

Table 14.1. *Share prices and market capitalization of Telefonica (Spain)*

End period	Share prices (Euro)	Market capitalization (Euro 1,000m.)
1995	3.36	9.49
1996	6.04	17.02
1997	8.71	24.56
1998	12.64	38.87
1999	24.80	80.91

Table 14.2. *Subsidiaries and participations of Telefonica in Spain*

Company name	% Shares
Amper, s.a.	6.1
Fastibex, s.a.	5.5
Telefonica Publicidad e Informacion, s.a.	63.0
Terra Networks, s.a.	68.5

the Spanish stock markets. The company is listed on all major Stock Exchanges: London, Paris, Frankfurt, Tokyo, and New York.

Although telecommunication is an increasingly competitive industry, the market value of Telefonica has grown above average compared to similar companies in other EU countries. Table 14.1 shows this effect in terms of market capitalization. The ownership structure of the company is highly dispersed, with a stable core of three banks as large shareholders. Argentaria group, a former state-owned bank, controls 5.02 per cent of the outstanding shares at the end of 1999. Banco Bilbao Vizcaya, S. A., a private bank involved in a merger process with Argentaria, owns 3.22 per cent, and Caja de Ahorros y Pensiones de Barcelona, a Catalan-based Savings Bank, is the owner of 5.01 per cent. This means that a typical C3 measure of ownership concentration is below 15 per cent and all the owners belong to the banking sector.

A significant difference of Spanish listed companies from other EU countries is the absence of pyramidal structures to concentrate voting power. In that sense, Telefonica is a representative example for Spain. Some subsidiaries and corporate participations of Telefonica in Spain are presented in Table 14.2. The international expansion of Telefonica to Latin America involves Telefonica CTC Chile, Telefonica Argentina, CANTV, and the Brazilian companies Telesp fija, Telesp cellular, Telesudeste cellular and Teleleste cellular. The market capitalization of these companies by the end of 1999 was USD 20,492m.

The company has implemented a Good Practices Code, which sets the governance rules of the company, according to the contents of the Olivencia Report (which is similar to the Cadbury and other European Corporate Governance reports). The structure of the board of directors follows these recommendations. The composition of the board is as reported in Table 14.3. A characteristic feature in most Spanish listed

Table 14.3. *Board structure of Telefonica (Spain)*

Type of directors	Number
Executive directors	3
Representing significant shareholders	6
Independents	9
From companies with strategic alliances	2
Total board members	20

companies is the small amount of shares owned by members of the board of directors. For Telefonica the sum of all 20 directors' shareholdings (as personal ownership) is about 0.01 per cent. Telefonica amended its company statutes in June 1998. These modifications affect the following aspects which protect incumbent management from takeovers to a certain extent:

1. Increase of the minimum amount of shares to attend general meetings.
2. Limit on the maximum number of votes that a shareholder can exercise. No shareholder can vote more than 10 per cent of the outstanding shares, independent of the number of shares she owns (Art. 21). This is a voting cap, see QIII of Table 1.1.
3. Requirement of a minimum ownership of shares for the last three years to be eligible as a member of the board (Art 25). The exception to this rule is for executives of the company or in case of authorization of a 85 per cent majority of the board.
4. A board member can only be promoted to president, vice-president or CEO, if she/he has been a board member for at least three years. This rule can be exempted with the approval of 85 per cent of board members.

These Anti-takeover protections did not appear to have an impact on market value. This kind of protections are frequent among Spanish listed companies, even though there is no active market for corporate control. Most formal takeovers can be classified as friendly.

A final comment on governance issues refer to the 'Golden share' mechanism that the government retains for a ten years period starting after full privatization of Telefonica. This mechanism has not been used explicitly, although there were some rumours that it would be used in the KPN-Telefonica merger in 2000.

3. OWNERSHIP STRUCTURE AND PERFORMANCE

In Spain ownership structure is characterized by high concentration levels, important cross-shareholdings, and an increasing importance of foreign companies as investors. On average, for example, the two largest shareholders hold around 50 per cent of the equity in listed companies.

This structure motivates the Crespí (1998) paper, which, following the Demsetz and Lehn (1985) research on the causes and consequences of ownership structure, explains the Spanish ownership structure in terms of company size, noisiness in the environment, level of debt and the influence of a regulatory agency. Additionally, the panel data approach of this research allows the introduction of cyclical non-firm specific conditions as explanatory variable. The main conclusion is that size is not inversely related to ownership concentration, except for individual investors. Galve and Salas (1994) find that ownership concentration depends on the type of the controlling shareholder. Specifically, the influence of size on ownership concentration is positive only if other companies are the controlling owners.

Linking the ownership structure to performance Galve and Salas (1993) is the most often cited reference in Spain. Their conclusion is that majority control in family firms limits company growth, which is explained by upper limits in risk concentration. While there is higher efficiency in firms characterized by a large concentration of ownership than for non-concentrated ownership, this efficiency improvements do not show up in better performance because economies of scale cannot be achieved due to firm size constraints. Galve and Salas (1996a) show the average rate of return of family and non-family firms are basically equal. This reflects the trade-off between increased efficiency of the former and the lack of restriction on size for the latter. The implication of this analysis is that performance is evaluated within a two dimensional framework where size and ownership structure determine a set of possible solutions.

Connecting external with internal control variables like incentive compensation schemes, Salas (1992) presents a model where controlling shareholders exert supervision. Shareholder supervision can substitute for external devices like takeovers or administrative regulation. An empirical test of this theoretical framework is Crespí and Gispert (1998), who introduce alternative governance mechanisms as, for example, ownership concentration or debt to justify the pay for performance relationship.

4. TAKEOVERS AND THE MARKET FOR CORPORATE CONTROL

Takeover activity is important in Spain compared to other Continental European countries if one looks at aggregate numbers of the CNMV. Since 1990 more than 150 formal takeovers have been registered and supervised by the stock market agency. However, most of them are mergers or friendly acquisitions. The empirical research on takeover activity in Spain has focused on the financial implications of the transactions rather than on the disciplinary role and their influence as a governance mechanism. Fernandez-Blanco and Garcia-Martin (1995), with a sample of 35 listed companies using event-study techniques, find positive abnormal returns around the announcement date of the takeovers only for target shareholders but not for bidding shareholders. While target shareholders experience positive abnormal returns, these are lower than in other countries. The authors attribute this to methodological problems linked to the low frequency of transactions for some companies in the sample.

Vazquez-Ordas (1992) tries to determine the features that identify the Spanish firms subject to mergers. Inefficiencies in the management as measured by low price–earnings ratios, the ability to pay back short-term debt, and leverage increase the probability of being correctly classified as a target company.

Even though the market for corporate control is not very active, some large listed companies in Spain have modified their statutes to make takeovers more difficult. Crespí (1995) and Fernandez and Gomez (1997) evaluate the impact of the adoption of anti-takeover amendments, however, abnormal returns are insignificant. Crespí (1995) explores the impact of ownership concentration, sector of activity, and capital structure; however none of these explain differences in abnormal returns across companies.

Crespí (1993) and Arruñada (1992) focus on non-voting shares which introduce a deviation from 'one-share-one-vote' that current law permits. Arruñada (1992)—from an institutional view—and Crespí (1993)—from a case study perspective—show that current legal rules allow, to some extent, wealth transfers from non-voting to voting shareholders in case of opportunistic managerial behaviour. The Spanish Companies Act which allows for non-voting shares, however, imposes a minimum dividend to be paid to non-voting shares in addition to the dividend of ordinary shares. This compensates for the lack of voting rights. The additional dividends are based on the face value of shares.

5. THE ROLE OF THE BOARD OF DIRECTORS, AND MANAGERIAL COMPENSATION

Internal control mechanisms are those contractual arrangements or internal organizational devices that align the interests of the members of the organization with company objectives. At the first level there is the shareholders' board of directors. Fernandez, Gomez, and Fernandez (1998) look at cross-sectional attributes of boards such as size and composition (measured by the proportion of internal versus external board members) for a sample of Spanish listed companies. An interesting finding is the non-monotonically increasing relationship between board size and performance. Board composition also explains performance, i.e. external board members monitor internal members and company performance is positively affected by the presence of external board members.

Gispert (1998), using a panel of 113 listed companies, considers board characteristics as explanatory factors of disciplining actions in case of poor company performance. A Tobit specification shows that board turnover is higher when performance is poor; however board composition does not explain higher disciplinary attitudes.

Pay–performance incentives in remuneration packages are an alternative way of disciplining or motivating managers. Given the poor data available in Spain, it is only possible to test the influence of performance on aggregate board remuneration. Crespí and Gispert (1998) find a positive sensitivity of board remuneration to changes in company performance which is strongest when measured by accounting information. Contrary to the generally accepted hypothesis, ownership concentration does not seem to be a substituting governance device for incentive compensation.

6. FINAL REMARKS

As a conclusion, the governance mechanisms of large Spanish listed companies seem to behave very differently from the market-oriented systems in the UK and US. While takeovers have a positive wealth effect on target shareholders, recent research (Gomez 1998) does not find strong evidence for a disciplinary role of takeovers. Many companies adopt anti-takeover devices. Given the absence of an effective market for corporate control, this is difficult to explain by value-maximizing objectives; however, it is consistent with managerial motives.

Turning to internal control mechanisms, poor performance appears to explain the removal of board members. Company performance-compensation schemes—while present in Spain—do not behave as a substitute to direct ownership monitoring.

References for Chapter 14

Arruñada, Benito (1992), 'La conversión coactiva de acciones comunes en acciones sin voto para lograr el control de las sociedades anónimas: De cómo la ingenuidad legal prefigura el fraude. Revista Española de Financiación y Contabilidad', 21/71: 283–314.

Crespí-Cladera, Rafel (1993), 'Las ofertas de conversión de acciones ordinarias en acciones sin voto: aplicación al caso del Banco Guipuzcoano', *Moneda y Crédito*, 197: 167–96.

—— (1995), 'Protección de los administradores ante el mercado de capitales: Evidencia empírica en España', *XI Jornadas de Economía Industrial*, 45–58.

—— (1998), 'Determinantes de la estrucuctura de propiedad: Una aproximación al caso español con datos de panel', *Moneda y Crédito* 206 (June).

—— and C. Gispert-Pellicer (1998), 'Board Remuneration, Performance, and Corporate Governance in Large Spanish Companies', Workshop on Corporate Governance, Contracts, and Managerial Incentives, Berlin (July).

Demsetz, H. and R. Lehn (1985), 'The Structure of Corporate Ownership: Causes and Consequences', *Journal of Political Economy*, 93/6: 1155–77.

Fernández Alvarez, A. and S. Gómez Ansón (1997), 'Los acuerdos estatutarios antiadquisición: Evidencia en el mercado de capitales español', *Investigaciones Económicas*, 21: 129–38.

—— —— and C. Fernández Méndez (1998), 'The Effect of Board Size and Composition on Corporate Performance', in Balling *et al.* (eds.), *Corporate Governance, Financial Markets and Global Convergence*, Boston: Kluwer Academic Press, 1–14.

Fernandez Blanco, M. and C. J. Carcía Martín (1995), 'El efecto de la publicación de una opa sobre la rentabilidad de las acciones', *Revista Española de Economia*, 12/2: 219–40.

Galve Gorriz, C. and V. Salas Fumas (1993), 'Propiedad y resultados de la gran empresa española', Investigaciones Económicas, 27/2: 207–38.

—— —— (1994), 'Análisis de la estructura accionarial de la gran empresa', *Revista de Economia Aplicada*, 2/4: 75–102.

—— —— (1996a), 'Ownership and Governance Among Large Spanish Corporations', *ZfB-Ergänzungsheft*, 3/96: 65–77.

—— —— (1996b), 'Ownership Structure and Firm Performance: Some Empirical Evidence from Spain', *Managerial and Decision Economics*, 17: 575–86.

Gómez Ansón, S. (1988), 'Determinantes Del Reemplazo Del Equipo Gestor En El Mercado De Control Corporativo Español', mimeo, University of Oviedo.

Gispert, Carles (forthcoming), 'Board Turnover and Firm Performance in Spanish Companies', *Investigaciones Económicas*.

Salas Fumas, V. (1992), 'Incentivos y supervisión en el control interno de la empresa: Implicaciones para la concentración de su accionariado', *Cuadernos económicos del ICE*, 52/3: 127–45.

Vazquez Ordas, C. J. (1992), 'Perfil característico de las empresas españolas objetivo de fusiones', *Investigaciones Económicas*, 16/3: 489–99.

15

Turkey

BURCIN YURTOGLU

1. INTRODUCTION

Franks and Mayer (1998) characterize an 'insider system' of corporate governance by three features: (1) few listed companies, (2) a large number of substantial share stakes, and (3) large inter-corporate shareholdings. Outside investors, while able to participate in equity returns through the stock market, cannot exert much control. On the other side, the Anglo-Saxon system is a market oriented or 'outsider system' and is characterized by a large number of listed companies, a liquid capital market where ownership and control rights are frequently traded, and few inter-corporate shareholdings.

The Turkish system shares all the three features of the 'insider system' described above, it differs however from both of these systems in several aspects. First, few Turkish companies are traded.[1] Although the number of traded companies increased steadily from 80 in 1986 to 285 at the end of 1999, the market capitalization is around 12 per cent of the GDP over this period.[2]

Second, Turkish-traded companies exhibit highly concentrated and centralized ownership structures. Families, directly or indirectly, own more than 75 per cent of all companies and keep the majority control. The separation of ownership and control is mainly achieved through pyramidal or complex ownership structures and/or by building coalitions with other families or foreign firms.[3]

Third, an active market for corporate control does not exist given the limited openness and the concentrated ownership of the typical traded company. It is almost impossible to acquire a traded company without the consent of the controlling owner. There are also no signs that a market for large stakes operates in a way that disciplines poor management. The distinctive features of the Turkish case are its financial system and the presence of business groups. Almost every private bank is under the control of families who typically control a large number of other financial and industrial companies. Hence, the monitoring function of banks works in a way that reinforces the interests of the owner family.

In the absence of these mechanisms other elements of corporate governance are at work: families or coalitions of mutual trust, pyramidal and complex ownership structures play a substantial role. A central device for organizing the separation of ownership and control is the holding company. The small number of existing studies confirm that no matter how large and diversified the Turkish holding companies are, they are still owned and managed by the founder family (Bugra 1994).[4] Many of the largest corporations in Turkey are affiliated with a business group. The firms affiliated with a business group are linked to one another in two ways. The first may be described as a complicated web of interlocking shareholdings. The second way of organizing the group companies is to form a pyramidal group by spreading the voting rights of minority shareholders out over a large number of firms and concentrating those of the ultimate owner at the top of the pyramid.

These groups are the outcome of investments by a single family or a small number of allied families who, once having established the core of the group, keep them together as a coherent body among which resources and personnel may be shifted as needed. Banks constitute a special feature of the Turkish business group even though the extent and importance of their role is not comparable to the Japanese and German cases.

2. CORPORATE GOVERNANCE IN TURKEY

The next section summarizes briefly the legal environment surrounding the relationship between large stakeholders and minorities. Then, we summarize the findings in Yurtoglu (2000) concerning the concentrated direct and ultimate ownership and the role of coalitions in the ownership structure of the listed firms. We also give a brief summary of the structure of the board of directors and look at the relationship between ownership structure and performance. The final section concludes.

2.1. *Shareholder rights*

There are at least three ways around the 'one-share-one-vote' principle in Turkey. First, companies can issue shares with different voting rights and with different rights in getting collateral in liquidation (Company Law: §401). Secondly, the owners can reduce their cash flow rights below their control rights by using pyramids. Finally, the ultimate owners can enforce their control via cross-shareholdings.

Regarding anti-director rights the Turkish investor has to abstain from several rights enjoyed in the Anglo-Saxon countries (La Porta *et al.* 1998). A shareholder cannot attend and vote unless she has lodged her shares with the company one week before the time of the meeting (§360). Shareholders are not allowed to mail their proxy vote directly to the company (§360). Shareholders can call an extraordinary shareholders' meeting to challenge the management. The percentage of share capital necessary for this action is 10 per cent and can be reduced by the company charter (§366). The shareholders are entitled to the pre-emptive right to buy new issues of stock (§394).

2.2. *Ownership structure of the Turkish listed companies*

Yurtoglu (2000) studies the ownership structure of 257 Turkish companies whose shares are traded on the Istanbul Stock Exchange in 1997. The average listed firm is quite large with 910 employees. Among the 179 manufacturing companies 146 were among the largest 500 Turkish manufacturing firms in 1996. The 16 banks are among the largest 20 banks in Turkey. The average age of the sample companies is 26. The average company has traded for about six years. A company has on average share stakes in six other companies.

2.3. *Direct ownership*

Equity ownership in Turkey is highly concentrated. The percentage of a company's outstanding equity held by the largest shareholder (C1) ranges from 1.1 to 98.2 per cent around a mean value of 44.6 per cent (see part A of Table 15.1). The five and ten largest shareholders together hold on average 67.3 and 69.2 per cent of the outstanding equity, respectively. In 207 out of the 257 companies there are five (or fewer) large

Table 15.1. *Summary statistics on ownership and control measures in Turkey*
A. Summary statistics on direct ownership concentration

Variable	Number	Mean	Standard deviation	Median	Minimum	Maximum
C1	257	44.65	20.34	41.23	1.10	98.17
C5	257	67.35	17.38	69.64	2.83	98.17
C10	257	69.16	17.09	72.57	3.48	98.52
Dispersed	257	29.94	16.72	27.00	1.76	96.38

B. Statistics on voting rights, cash flow rights, and the control leverage factor

Type of owner	Frequency	Ultimate ownership (cash-flow rights) Mean	Total control (voting rights) Mean	Control leverage factor Mean	Max.
Holding companies	11	62.8	62.8	1.00	1.00
Non-financial companies	6	52.1	52.1	1.00	1.00
Banks	10	52.5	64.5	1.39	3.02
Individuals/families	198	53.8	60.3	1.32	12.04
Foreign	15	50.7	56.4	1.18	2.10
State/state agencies	11	69.6	69.6	1.00	1.00
Managers	1	49.2	49.2	1.00	1.00
Foundations	3	51.5	62.1	1.40	2.21
Labour unions/ co-operatives	2	76.9	76.9	1.00	1.00

Notes: C1, C5 and C10 measure the percentage of a company's outstanding equity held by the largest, five largest and ten largest shareholders, respectively. 'Dispersed' measures the percentage of outstanding equity held by a large number of small investors. Majority (minority) control is defined as ultimate ownership above (below) 50 per cent.

shareholders with at least 50 per cent of the outstanding equity under their control. The mean value of the percentage of outstanding equity not held by the large shareholders (dispersed shareholdings) is 29.9 per cent.

Holding companies are the most important shareholders and have ownership stakes in 143 companies with an average stake of 36 per cent. Non-financial companies come next with investments in 139 companies. The average stake of a non-financial company is about 32 per cent. In 128 companies families or individuals have ownership stakes with an average stake of about 27 per cent. Financial companies (mainly banks and insurance companies) are not as important as the first three owner categories discussed above. In total, they have ownership stakes in 62 companies, banks being the largest investor category with an average stake of about 32 per cent. Foreign firms have ownership stakes in 40 companies. Their stakes are large on average compared to other investors with a mean value of 37 per cent. Managers have ownership stakes in only 11 listed companies and the managerial shareholdings are very small around a median of less than 1 per cent. Foundations and Pension funds have ownership stakes in 29 and 19 companies, respectively. These two categories are not independent actors and are best understood with their legal relationships to (mainly) holding companies.

2.4. *Ultimate ownership*

After taking account of the pyramidal and complex ownership structures, family ownership becomes the most important category. Families ultimately control 198 of the 257 companies in the sample (see part B of Table 15.1). They hold on average 53.8 per cent of the equity capital. This figure is substantially higher than the average direct shareholdings of families (27.1 per cent). On average families control about 60 per cent of the direct voting rights of a company although their ultimate cash flow rights are 53.8 per cent. Their control leverage factor is therefore equal to 1.32.

We do not have data on the identities of ultimate owners in 27 companies. Consequently, holding companies, non-financial companies, and banks appear now as ultimate controlling owners of 11, 6, and 10 companies, respectively. The Turkish state is the ultimate owner of 11 companies. The mean and median values of the ultimate ownership stakes of the state are about 70 per cent.

Foreign investors have ultimate control in 15 listed companies although they have a direct ownership stake in 40 listed companies. They ultimately control 56.3 per cent of the equity capital owning 50.6 per cent of the capital on average. The average control leverage factor of foreign firms is 1.18.

2.5. *Minorities and coalitions*

In 81 traded companies there are sizeable stakes held by a shareholder other than the ultimate controlling owner. The average stake is about 17 per cent. It is interesting to note that these stakes cluster around 10 per cent of the voting rights; an amount just enough to call an extraordinary shareholders' meeting to challenge the management. The majority of these stakes are found in companies where the ultimate owner is a family or a foreign company. The most frequent and sizeable relationships are among families (26 cases with an average stake of 12.7 per cent) and between families and foreign firms (21 cases with an average of 22.1 per cent participation in the voting rights by a foreign firm and four cases where the ultimate owner is a foreign firm and families having on average 12.3 per cent of the voting rights).

2.6. *Boards of directors*

Section two of the Company Law concerning joint stock companies deals with the boards of directors, laying down several points similar to those listed in La Porta *et al.* (1998) for countries with legal systems based on the French origin. Within this legal setting the boards can function in various ways, but most of them are composed of the controlling shareholders who are engaged in managing the company.

The previous sections provide evidence that the typical listed company is owned and controlled by a founder family or a coalition of families. Data on the board of directors are also consistent with this observation. In 206 companies there is at least one board member who is also a member of the controlling family. On average more than one-third of all board members are large shareholders. The percentage of large shareholders on the board of directors decreases with the board size. In companies with less than six board members half of the board consists of large shareholders.

The median size of the board of directors is seven. Only 20 companies have three board members, the minimum number specified by the law. Board size is positively related to firm size and to the number of subsidiaries of the company and negatively related to the percentage holdings of the largest direct shareholder. There are significant differences across industries. Holding companies and financial companies have larger boards than the manufacturing companies. There are, however, no statistically significant differences in board size across ultimate owner categories.

2.7. *Ownership structure and performance*

Yurtoglu (2000) finds a statistically significant negative relationship between three widely used performance measures (return on assets, market-to-book ratio, and dividend pay-out ratio) and ownership concentration after controlling for industry effects and size. The estimates imply that while the effect of the largest direct shareholder is small, increasing control leverage has a substantially negative impact on market valuation, possibly implying opportunistic behaviour by owners towards minority shareholders. The results also underline the existence of significant agency costs in pyramidal ownership structures where ownership and control rights are not aligned.

2.8. *An example*

This section portrays the governance of Arcelik A.S., the largest private sector company in Turkey. Arcelik was founded in 1955 and has become the seventh largest consumer durables manufacturer of Europe in 1997. It has 3,752 employees and 1998 sales of

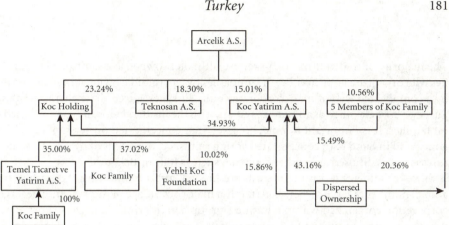

Figure 15.1. *Ownership structure of ARCELIK A.S. (Turkey)*

USD 880m. Arcelik is one of the 92 affiliated companies of the Koc Group which is the largest business group in Turkey. Figure 15.1 details the ownership structure of Arcelik. There are four major shareholders of Arcelik holding a total of 67 per cent of the shares.[5] The dispersed shareholdings amount to 20.4 per cent. The largest shareholder is the holding company of Koc Group with about 24 per cent of the voting rights. The second largest shareholder, Teknosan, is not a member of the Koc Group, however, it belongs to another family (Burla Brothers) with whom Koc Group has been in contact since the early days of its foundation (Sönmez 1992). The third largest shareholder of Arcelik is a group member which has cross-shareholdings with several other Koc Group affiliates. Five members of the Koc family, the founder of the Koc Group, hold about 11 per cent of the voting power directly. Pyramiding devices are also at work. The Koc family has a 37 per cent direct stake in Koc Holding and another 35 per cent stake via its full ownership in *Temel Ticaret A.S.*, which in turn has a 35 per cent stake in Koc Holding.

The voting rights in Arcelik associated with the Koc family amount to 58.04 per cent. This figure is the sum of the 10.56 per cent directly held by the Koc family members, the 23.24 per cent stake of Koc Holding (since it is controlled by the family), and the 15.01 per cent stake through Koc Yatirim A.S. (since it is also controlled by the Koc family).[6] To calculate the corresponding cash flow rights, one has to multiply the fraction of Koc family ownership in all companies that have an ownership relationship with Arcelik. For example, the cash flow rights of the Koc family through Koc Holding are equal to 16.73 per cent (=23.24 per cent * (35.00 per cent+37.02 per cent)). By adding the corresponding cash flow rights in Koc Yatirim, we find that the total cash flow rights amount to 37.2 per cent. So, the control leverage factor is equal to 1.56.

Looking at the board of directors of Arcelik, we can also confirm the influence of the Koc family. Four of the nine board members belong to the Koc family, the remaining five being executives from affiliated firms that are controlled by the Koc Group.

3. CONCLUSION

The majority of traded firms in Turkey are ultimately owned and controlled by families who organize a large number of companies by a pyramidal ownership structure or by a complicated web of inter-corporate equity linkages. Given these characteristics, Turkey can be classified as an 'insider system', with the insiders being the country's richest families. It is important to note, however, that concentrated ownership has so far gone hand in hand with concentrated voting rights, i.e. the extent of pyramidal structures is not as diffused as in other countries such as Italy or Belgium.

Since cash flow and control interests are aligned, direct monitoring of managers by a small number of large owners is certainly a major advantage of this system. The large corporations organized within a business group can in principle neglect short-term considerations and pursue long-term growth strategies. Since most of the business groups operating in Turkey have formed a bank early on or acquired a bank in later stages of their development, they are also functional substitutes to external capital markets. Consequently, the typical company of a business group operates under a reduced set of constraints relative to an independent firm in the same country.

There are, however, at least three disadvantages of concentrated ownership. First, concentrated ownership reduces diversification possibilities and liquidity. Selling larger fractions of the company increases the scope for diversification by the initial owners whose portfolios generally consist of equity in other family businesses organized around the holding company. Second, concentrated ownership puts the interests of small shareholders at a risk. The existence of a business group raises the probability of rent extraction through the following mechanism. While the minority shareholders are interested in the returns from their investment in a subsidiary company, the ultimate owner focuses on the benefits from the group as a whole and not necessarily the benefits derived from one particular member company. In general, the ultimate controlling owners are more interested in profits coming from companies where their shareholdings are higher. The ultimate owners might try to transfer resources from other subsidiaries using transfer pricing that increase the group's benefits. Given this possibility rational minority shareholders will demand a premium on the shares issued or exit by selling their shares, since these are the only available mechanisms to protect their interests. These considerations suggest that the ownership structure of these companies depends on the characteristics of the business group. The fraction of the shares sold to outside investors is determined not only by the needs of the individual company, but also by the external capital requirements of the group as a whole.

The third disadvantage of this system is the increased likelihood of overall concentration in the product market (Scott 1982). Inter-corporate equity linkages may foster collusive behaviour and act as a barrier to entry. Furthermore, inter-corporate equity linkages reduce the transparency needed to use competition policy to increase the overall efficiency of the economy. The separation of ownership and control implied by the business group system and the high concentration of ownership makes hostile takeovers impossible and deprives the capital market of its usual functioning in the efficient allocation of capital.

A broader discussion of these problems goes beyond the scope of our present data set and therefore of this report. However, facts assembled here constitute a background for the design of specific monitoring and regulatory devices for large traded companies in Turkey.

Notes

1. Data obtained from the State Institute of Statistics of Turkey indicate 51,701 active stock corporations in 1997 in Turkey. The number of listed companies in the same year was, however, below 1,000, out of which only 274 were traded.
2. This ratio reaches an all-time high of 32 per cent at the end of 1997, a number which puts Turkey to the middle of the Continental European ranking (Renneboog 1998).
3. In this respect, Turkey is much closer to Italy (Bianchi and Casavola 1995) than, say, to Germany (Gugler 1998).
4. Bugra (1994) gives a rigorous account of the importance of the holding companies in Turkey. Sönmez (1992) studies the development and main activities of several holding companies. Sen (1995) explores the same issue by looking at the business groups as a social class.
5. There are four other direct owners of Arcelik which hold less than 10 per cent of the shares. The largest of them is a pension fund designed for the employees of the Koc Group with 5.6 per cent of the votes. The remaining owners are other firms that belong to the Koc Group. We do not follow the ownership relations through these owners to keep the figure as simple as possible.
6. The discrepancy is due to the stakes below 10 per cent which are not shown in Figure 15.1. We do, however, consider them in our calculations.

References for Chapter 15

Bianchi, M. and P. Casavola (1995), 'Piercing the Corporate Veil: Truth and Appearance in Italian Listed Pyramidal Groups', Working paper Banca D'Italia, presented at the Corporate Governance and Property Rights Workshop in Milan 16–17 June.

Bugra, A. (1994), *State and Business in Modern Turkey*, New York: State University of New York Press.

Franks, J. and C. Mayer (1998), 'Bank Control in Germany: Takeovers and Corporate Governance', *Journal of Banking and Finance*, 22: 1385–404.

Gugler, K. (1998), 'Corporate Ownership Structure in Austria', *Empirica*, 25: 285–307.

La Porta, Rafael, Florencio Lopez-de-Silanes, Andrei Shleifer, and Robert Vishny (1998), 'Law and Finance', *Journal of Political Economy*, 106: 1113–55.

Renneboog, L. (1998), 'Shareholding Concentration and Pyramidal Ownership Structure in Belgium', in M. Balling, E. Hennessy, and R. O'Brien (eds.), *Corporate Governance, Financial Markets and Global Convergence*, Boston: Kluwer Academic Publishers.

Scott, J. J. (1982), 'Multimarket Contact and Economic Performance', *Review of Economics and Statistics*, 64: 368–75.

Sen, M. (1995), 'The Anatomy of the Big Bourgeoisie in Turkey', *Toplum ve Bilim*, 66: 46–68.

Sönmez, M. (1992), *Holdings in Turkey* (Türkiye'de Holdingler), Ankara: Arkadas Yayinevi.

Yurtoglu, B. (2000), 'Ownership, Control and Performance of Turkish Listed Companies', *Empirica*, 27: 193–222.

16

United Kingdom

MARC GOERGEN AND LUC RENNEBOOG

1. INTRODUCTION

The UK is very different from most other countries, such as the Continental European countries and Japan, in terms of corporate governance and ownership. First, there is a much larger number of UK firms that are quoted on the stock exchange: the total market capitalization of domestic listed firms amounts to 81 per cent of the GNP (these figures are adjusted for double counting due to cross-shareholdings between companies). In comparison, the total market values of quoted German and Japanese firms are only about 14 and 37 per cent of GNP respectively (Prowse 1995). On average, British companies also go public at a much earlier point in their life cycle than their German counterparts. The average age of firms at the time of their initial public offering is only 14 years in the UK, but 53 years in Germany. Surprisingly, however, the difference in size is much less pronounced, as UK IPOs are only half as large as German IPOs, measured by market capitalization (Goergen 1998).

Second, the separation of ownership and control—as defined by Berle and Means (1932)—exists in most listed British firms. Franks and Mayer (1995) report that about 84 per cent of the top 200 quoted UK firms do not have any shareholder controlling more than a quarter of the voting equity, compared to 15 per cent of German firms. Similarly, only 10 per cent of listed British companies are majority-owned, whereas in Germany the proportion of majority-owned companies is 25 per cent (Prowse 1995). Goergen (1998) finds that pre-IPO shareholders of British firms on average tend to lose majority control two to three years after the flotation, whereas pre-IPO shareholders of German firms lose majority control only after five to six years.

Goergen and Renneboog (forthcoming b) show that for a random sample of 200 listed UK firms directors (both executive and non-executive directors) are the second largest group of shareholders—institutional investors being the largest group—holding a total 10 per cent. The figures are for 1992. The percentages held by executive directors and non-executive directors are 5.8 and 4.1 per cent respectively. The single-board system further reinforces the power of executive directors. Franks, Mayer, and Renneboog (1998) show that 23 per cent of listed UK firms do not separate the roles of chairman and CEO. Hence, the main agency problem faced by shareholders is the potential expropriation by the management. The Cadbury (1992), Greenbury (1995) and

Hampel (1998) reports have tried to reduce managerial power. All reports advocate the independence of non-executive directors and the separation of the functions of chairman and CEO. Given the control and ownership characteristics of the average UK firm, most empirical research on the link between performance and ownership in UK firms focuses on the role of managerial equity ownership.

Third, the UK is the only European country with an active market for corporate control. Outside the UK and the USA, hostile takeovers are very rare and managerial failure seems to be corrected via internal mechanisms such as large-shareholder monitoring. Franks and Mayer (1996) report 80 hostile takeovers in the UK in 1985–6 alone, compared to only three hostile takeovers in Germany since World War II.[1]

Section 2 of this chapter discusses the effects of owner control and managerial control on corporate performance. A distinction is made between studies on large, quoted companies and those on smaller or unlisted companies. As an example of control structures in the UK, Vodafone Airtouch plc., is presented. Section 2 also reviews recent evidence on initial public offerings (IPOs) in the UK. In section 3 we review the two main mechanisms of disciplining badly performing managers in the UK, the market for corporate control and board dismissal, as well as an additional, indirect mechanism, i.e. audit reports. Section 4 addresses an important agency problem in the UK, excessive, non-performance related managerial remuneration. Section 5 reviews empirical studies on the role of institutional investors, and other large shareholders, in the UK and their effect on company performance. Section 6 discusses the UK studies on the determinants of corporate ownership. Finally, section 7 concludes this chapter.

2. DIRECT MONITORING VERSUS DISPERSED OWNERSHIP: OWNER-CONTROLLED VERSUS MANAGER-CONTROLLED FIRMS

2.1. *An example of control in the UK: Vodafone Airtouch plc.*

In January 2000, after the decision to merge with the Mannesmann subsidiary Airtouch Inc, Vodafone became the UK's largest firm and has many characteristics of the typical governance and ownership characteristics of the typical UK corporation. As Vodafone's shares are listed on the London Stock Exchange,[2] it has to make a statement about its level of compliance with the Combined Code on Corporate Governance. Apart from some minor exceptions, Vodafone adhered to the Code during the financial year ending on 31 March 1999. The board comprises more independent (non-executive directors) than executive directors (5 versus 4) and the functions of chairman and CEO are separated. (After the completion of the merger the board size is to increase to 14, half of the directors are to be appointed by Vodafone, the other half by Airtouch.) Furthermore, the company has set up a nominations committee, a remuneration committee and an audit committee as recommended by the Code. More than 85 per cent of the shares in Vodafone are held by banks or through nominee accounts (see Table 16.1). The beneficial holders behind these nominee accounts are mostly institutional investors. The only significant shareholdings in the company are all owned by institutional

Table 16.1. *Vodaphone Airtouch plc. type of shareholders, 31 March 1999 (UK)*

	Number of accounts	Percentage of equity issued
Private individuals	36,264	3.9
Banks or nominee accounts	16,457	85.5
Investment trust and funds	595	0.1
Insurance companies	21	0.2
Industrial and commercial companies	701	0.9
Other corporate bodies	594	1.8
Pension funds and trustees	34	0.9
Bank of new nominees— ADRs	1	6.7
TOTAL	54,667	100.0

Source: Vodafone Airtouch plc.

investors and add up to 17 per cent of the equity. The significant stakes are: a 5.8 per cent holding by Mercury Asset Management Limited, a 5.1 per cent holding by Schroder Investment Management Limited, a 3.1 per cent holding by Legal and General Investment Management Limited, and a 3.0 per cent holding by Prudential Corporation group of companies. The sum of the shares beneficially held by the directors was 477,948 out of a total of 3.1 billion outstanding shares.

2.2. *The case of listed companies*

The most extensive UK study on ownership structure and performance is the Leech and Leahy (1991) study, based on a sample of 470 UK listed companies. Leech and Leahy use two types of measures of ownership concentration. The first type is concentration ratios (e.g. a Herfindahl index of all stakes, and the combined holding of the largest five shareholders) and the second type is control-type dummies (e.g. largest shareholding exceeds 10 per cent, the degree of control[3] of the largest shareholder exceeds 90 per cent). The six different measures of performance they use are a valuation ratio (market value of equity over book value of equity), the trade–profit margin, the return on equity, the growth rate of sales, the growth rate of net assets, and the salary of the highest-paid director. Their findings suggest that if concentration is measured by the control-type dummies, ownership control is associated with a higher valuation ratio, profit margin, return on equity and higher growth rates of sales and net assets. However, the concentration ratios tend to suggest the opposite effect, i.e. that a higher degree of ownership dispersion produces a higher valuation ratio, profit margin, and growth rate of net assets.

Faccio and Lasfer (1999) analyse the link between firm value and managerial ownership for all the 1,650 non-financial companies listed on the London Stock Exchange (LSE) in 1996–7. When they investigate the subsample of low-growth firms, they detect no link between performance and insider ownership (as measured by the equity percentage owned by directors). In contrast, for high-growth firms, they show a non-monotonic relationship between performance and insider ownership: the relationship between performance and insider ownership is positive if directors own less than 20 per cent of the equity, the relationship is negative for insider ownership concentration between 20 and 54 per cent, and becomes positive again for board ownership exceeding 54 per cent.

Short and Keasey (1999) undertake a study similar to the ones by Morck, Shleifer, and Vishny (1988) and McConnell and Servaes (1990): for a random sample of 225 firms listed on the LSE[4] they test whether there is a non-linear link between performance and ownership. Their data suggest that managers of British firms become entrenched at higher levels of ownership than managers of US firms. Morck, Shleifer, and Vishny found that managerial ownership has a positive effect on firm value in the range of 0 to 5 per cent, has a negative effect between 5 and 25 per cent, and a positive effect above 25 per cent. In the UK, the ranges are 0 to 12 per cent, 12 to 41 per cent, and 41 to 100 per cent. Short and Keasey conclude that managers in the UK need higher stakes to insulate themselves from shareholder monitoring.

Unfortunately, Short and Keasey (1999) do not address the issue of the direction of causality between firm value and ownership. Agrawal and Knoeber (1996) and Kole (1996) have advocated a reversal of causality and have found some strong empirical support that ownership is determined by financial performance and not vice-versa. Himmelberg, Hubbard, and Palia (1999) provide additional evidence that managerial ownership is not exogenous. Their findings suggest that managerial ownership and firm value depend on common characteristics, some of which are unobservable. This presence of unobservable variables and the (wrong) assumption of exogeneity of ownership may explain why former studies (such as the one by Morck, Shleifer, and Vishny 1988) have found a link between managerial shareholdings and firm value. Therefore, it is not clear whether Short and Keasey's results are merely due to their assumption about the direction of causality (see also Goergen 1998).

2.3. *The case of small companies and unlisted companies*

Keasey, Short, and Watson (1994) find a non-linear relationship between performance and directors' ownership for a sample of 72 quoted and unquoted small and medium-sized firms. The return on total assets augments with increasing managerial ownership as long as managerial ownership is below 68 per cent, but with decreasing managerial ownership at very high levels of ownership when management is strongly entrenched. However, the authors do not take into account the relative control power, since they ignore equity holdings by other types of shareholders and do not control for the fact whether the firm is quoted or not.

Hay and Morris (1984) analyse the contribution of unquoted firms to the British economy. Out of their sample of 54 unquoted companies, only one is not a close company. By definition '... a company is close if it is either under the control of five or fewer participators, or under the control of its directors, or the ultimate destination of 50 per cent or more of the company's income, assuming full distribution, would be five or fewer participators, or participators who are directors' (Hay and Morris 1984: 82). Hay and Morris find that in general unquoted firms have higher profit rates and grow faster than quoted firms. They also report that unquoted companies tend to use more short-term financing and retention and use comparatively less equity and long-term debt than the quoted ones. However, Hay and Morris also interviewed a subsample of their companies and did not find any qualitative evidence that the management of unquoted firms has different priorities regarding growth and profit than the management of quoted ones.

Mayer *et al.* (1998) corroborate Hay and Morris's (1984) findings on the use of different sources of finance, but find contradictory results for company performance. According to Mayer *et al.*, quoted firms are more profitable than unquoted firms, but tend to invest a smaller proportion of their profits given their higher dividend payout. Furthermore, the authors' findings suggest that listed companies have a less flexible dividend policy than unlisted ones: the former have a lower frequency of dividend omissions, a higher dividend payout ratio and a lower ratio of investments to profits. Hence, there may be some evidence that quoted businesses suffer from costly dividend signalling.

2.4. *The case of initial public offerings*

To study how control evolves in listed companies, Goergen and Renneboog (forthcoming *a*) estimate a multinomial logit model predicting the likelihood of four different control states for a sample of UK and German IPOs six years after going public. In each of the firms, the largest shareholder immediately prior to the IPO is an individual or a family. The four possible states of control are: (1) remaining under the control of the initial shareholders; (2) becoming widely held (i.e. there is no shareholder owning more than 25 per cent of its voting shares); (3) being taken over by a firm which is (ultimately) closely held; (4) being taken over by a firm which is (ultimately) widely held. The explanatory variables in the multinomial logit model are the market capitalization of the firm, a dummy capturing whether or not the founder or the founding family were holding shares in their company immediately before the IPO, company risk (measured by the standard deviation of the monthly stock returns), the average annual growth rate of total assets over the first five years after the flotation, a dummy variable set to one if the company issued non-voting shares in the IPO, and a profit rate (defined as the annual cash flow standardized by book value of total assets).

The model predicts the correct state of control for 80 per cent of the sample. The likelihood that an IPO will be widely held rises if the founder is no longer a shareholder at the moment of the public offering and if the firm is growing rapidly. German and UK IPOs that are risky and have poor performance—firms which may have a compelling need for enhanced monitoring—tend to end up with concentrated ultimate control. Moreover, for the German IPOs, the probability that the firm is controlled by a new large shareholder augments when non-voting shares are issued at flotation and when the company grows fast. Profitable, non-risky, large companies tend to be widely held six years after being listed. Finally, founders are more likely to maintain control over smaller, profitable companies with a moderate risk and a moderate growth. Goergen (1999) investigates whether the long-run underperformance in UK and

German IPOs results from increasing agency conflicts between management and the major (original) shareholders which gradually reduce their ownership stakes. Still, no support is discovered for this hypothesis.

Retaining control power is put forward as an explanation for underpricing in the UK by Brennan and Franks (1997). For a sample of 68 UK IPOs in 1986–9, they find a positive relationship between underpricing and over-subscription of the shares issued. They develop a model where the initial shareholders deliberately underprice to cause over-subscription. Using a share rationing scheme, they discriminate in favour of small investors, such that, when the shares are allocated to obtain maximum dispersion of ownership, they keep control over their firm after the IPO.

3. DISCIPLINING MECHANISMS FOR BADLY PERFORMING MANAGERS

3.1. *The market for corporate control*

Given the high dispersion of ownership in the UK, the market for corporate control is expected to be the main mechanism for the correction of managerial failure. Manne (1965) was the first to advance the disciplining role of hostile takeovers.

However, two recent empirical studies by Franks and Mayer (1996) on the UK and Schwert (2000) on the USA have questioned the validity of Manne's thesis. Both studies agree that the pre-takeover performance of targets of hostile bids is not significantly different from the one of targets of friendly bids. In addition, the authors find that the performance of targets of hostile bids is not significantly different from the one of non-merging firms. Still, the fact that the incidence of takeovers of poorly performing companies is modest, does not mean that hostile takeovers are negligible as a corporate governance mechanism. When hostile takeovers of poorly performing firms do take place, 88 per cent of the directors are replaced in a two-year period subsequent to the takeover. Hence, the mere threat that a poorly performing firm may be subject to a hostile takeover may by itself be a powerful disciplinary mechanism.

3.2. *Board turnover and corporate restructuring*

Lai and Sudarsanam (1997) analyse the choice of recovery strategies made by different types of stakeholders in badly performing firms. Their sample consists of 297 UK firms whose share-price performance dropped from the top 50 per cent of all the firms listed on the LSE to the bottom 20 per cent in the year of the decline. Their period of study ranges from 1989 to 1994. Lai and Sudarsanam distinguish between four different recovery strategies: (1) operational restructuring, (2) asset restructuring (cash generation, acquisitions, and capital expenditure), (3) board turnover, and (4) financial restructuring (dividend cuts/omissions and debt restructuring). They investigate whether the choice of a recovery strategy is determined by specific corporate governance variables. They distinguish among managerial equity ownership, control by relatives of the management, institutional ownership, and ownership by other outside shareholders (like industrial corporations or families and individuals not related to the management). The degree of leverage is also recorded because a high gearing may trigger creditor monitoring. Internal governance variables include whether or not the functions of the CEO and chairman are combined, and the proportion of non-executives on the board of directors. For their sample, Lai and Sudarsanam report an average leverage of 29 per cent, managerial ownership of 20 per cent (median of 10 per cent), institutional ownership of 12 per cent, and non-institutional ownership of 7 per cent. Average ownership by shareholders related to the management is close to zero. In 44 per cent of the sample companies the roles of the CEO and chairman are combined in one person.

Lai and Sudarsanam find that on the whole there is a higher incidence of recovery activities in their sample than in the population of firms listed on the LSE. Results from univariate tests show that manager-controlled[5] firms are less likely to discipline through executive management turnover and operational restructuring than other firms when performance falls. Firms controlled by debt-holders prefer to choose operational, asset, and financial restructuring. Furthermore, debt-holders do not seem to generate management changes even in the wake of poor performance. Widely held underperforming firms in which the positions of chairman and CEO are combined are also less likely to experience a management change. The probit models which measure the likelihood of the different types of restructuring largely confirm that debt-holders prefer cash-generating actions (like asset sales) to tackle the company's underperformance, but they are indifferent to board changes. Also, board changes are more likely to be instigated by non-executives, but are less likely to happen in firms which are neither shareholder- nor debt-holder-controlled and have a combined chairman/CEO.

A similar study by Franks, Mayer, and Renneboog (1998) focuses on who disciplines poor management. The efficiency of several corporate governance mechanisms in disciplining underperforming management is estimated and compared for a random sample of 250 quoted UK firms over the period of 1988 to 1993. Firms are classified into deciles of performance based on abnormal share price performance, return on equity, cash flow margin, and dividend changes. The relationship between executive turnover and performance is non-monotonic with high executive board turnover and CEO turnover being concentrated in the lowest decile companies. From Tobit regressions of board turnover on performance, ownership structure, capital mix, board structure variables, and performance interaction variables, they conclude the following. First, executive directors successfully use their voting power as shareholders to entrench their position on the board. Second, there does not seem to be a significant relationship between board turnover and different types of shareholder, except for increase in ownership by industrial companies when performance is poor. Third, in contrast to Lai and Sudarsanam (1997), they report a strong relationship between board turnover and leverage. Fourth, executive board turnover is higher for firms with low interest coverage. Fifth, managerial disciplining augments when the company is refinanced via an equity issue with rights issues. Poor performance with financing needs seems to be the ideal time for shareholders to request corporate board restructuring. Sixth, although takeovers in the poorly performing subsample are rare, they account for high executive turnover when they do occur. Finally, the study also reports high board restructuring in the companies with an interest–coverage ratio of less than 2, when a company has typically lost investment grade. Still, although low-interest coverage combined with high leverage may indicate increased creditor monitoring, a detailed analysis of 34 case studies reveals that corporate monitoring takes place by shareholders rather than by debt-holders.

Faccio and Lasfer (1999) study the relationship between managerial ownership, the structure of the board and firm value for a sample that includes all the 1,650 non-financial companies listed on the LSE in 1996–7. They hypothesize that managers seek entrenchment with high levels of corporate ownership which make them largely immune to monitoring by non-executive directors. In such companies, the roles of the chairman and chief executive officer are combined and fulfilled by an executive director.

In the Faccio and Lasfer study, managers own on average 17 per cent of the shares. In 88 per cent of their sample, the roles of CEO and chairman are combined and non-executives constitute 43 per cent of the board. Although, the Cadbury (1992) report emphasizes the importance of non-executive directors, Lasfer and Faccio's results for the year 1996–7 do not suggest that the proportion of non-executives is increasing. Their figure of 43 per cent is identical to the one by Conyon (1994) for the year 1993 and only marginally larger than in the Franks, Mayer, and Renneboog (1998) study.

Faccio and Lasfer find a non-linear relationship between the probability of separating the roles of chairman and CEO and managerial ownership. Firms whose managerial ownership is below 19 per cent or is between 10 and 46 per cent are more likely to split the two roles, which is considered as a signal to adopt better corporate governance mechanisms. Likewise, there is a non-linear relationship between the likelihood of having a non-executive chairman and ownership by the management. The probability of having a non-executive chairman increases with very low levels of management ownership (between 0 and 0.40 per cent), however, this probability decreases when managerial ownership is in excess of 12 per cent. Furthermore, the proportion of non-executive directors is positively related to management ownership at low levels of ownership (between zero and 1 per cent), but is negatively related to management ownership at high levels of ownership (in excess of 46 per cent). Consequently, the Faccio and Lasfer study concludes that managers entrench themselves by reducing the monitoring capabilities of the board.

Peasnell, Pope, and Young (2000) also analyse the relationship between managerial ownership and the proportion of outside directors. Their sample consists of all the non-financial and non-utilities firms among the largest 1,000 firms listed on the LSE in the pre-Cadbury year 1991 and the post-Cadbury year 1995. They find a U-shaped, convex relationship between managerial ownership and the proportion of non-executive directors. The turning point of the U-shaped function is 42 per cent in 1991 and 33 per cent in 1995. Although the proportion of outside directors increases with high executive ownership it does not attain the same level it attains at managerial ownership below 10 per cent. The study further investigates whether having a large number of independent non-executive directors reduces the amount of earnings management which is expected to go to the executive directors. Earnings management to disguise losses or decreases in earnings may have a favourable impact on managerial compensation and may also decrease the risk of board dismissals. As a result of earnings management, non-executive directors may suffer loss of their reputation as efficient monitors. It is therefore in the interest of the non-executives to reduce earnings management within the firm. *Ceteris paribus*, Peasnell, Pope, and Young expect that the larger the proportion of non-executives on the board, the less pronounced the earnings management. They also test whether audit committees reduce the use of earnings management. For a sample of 559 firms listed on the LSE between July 1993 and May 1996, there is evidence that the higher the proportion of outside directors the lower will be the use of earnings management to disguise losses or reduced earnings. This relationship is strengthened by the presence of an audit committee.

The role of shareholder voting coalitions formed in order to discipline incumbent management is analysed by Crespí and Renneboog (1999). Shapley values capturing the relative power of shareholder coalitions by category of owner have higher explanatory power in disciplinary executive turnover models than percentages ownership concentration and than other power indices reflecting the voting power of individual owners. There is evidence of successful executive director resistance to board restructuring if these executive directors can combine their ownership stakes to form a substantial block of voting power. Non-executive directors seem to support incumbent management. Poor performance is penalized by industrial and commercial companies with large relative voting power. The voting power of insurance companies is positively related to executive director turnover, but this voting power is used to remove management for reasons other than performance, which may be of strategic nature. Investment/pension funds and funds managed by banks do not play a role in the management substitution process. A large number of share blocks change hands, and new shareholders—industrial companies, individuals, and families—are related to increased executive director turnover. Still, these changes in share stakes do not constitute a market in (partial) control since there is no systematic evidence that these changes are triggered by poor performance with the notable exception of industrial companies. There is also little evidence that adjusting the board composition to allow for more independence for non-executive directors leads to higher managerial removal. In contrast, high gearing facilitates substitution of executive directors, especially if the company needs to be refinanced.

3.3. *Audit reports*

In the UK, given the low levels of ownership concentration, an important monitoring device of managers may be audit reports. Audit reports are important as they may act as an external, independent endorsement of the management. Lennox (1998) argues that unfavourable audit reports—so-called modified audit reports—should have an impact on executive remuneration and board turnover. Companies may receive modified audit reports, because they have financial difficulties and/or use unorthodox accounting policies. The sample consists of 56 UK firms that received at least one unfavourable audit report during the period 1987–94. Firms had to have four years of clean reports before the year of the modified report—year 0—and could have a clean or modified report in year +1.

Lennox firstly hypothesizes that there should be a negative correlation between unfavourable audit reports and managerial compensation and a positive one between unfavourable audit reports and executive board turnover. Secondly, he argues that unfavourable audit reports exposing managerial accounting manipulation (unorthodox accounting techniques) should have a higher impact on compensation and turnover than audit reports that are unfavourable for reasons that are not under the control of the management (going-concern problems). Finally, first-time unfavourable audit reports should convey more information to shareholders and financial markets than repeated unfavourable reports, for two reasons. Firstly, auditors may be reluctant to issue first-time unfavourable audit reports, in order to avoid losing their clients. Secondly, they may also be reluctant to do so in order to avoid litigation by investors if the causes for the first-time unfavourable report were already apparent in previous years. Therefore, one should expect a stronger correlation between executive compensation/turnover and first-time unfavourable reports than between the former and repeated bad reports.

Lennox finds evidence of a positive correlation between unfavourable reports and CEO turnover and of a negative relationship between CEO remuneration (after correcting for performance) and modified reports. When reports are unfavourable due to questionable accounting policies, the relationship to CEO turnover is more significantly negative than when reports are unfavourable because of financial distress. Only the surprise factor of first-time unfavourable reports has an impact on CEO turnover, since CEOs do not seem to be disciplined in case of repeated unfavourable reports. The findings also indicate that bad audit reports have a negative impact on managerial compensation (after correcting for performance). The impact is only significant for non-going-concern issues and for newly unfavourable reports.

4. MANAGERIAL REMUNERATION

The few studies that use ownership characteristics to explain managerial remuneration tend to agree that there is no relationship between the two. Leech and Leahy (1991) regress the salary of the highest paid director on measures of ownership concentration, but do not find a significant correlation. Conyon and Leech (1994) investigate the large increases in managerial remuneration during the first half of the 1980s. In line with most US studies, top executive compensation depends only weakly on the firm's performance, but is strongly influenced by the firm's size. There is some evidence that firms with a higher ownership concentration have lower levels of top executive pay, but there is no significant difference in the growth of top executive pay during the 1980s. Conyon and Leech do not find any influence of monitoring by investors on managerial remuneration. Similarly, there is no link between separation of the functions of CEO and chairman and directors' pay. Likewise, Chan (1997) does not detect any link between top executive pay and insider and outsider ownership for the 50 largest listed UK firms during 1992–6.

In a study comprising the 1980s and most of the 1990s, Conyon, Gregg, and Machin (1994) and Conyon (1997, 1998) test the twin agency predictions that directors' pay is not related to performance in the 1980s but positively related to corporate performance in the 1990s. They find no link between compensation and performance for both periods. Furthermore, CEO turnover is negatively associated with firm profitability. The CEO turnover model predicts a negative association with predated shareholder returns which is consistent with the view that CEOs are disciplined by the threat of dismissal.

Conyon and Murphy (1999) compare the level and composition of CEO compensation in the UK and US and find that in both countries total compensation is higher for CEOs who also fulfil the task of chairman. However, for the combined CEO/chairman the relationship between managerial remuneration and performance is also higher, mainly via ownership stakes.

5. INSTITUTIONAL INVESTORS AND OTHER LARGE SHAREHOLDERS

5.1. *The importance of institutional investors as owners of equity*

In 1994 approximately 50 per cent of UK shares were beneficially owned by pension funds (28 per cent) and by insurance companies (22 per cent) (Stapledon 1996). This is in marked contrast to other European countries such as, for instance, Germany, where non-bank financial institutions hold only about 12 per cent of the shares (Franks and Mayer 1995). The large proportion of equity held by institutional investors is an important characteristic of ownership in the UK. Over the last decades, non-bank institutional ownership has increased from 16 per cent in 1963 to 50 per cent in 1994 to the detriment of individual ownership which has dropped from 54 per cent to 20 per cent (Stapledon 1996).

Recently, pension funds have been publicly criticized for their 'absenteeism' at AGMs. Stapledon (1996) reports that in 1994 only 28 per cent of the pension schemes voted at all times, the rest never voted (21 per cent) or voted only in certain circumstances (51 per cent). Given their apparent dislike of direct monitoring and their preference for disinvesting out of badly performing firms, institutional investors have also been accused of exerting too much pressure on firms to produce short-term profits and abandon long-term projects (see Marsh 1990, and Miles 1993 for the contrasting views on short-termism in the UK).

The Cadbury (1992), Greenbury (1995), and Hampel (1998) corporate governance committees have urged institutional investors to become more actively involved in their companies. Institutions may take a passive stance, as they may lack the required monitoring expertise. This may be the reason why, for instance, occupational pension funds do not improve firm value (Faccio and Lasfer 1999). Furthermore, the Newbold Inquiry of 1999 reports that the voting procedure for institutions represents 'a tortuous process' because the proxy forms are held by custodians and not by the fund managers themselves (Stapledon and Bates forthcoming).

However, surveys on the voting behaviour of investment funds reveal that vote casting by institutions has been growing rapidly. Many institutional investors have now established voting policies (see e.g. Mallin 1999). Voting by investment funds increased significantly over the 1990s: 20 per cent of funds voted in 1991 (ISC 1991), 35 per cent in 1995 (Mallin 1995), and 41 per cent in 1997 (MVA 1998). Pension funds vote more often with 44 per cent in 1993 (ISC 1993), and 59 per cent in 1996 (Mallin 1996). The vast majority of insurance companies vote: 70 per cent voted in 1993 (ISC 1993), and 87 per cent in 1996 (Mallin 1996).

5.2. *Identity of shareholders and performance*

Most papers studying the link between ownership and performance for UK firms focus on managerial ownership (e.g. Keasey, Short, and Watson 1994) or use general measures of ownership concentration and do not normally distinguish between the different types of shareholders (e.g. Leech and Leahy 1991), as large share stakes are rare.

In contrast, Goergen (1998) investigates the relationship between financial performance and ownership by different types of shareholders in recently floated British and German companies. He distinguishes between six different types of shareholders: families, domestic companies, foreign companies, banks, non-bank institutional investors, and charities. Companies are followed up over a period of six years after the IPO. A panel-data model is estimated explaining current performance by ownership concentration and the type of the largest shareholder of the previous year. Goergen does not find any significant link between a firm's performance and the type of its major shareholder. Short and Keasey (1999) also try to explain firm value by managerial ownership, institutional ownership, and ownership by other block-holders. They do not find that firm value depends on institutional ownership and ownership by other shareholders on the other side for a random sample of 225 firms.

6. DETERMINANTS OF OWNERSHIP CONCENTRATION

In most ownership and performance studies, ownership is treated as an exogenous variable. However, an increasing number of studies assume ownership concentration to be endogenous, i.e. to be determined by the characteristics of the firm. Leech and Leahy (1991) find that a firm's ownership concentration index depends negatively on its size, its level of product diversification (i.e. a highly diversified firm tends to have a less concentrated ownership), and its CAPM beta. They also estimate a probit model using different control dummies as the dependent variable. Their results suggest that smaller firms and firms with a lower CAPM beta are more likely to be owner-controlled rather than manager-controlled.

For his sample of UK IPOs, Goergen (1998) finds that ownership concentration six years after the IPO is higher for firms whose initial owners had low liquidity needs at the time of the IPO, for firms whose business environment is characterized by a low risk and for firms whose founder(s) still held shares in their company at the moment of the flotation. He does not detect a relationship between concentration and firm size.

7. COMPARING CORPORATE GOVERNANCE SYSTEMS: UK VERSUS THE REST OF THE WORLD

As the UK is an exporter of corporate governance reform to the rest of the world (Cheffins 2000), there is need for more comparative empirical research on the strengths and weaknesses of different corporate governance mechanisms (Renneboog *et al.* forthcoming). La Porta *et al.* (1997, 1999) argue that legal and regulatory factors are more fundamental characteristics of countries than ownership. In most countries, legal systems have a long history and have shaped the development of accompanying institutions. La Porta *et al.* (1997) characterize countries' legal systems as being of English, French, German, or Scandinavian origin. They argue that common law countries (English) protect both shareholders and creditors the most, French civil law countries the least, and German and Scandinavian civil law countries somewhere in the middle. Whereas Hansmann and Kraakman (forthcoming) make a case for the superiority of the Anglo-American corporate governance system, Bratton and McCahery (forthcoming) show that the weaknesses of specific corporate governance devices may often be offset by the strengths of other devices.

Carlin and Mayer (1999) examine the effects of differences in corporate and financial systems on industrial activity, more specifically on growth, fixed capital formation, and R&D. They distinguish among countries and industries using bank–firm relations, the development of securities markets, the concentration of ownership and the degree of shareholder and creditor protection of legal systems. There is a strong relationship of market systems and legal protection of investors—both of which are characteristic for the UK—with growth of equity-financed and skill-intensive industries. Whereas no evidence for a role of bank–firm relations (as prominent in Germany for example) is uncovered, a positive role for ownership concentration (as in Continental Europe) in equity-financed and skill-intensive industries is found. For low-income countries, market transparency promotes growth in equity-dependent industries, development of the banking system supports bank-dependent industries and dispersed ownership diminishes agency problems in equity-dependent and skill-intensive industries. Although close relations between banks and industry may have significantly increased growth in countries with high bank ownership, close bank–firm relations are not associated with higher growth of bank-financed industries in developed countries.

Carlin and Mayer (1999) suggest that policies concerning the structure of financial and corporate systems should be sensitive to countries' industrial composition and stages of economic development. In the early stages of development, policy may be best focused on the creation of efficient banking systems and the control of ownership concentrations. At later stages, some activities may benefit from greater information disclosure and the commitments that concentrated owners can provide.

8. CONCLUSION

In terms of corporate governance and ownership, the UK is closer to the USA than to Continental European countries or Japan. The UK has a relatively large number of listed companies which have a widespread ownership. As young companies seek a stock exchange listing, the average percentage of managerial ownership is high relative to Continental Europe. Furthermore, institutional investors hold the bulk of the equity capital. UK firms have a one-tier board of directors, the majority of which is constituted by executive directors. Several codes of good corporate governance intend to strengthen the independence of non-executive directors.

The hostile takeover market performs an important monitoring role. Although hostile takeovers do not particularly focus on poorly performing firms (as the incidence is lower than for other types of companies), poorly performing acquired companies are subjected to substantial board, asset, and financial restructuring. There is not much evidence that the market for partial control (large share blocks below 30 per cent, the mandatory takeover threshold) has a disciplinary role.

Although vote casting on annual meetings by investment and pension funds as well as funds managed by insurance companies has grown significantly, there is little evidence that institutions perform a disciplinary role. This may be due to a deliberate arm's length approach in order not to violate insider trading regulations. There is strong evidence that high managerial ownership entrenches management, as it is then immunized against disciplinary actions by internal and external corporate governance mechanisms. There is some evidence that shareholders (like executive directors or industrial companies) form voting coalitions in order to oppose or perform disciplining of underperforming management.

There is not much evidence that an increase in the number of non-executive directors increases the independence of the board, since non-executive directors appear to vote with the incumbent management. However, separating the roles of CEO and chairman, such that the chairman is a non-executive director, has a significant impact on the effectiveness of monitoring and disciplining of management. Internal audit, remuneration, and nomination committees have not contributed to efficient corporate control. In contrast, unfavourable reports by external audit firms entail a high probability of CEO dismissal.

Although linking top management's remuneration to performance is important to reduce the potential agency conflicts between management and shareholders, there is little evidence of a positive relationship between remuneration and performance for the 1980s and the first half of the 1990s. However, managers in large companies are consistently paid more than managers in small or medium companies. Only recently, since the publication of the Greenbury report (1995), has there been any evidence of a positive pay–performance relationship.

All in all, the degree of capital market development in the UK combined with its good creditor and shareholder protection appears to be well suited to stimulate growth in equity-financed and skill-intensive industries.

Notes

1. The fourth and most recent hostile takeover in Germany was the takeover of Mannesmann AG by Vodafone plc.
2. Vodafone's shares are also listed on the New York Stock Exchange under the form of American Depository Receipts (ADRs).
3. The degree of control of a large stake is determined by using Cubbin and Leech's (1983) voting model. The model calculates the probability that a large shareholder obtains the support of a majority in a contested vote. This probability reflects the degree of control.
4. Their sample excludes financial firms, firms from the oil and gas industries, privatized firms, firms from the broadcasting industry, and firms that do not comply with the typical 'one-vote-one-share' pattern of UK firms.
5. A firm is manager-controlled if managerial ownership plus ownership by shareholders related to the management is in the top quartile of all the sample firms and their leverage is not in the top quartile. If the latter is the case, the firm is said to be debt-holder-controlled.

References for Chapter 16

Agrawal, A. and C. Knoeber (1996), 'Firm Performance and Mechanisms to Control Agency Problems between Managers and Shareholders', *Journal of Financial and Quantitative Analysis*, 31: 377–97.

Bratton, W. and J. McCahery (forthcoming), 'Comparative Corporate Governance: the Case against Global Cross-reference', in Renneboog, McCahery, Moerland, and Raaijmakers, *Convergence and Diversity in Corporate Governance Regimes and Capital Markets*.

Brennan, M. and J. Franks (1997), 'Underpricing, Ownership and Control in Initial Public Offerings of Equity Securities in the UK', *Journal of Financial Economics*, 45: 391–413.

Carlin, W. and C. Mayer (1999), 'How Do Financial Systems Affect Economic Performance?', Working paper, University of Oxford.

Cadbury, A. (1992), *Report of the Committee on the Financial Aspects of Corporate Governance*, London: Gee & Co.

Chan, K. (1997), 'Top Executive Compensation, Corporate Ownership Structure and Capital Structure: An Empirical Study', unpub. MSc diss. UMIST, Manchester.

Cheffins, B. (forthcoming), 'Corporate Governance Reform: Britain as an Exporter', Hume Papers on Public Policy, 8.

Conyon, M. (1994), 'Corporate Governance Changes in UK Companies Between 1988 and 1993', *Corporate Governance*, 2: 97–109.

—— (1997), Corporate Governance and Executive Compensation, *International Journal of Industrial Organization*, 15/4: 493–509.

—— (1998), 'Directors' Pay and Turnover: An Application to a Sample of Large UK Firms', *Oxford Bulletin of Economics and Statistics*, 60/4: 485–507.

—— and D. Leech (1994), 'Top Pay, Company Performance and Corporate Governance', *Oxford Bulletin of Economics and Statistics*, 56: 229–47.

—— and K. Murphy (1999), 'The Prince and the Pauper? CEO Pay in the US and the UK', Paper presented at the Eindhoven Conference on Convergence and Diversity in Corporate Governance Regimes and Capital Markets, mimeo, University of Warwick and University of Southern California.

—— P. Gregg, and S. Machin (1994), 'Taking Care of Business: Executive Compensation in the United Kingdom, *Economic Journal*, 105/430: 704–14.

Crespí, R. and L. Renneboog (1999), 'United We Stand: Corporate Monitoring by Shareholder Coalitions in the UK', Working paper CentER, Tilburg University.

Cubbin, J. and D. Leech (1983), 'The Effect of Shareholding Dispersion on the Degree of Control in British Companies: Theory and Measurement', *Economic Journal*, 93: 351–69.

Faccio, M. and M. Lasfer (1999), 'Managerial Ownership, Board Structure and Firm Value: The UK Evidence', mimeo, Università Cattolica del Sacro Cuore and City University Business School.

Franks, J. and C. Mayer (1995), 'Ownership and Control', in H. Siebert (ed.), *Trends in Business Organization: Do Participation and Cooperation Increase Competitiveness?*, Tübingen: Mohr.

Franks, J. and C. Mayer (1996), 'Hostile Takeovers and the Correction of Managerial Failure', *Journal of Financial Economics*, 40: 163–81.

—— and L. Renneboog (1998), 'Who Disciplines Bad Management?', Discussion paper, 98130, CentER, Tilburg University.

Goergen, M. (1998), *Corporate Governance and Financial Performance: A Study of German and UK Initial Public Offerings*, Cheltenham: Edward Elgar.

—— (1999), 'Insider Retention and Long-Term Performance in German and UK IPOs', mimeo, UMIST, Manchester.

—— and L. Renneboog (forthcoming *a*), 'Prediction of Ownership and Control Concentration in German and UK Initial Public Offerings', in Renneboog, J. McCahery, P. Moerland, and T. Raaijmakers (eds.) (forthcoming), *Convergence and Diversity in Corporate Governance Regimes and Capital Markets*.

—— —— (forthcoming *b*), 'Strong Managers and Passive Institutional Investors in the UK', in F. Barca and M. Becht, *The Control of Corporate Europe*, Oxford: Oxford University Press.

Greenbury Committee (1995), *Final Report of the Study Group on Directors' Remuneration* (Greenbury Report), London: Gee Publishing Ltd.

Hampel Committee (1998), *Final Report of the Committee on Corporate Governance* (Hampel Report), London: Gee Publishing Ltd.

Hansmann, H. and R. Kraakman (forthcoming). 'The End of History for Corporate Law', in Renneboog, McCahery, Moerland, and Raaijmakers (eds.), *Convergence and Diversity in Corporate Governance Regimes and Capital Markets*.

Hay, D. and D. Morris (1984), *Unquoted Companies: Their Contribution to the United Kingdom Economy*, London: Macmillan.

Himmelberg, C., R. Hubbard, and D. Palia (1999), 'Understanding the Determinants of Managerial Ownership and the Link Between Ownership and Performance', *Journal of Financial Economics*, 53: 353–84.

ISC (Institutional Shareholders Committee) (1991), 'The Responsibilities of Institutional Shareholders in the UK', London: ISC.

—— (1993), 'Report on Investigation of Voting Rights by Institutions', London: ISC.

Keasey, K., H. Short, and R. Watson (1994), 'Directors' Ownership and the Performance of Small and Medium Sized Firms in the U.K.', *Small Business Economics*, 6: 225–36.

Kole, S. (1996), 'Managerial Ownership and Firm Performance: Incentives or Rewards?', *Advances in Financial Economics*, 2.

Lai, J. and S. Sudarsanam (1997), 'Corporate Restructuring in Response to Performance Decline: Impact of Ownership, Governance and Lenders', *European Finance Review*, 1: 197–233.

La Porta, R., F. Lopez-de-Silanes, A. Shleifer and R. Vishny (1997), 'Legal Determinants of External Finance', *Journal of Finance*, 52: 1131–50.

—— —— —— ——(1999), 'Corporate Ownership Around the World', *Journal of Finance*, 54: 471–517.

Leech, D. and J. Leahy, (1991), 'Ownership Structure, Control Type Classifications and the Performance of Large British Companies', *Economic Journal*, 101: 1418–37.

Lennox, C. (1998), 'Modified Audit Reports, Executive Compensation and CEO Turnover', mimeo, University of Bristol.

McConnell, J. and H. Servaes (1990), 'Additional Evidence on Equity Ownership and Corporate Value', *Journal of Financial Economics* 27: 595–612.

Mallin, C. (1995), 'The Role of Institutional Investors in Corporate Governance', Research Board monograph, Institute of Chartered Accountants in England and Wales, London.

—— (1996), 'The Voting Framework: A Comparative Study of Voting Behaviour of Institutional Investors in the US and the UK', *Corporate Governance: An International Review*, 4.

—— (1999), 'Corporate Governance: Financial Institutions and their Relations with Corporate Boards', Working paper, Nottingham Business School.

Manne, H. (1965), 'Mergers and the Market for Corporate Control', *Journal of Political Economy*, 73: 110–20.

Marsh, P. (1990), *Short Termism on Trial*, London: Institutional Fund Managers Association.

Mayer, C., I. Alexander, L. Correia da Silva, and M. Goergen (1998), 'Stock Markets and Corporate Performance: A Comparison of Publicly Listed and Private Companies', mimeo, University of Oxford, LEA, Oxford Economic Research Associates Ltd, and UMIST.

Miles, D. (1993), 'Testing for Short Termism in the UK Stock Market', *Economic Journal*, 103: 1379–96.

Morck, R., A. Shleifer, and R. Vishny (1988), 'Management Ownership and Market Valuation: An Empirical Analysis', *Journal of Financial Economics*, 20: 293–315.

MVA (Manifest Voting Agency) (1998), 'Proxy voting 1997 Survey', Mandate 3, Manifest Voting Agency Ltd.

Peasnell, K., P. Pope, and S. Young (1999), 'Board Composition and Earnings Management: Do Outside Directors Constrain Abnormal Accruals?', Working paper 99/006, University of Lancaster.

—— —— —— (2000), 'Managerial Equity Ownership and the Demand for Outside Directors', Working paper 99/007, University of Lancaster.

Prowse, S. (1995), 'Corporate Governance in an International Perspective: A Survey of Corporate Control Mechanisms Among Large Firms in the U.S., U.K., Japan and Germany', *Financial Markets, Institutions Instruments*, 4/1: 1–63.

Renneboog, L., J. McCahery, P. Moerland and T. Raaijmakers (forthcoming), *Convergence and Diversity in Corporate Governance Regimes and Capital Markets*, Oxford: Oxford University Press.

Schwert, W. (2000), 'Hostility in Takeovers: In the Eyes of the Beholder?', *Journal of Finance*, 60: 2599–640.

Short, H. and K. Keasey (1999), 'Managerial Ownership and the Performance of Firms: Evidence from the UK', *Journal of Corporate Finance*, 5: 79–101.

Stapledon, G. (1996), *Institutional Shareholders and Corporate Governance*, Oxford: Clarendon Press.

—— and J. Bates (forthcoming), 'Enhancing Efficiency in Corporate Governance: How Recognizing the Nature of Modern Shareholding Can Lead to a Simplified Voting Process', in Renneboog, McCahery, Moerland, and Raaijmakers (eds.), *Convergence and Diversity in Corporate Governance Regimes and Capital Markets*.

Study Group on Directors' Remuneration ('Greenbury Committee') (1995), *Code of Best Practice*, London: Gee Publishing.

17

Conclusion and policy implications

KLAUS GUGLER

This book has reviewed the main aspects of the corporate governance debates in the USA, Europe, and Japan. The Appendix to this chapter summarizes our main findings. While the 'answers' to the research questions are well backed by the evidence, they necessarily reflect at least in part the opinions of the authors.

First, the evidence is more on the positive side of direct shareholder monitoring. Large shareholders are active monitors in the corporations they control. They have both the incentives and the means to discipline management. In Austria, Belgium, Germany, and also the USA, the preponderance of studies do find beneficial effects of large shareholders for firm performance. However, there are also many studies that find insignificant and/or unclear results, such as in France, Japan, the Netherlands, Spain, or the UK. In Turkey, large shareholders may even be detrimental to the performance of companies.

Second, many predominantly Continental European studies assert that there is a level of ownership concentration beyond which owner-managers get entrenched and extract rents from other, smaller shareholders. Expropriation of minority shareholders appears to be consistently worse in countries with weaker shareholder protection and illiquid securities markets such as in Italy, Spain, Turkey, Germany, or Austria. There is also the suspicion expressed by many authors that pyramidal groups may—among other things—serve the purpose of extracting rents from small shareholders. Moreover, although investor protection is quite stringent in the USA or UK, some studies find managerial entrenchment in these countries.

While legislation reform has rectified the most evident abuses of shareholder rights in recent years, some countries are lagging behind. In Belgium, for instance, minority shareholders or a group of minority shareholders owning at least 1 per cent of the equity capital or shares with a value of not less than BEF 50 m. can initiate a minority claim and ask the court to appoint one or more experts who can scrutinize the company's accounting and its internal operations since 1991. On the other hand, in Germany a 75 per cent majority may legally make a binding tender offer to minority shareholders below market value. Similar regulations are in place in Austria.

A step in the right direction would be increased minority shareholder rights and better standards concerning company disclosure requirements. Reform in this area is surely needed. The task of prudential company legislation is to secure the benefits of large shareholders as effective monitors of management and, at the same time, to prevent them from consuming excessive private benefits from control. Stricter protection of minority shareholders is proposed. Only the prospect of a fair return will induce small and minority shareholders to invest in companies' stocks. High disclosure and accounting standards provide the necessary transparency for small shareholders to feel comfortable investing in equity markets. Disclosure requirements for pyramidal groups, the structure of ownership and voting rights, and legal separation devices should be mandatory and enforcement should be strict.

Third, we have seen that takeovers are an incomplete mechanism to solve the basic agency problem in the large public corporation. The markets for corporate control are very active in the USA or UK, however, nearly non-existent in Continental Europe or Japan. Due to the concentrated ownership of shares and anti-takeover regulations, statutes, and sentiments in many countries, hostile takeovers are not possible without support by incumbent block-holders. Large shareholders and/or banks must generally be courted to support the bid for it to succeed. Large block trades and subsequent control transfers only partially substitute for an active market for corporate control. Other control devices such as direct shareholder monitoring, the dual board structure, creditor monitoring, and/or the main bank system substitute for hostile takeovers.

The question remains whether state legislation should step in to reduce the probability of (hostile) takeovers occurring. Policy recommendations must be linked to the objectives of bidder firms. Whether principals (shareholders) can cope with their agents (managers) concerning acquisition activity certainly is a function of the ownership and control structure of the bidding and target firm. Certain restrictions on bidding firm managers would improve the role of the takeover process in corporate governance. Anti-takeover amendments of potential targets, however, reduce shareholder wealth. In any case, one could strengthen alternative mechanisms of control while not constraining hostile takeovers by regulation. Extreme views of either prohibiting hostile takeovers, or viewing hostile takeovers as the main control device, are too simplistic.

Particularly from a Continental European standpoint, where investor protection is lagging, takeover legislation must also be concerned with the interests of small shareholders. In Italy, Belgium, Denmark, and France laws were passed that every acquisition of more than 30 per cent of the stock of one company be followed by a tender offer to all voting shares at the same price. While these laws may reduce the probability of takeovers occurring, they prevent an unequal treatment of shareholders in takeovers. In Austria, however, the price offered to dispersed shareholders can be marked down by 15 per cent relative to the block price.

Fourth, US and UK studies question efficiently designed compensation packages. The UK evidence shows that compensation is more closely related to firm size than to firm performance. While recent studies for the USA do find a strong relationship between pay and performance mainly due to the effects of stock options, the evidence on relative compensation schemes is on the negative side. Unfortunately, little systematic evidence is available for other countries, since disclosure rules do not force companies to release the relevant information. Generally, there is the feeling of many authors that pay–performance schemes will gain in importance in Continental Europe, too.

One reason for inefficient compensation contracts may be that manager-dominated boards decide about key elements of the contract between the principals (shareholders) and the agents (managers). The evidence suggests that—in the face of weak boards—shareholders themselves may decide about proposals on compensation packages in general meetings. At least, better transparency regarding the level and the structure of compensation contracts—especially in Continental Europe—is necessary.

Fifth, and particularly in Continental Europe, the identity of large and controlling equity owners matters. There are, however, very few studies in this field so general statements are necessarily preliminary. While the effects of close bank–firm relationships and shareholdings of institutional investors on firm profitability are ambiguous, the evidence concerning state ownership is on the negative side. Some studies confirm beneficial effects of bank involvement concerning other dimensions of performance, e.g. financial constraints or distress. This is also evident in the 'contingent governance' system of Japan, where main banks are particularly dominant. The evidence concerning incentives of institutional investors reflects theoretical ambiguities. In view of the rapidly increasing importance of institutional holdings, the lack of established empirical evidence is particularly worrying.

The key to more efficient corporate governance arrangements is to have private savings channelled to stock exchanges, and at the same time not lose control and give rise to managerial discretion. Institutional investors can provide one part of the answer. The second part—efficient control and governance in these institutions themselves—must be provided by prudent regulation. As the problem seems to be that institutional investors are not too active but too passive, restrictions of their holdings in individual companies must be questioned. The UK Hampel Committee, the successor to the Greenbury Committee, considers the introduction of compulsory voting for institutional shareholders as is the case in the USA. Generally, excessively stringent restrictions of holdings in individual firms provide only insufficient incentives to fund managers to participate in active monitoring and to exert the 'voice' rather than the 'exit' option. Reconsideration of overly restrictive legislation in this field is warranted. Good corporate governance needs the right incentives, concentrated holdings of residual claims provide them.

Finally, there is the question of whether board structure has an effect on firm performance, and, therefore, how boards should be designed. The board of directors (or supervisory board in countries with a two-tier structure) plays a potentially very important role. If the CEO is also the chairman of the supervisory board, no effective monitoring or disciplining is to be expected. For example, Franks, Mayer, and Renneboog (1998) find for 250 UK companies for the 1988 to 1993 period that the separation of CEO and chairman leads to greater CEO replacement when performance is poor.

Likewise, board members are mostly also agents and the right incentives need to be given. In France, for example, the CEO/chairman has to own shares in the company. In the Netherlands, there is evidence that the structured regime, which implies a transfer of control rights from shareholders to board members, has a negative effect on firm performance. Although the economic effects of co-determination are still largely unexplored, workers on the supervisory board may have the incentive to exert a considerable monitoring function as is the case in Germany and Austria. However, there may also be detrimental effects of co-determination for efficient governance (see Pistor 1998, and Roe 1998 for plausible effects of co-determination).

It is commonly held that supervisory boards are less effective monitors than intended by the law. Roe (1998) enumerates as reasons the large size of the supervisory board, infrequent board meetings, sparse information flow to the board, low incentives to actively monitor management, and co-determination, which gives shareholders and management incentives to weaken the board. As Roe (1998) argues, block-holders would not get a fair price for their stock if a diffusion of ownership left firms either with labour-dominated or weak boards. More evidence is surely needed to arrive at a fuller picture.

While the US and UK debate centres around the manager–shareholder conflict, Continental European and Japanese corporate governance is more concerned with the large shareholder–small shareholder conflict. The former debate poses questions such as whether the takeover process is a good mechanism to constrain management, or how to efficiently design compensation packages. The latter discussion is more concerned with questions like whether minority shareholders should be better protected against large shareholders and whether the identity of owners matters. Of course, all these questions are interrelated contributing to the complexity of the analysis. As a general and therefore abstract policy guide, any corporate governance reform should be gradual, taking into account the endogenous nature of corporate governance and the national specificities of existing corporate governance arrangements.

As already mentioned, due to the tremendous ownership and voting power concentration in Continental Europe, there is an important conflict of interest between large controlling shareholders and weak minority shareholders. To understand corporate governance and sometimes its failures in these countries, it is necessary to analyse this conflict. However, it is also equally important to recognize the growing importance of the large public corporation in Europe. Large scale privatization of former state-owned quasi-monopolies contribute to this development. This privatization process in Europe (France, Germany, Austria, not ignoring the Eastern European countries!) makes the role of the state as entrepreneur less important, however at the same time poses new challenges as to how to design the relationship between ownership and control. The associated conflict between management and owners will, therefore, grow in importance. Institutional investors like pension or mutual funds will play a key role in channelling private savings to productive investment as is already the case in the USA and UK. Regulation of institutional investors will be the key to successful reform of the European capital markets.

This book has several general messages, bearing with them policy implications and recommendations:

(1) Relying on one or a few tools to solve agency conflicts is not optimal. Economic theory postulates that the various mechanisms for solving agency problems should be employed up to the zero marginal profit condition. A central message of this book is that all constellations of ownership and control structure involve costs and benefits,

i.e. the trade-offs in Table 1.1. Relying solely on the takeover mechanism is, for instance, not optimal. Excessive ownership concentration implies illiquid securities markets, low diversification opportunities, suboptimally risky investment projects, and possibly conflicts of interest between large and small shareholders. Sole reliance on this mechanism is also not optimal. The right mix of direct monitoring by shareholders and board of directors, efficiently designed managerial compensation packages, and competition in the managerial and product markets yield a better solution than relying excessively on one device.

(2) The costs and benefits of the various control devices depend on the kind of economic activity, i.e. the industry. The question is, which assets would be better employed in an organization characterized by the separation of ownership and control, and in which assets are better controlled by direct large shareholder monitoring. If, for example, investment in research and development is a 'complex' and a very risky undertaking, the benefits of separating the decision and control functions may outweigh the associated agency costs. Well-functioning capital and equity markets should put up the needed financial funds to guarantee an optimal level of investment in these activities. Investors should have the opportunity to diversify their risks across a large number of stock corporations implying a rather small stake in each one. Since monitoring is a public good and dispersed shareholders have little incentive and ability to monitor management, (takeover) markets, boards, and efficient contracts should provide this service, particularly in industries characterized by complexity, uncertainty, and high sunk costs.

(3) Corporate governance regulation and other legislation are intimately linked to each other. Anti-trust policy, competition policy, and regulations about corporate governance influence each other and must be viewed in conjunction. If competition in product markets is weak, managerial discretion over free cash flows is more likely. Accordingly, corporate governance becomes more important in monopolistic or oligopolistic environments.

(4) The basic trade-offs encountered in corporate governance are similar in type across countries, although they vary in intensity. This book makes the case for gradual steps for corporate governance reform incorporating national specificities in some areas however opts for immediate measures where failures of the current system are evident. Enhanced transparency and disclosure rules, and better representation of minority shareholders are certainly imminent in Continental Europe.

Appendix. A summary of answers to the basic corporate governance research questions

Question 1. *Is there a relation between direct shareholder monitoring and performance?*

Austria	Most authors confirm that direct shareholder monitoring is beneficial and/or that dispersion of ownership claims reduces the profitability of the corporation.
Belgium	Disciplinary actions against management are taken when market-adjusted share returns are negative and when the company generates operating earnings' losses or resorts to substantial cuts in dividends in the years prior to the restructuring. There is also evidence that companies with levels of and changes in ROE and cash flows below those of industry peers are subjected to increased monitoring. Shareholder monitoring is beneficial, but it is not the shareholders owning the direct equity stakes which monitor but the ultimate shareholder in a control chain (Renneboog 2000; Goergen and Renneboog 2000).
Germany	There is some evidence that monitoring depends on performance. Franks and Mayer (1996*b*) find that changes in block ownership are more likely after periods of poor performance. These changes, however, do not significantly affect the composition of managing and supervisory boards.
France	Empirical evidence on the shareholders' monitoring influence on firms' performances is inconclusive: Romieu and Sassenou (1996) find a positive influence while Charreaux (1997) and Kremp and Sevestre (2000) find mixed results. The results depend on the performance measure considered.
Italy	There is no direct evidence on this point, because, until recently, there were basically no management-controlled companies.
Japan	Nakatani (1984), Weinstein and Yafeh (1998), and Hoshi and Itoh (1991) find lower profitability of firms in closely held corporate groups (*keiretsu*) than less-affiliated firms. Prowse (1992) finds an insignificant relationship between concentrated ownership and several performance measures.
The Netherlands	Van Kampen and Van de Kraats (1995) find insignificant and unclear results.
Spain	There is no significant empirical evidence that family majority-controlled firms have better performance than non-concentrated ownership firms. Galve and Salas (1993) find higher efficiency for non-concentrated ownership firms, and limits on size and risk concentration of family-controlled groups.
Turkey	Yurtoglu (2000) finds that several performance measures are negatively correlated with concentrated direct shareholdings.
UK	The UK evidence is inconclusive. Some studies find a relationship between performance and managerial ownership whereas others do not. Also, the studies that find a link do not agree on the form of the link.
USA	The preponderance of studies find beneficial effects of large shareholder monitoring and owner control. However, there may be reverse causality of ownership and performance with causation running from performance to ownership structure.

Note: The answers to the research questions reflect the opinions of the authors.

Question 2. *Are block-holders beneficial or is there entrenchment and rent extraction?*

Austria	Ownership concentration seems to be excessive in Austria. Gugler (1998) finds that ownership concentration and profitability are negatively related. This suggests entrenchment and rent extraction.
Belgium	Control is usually levered by pyramidal and complex ownership structures and there is an important market for share stakes. However, little relation is found between ownership structures and the disciplining of top management in listed industrial and commercial companies. The presence of large industrial shareholders (and to a lesser extent of family shareholdings) is related to high executive board turnover when performance is poor, whereas no evidence is found for a monitoring role by large holding companies. (Renneboog 2000, Goergen and Renneboog 2000)
Germany	Several studies test whether bank control and block ownership affects firm performance. Unfortunately, their results diverge substantially and depend strongly on the sample, period, and methodology used.
France	Ownership concentration is very high, which may explain the difficulty in finding a clear relationship between ownership concentration and performance (Charreaux 1997). However, Kremp and Sevestre (2000) find a slight positive effect. Paquerot (1997) finds evidence of entrenchment with no clear influence on firms' performance, while Romieu and Sassenou (1996) find a positive influence of the capital share owned by the manager on the average return per share.
Italy	Various studies (Zingales 1994; Caprio and Floreani 1996; Bianco, Casavola, Ferrando 1997) find evidence of entrenchment and rent extraction.
Japan	Shareholding main banks charge higher interest to firms in a *keiretsu* group (Weinstein and Yafeh 1998) as a compensation for rescue operation (Hoshi, Kashyap, and Sharfstein 1991; Asako 1991; and Okazaki and Horiuchi 1992) and takeover defence.
The Netherlands	Van Kampen and Van de Kraats (1995) find insignificant and unclear results.
Spain	Only indirect empirical evidence suggests that (block-holder-supported) management entrenchment holds. Powerful anti-takeover provisions, large cross shareholdings, golden parachute contracts, and lack of transparency of board compensation are examples of this trend.
Turkey	Yurtoglu (2000) presents evidence consistent with rent extraction and entrenchment of large shareholders. Pyramidal structures serve mainly this purpose.
UK	Franks, Mayer, and Renneboog (1998) report that managers, being the second most important type of shareholder in listed UK firms, use their votes to entrench their position on boards in the wake of bad financial performance.
USA	Some authors (e.g. Morck *et al.* 1988) find managerial entrenchment. Stringent investor protection rights prevent substantial rent extraction by large corporate insiders (La Porta *et al.* 1997).

Note: The answers to the research questions reflect the opinions of the authors.

Question 3. *Are takeovers important as a disciplinary device? Are they beneficial?*

Austria	Hostile takeovers are unimportant as a disciplinary device. There are many large block trades; however, there is no systematic evidence about their effects. Internal control devices, such as large shareholder monitoring, are the primary means of control.
Belgium	Since 1989, hostile takeovers are virtually ruled out. Legislation allows for the use of poison pills. Furthermore, given the high concentration of ownership in most companies, hostile takeovers without an *ex ante* toehold stake are almost impossible (Renneboog 2000; Goergen and Renneboog 2000).
Germany	While management can be bypassed (making an offer hostile), large shareholders and/or banks must generally be courted to support the bid for it to succeed. Since there are no immediate publication requirements for such negotiations, little is known about the consequences for the target firm.
France	There have been too few hostile takeovers to draw any conclusion about their possible impact on managerial behaviour.
Italy	Takeovers are not very common and rarely hostile (with a recent and notable exception). There is evidence for the past (Guelpa 1992; Caprio and Floreani 1996) that takeovers were not a disciplinary device, but more recent evidence (Bianco and Casavola 1998) suggests that this might be changing.
Japan	Internal monitoring by banks, large shareholders and family control are the main tools for controlling management. Hostile takeovers would distort the balance of power between shareholders and employees in contingent governance.
The Netherlands	No. For example, Kabir, Cantrijn, and Jeunink (1997) document a multitude of technical takeover defences and a negative correlation with ownership concentration. Bosveld and Goedbloed (1997) find one hostile takeover in the period 1960–96.
Spain	There is an important number of registered takeovers. However, only a few of them are hostile. Crespí and Gispert (1998) find evidence on higher board turnover around large block transfers (including takeovers). Their disciplinary role is not confirmed because those transfers are not a consequence of a company's poor performance.
Turkey	Hostile takeovers are non-existent among listed firms. Lack of data prevents studies covering non-listed firms.
UK	Franks and Mayer (1996a) find that the performance between the targets of hostile takeovers and that of friendly takeover targets, non-merging firms and the targets of failed takeovers are not significantly different. This suggests that targets of hostile takeovers are taken over for other reasons than bad performance.
USA	The market for corporate control is most important in the USA. However, takeovers are an incomplete mechanism to solve the basic agency problem in the large public corporation. The takeover premium is about 30–40 per cent.

Note: The answers to the research questions reflect the opinions of the authors.

Question 4. *Is there a positive pay–performance relationship (or are managers paid like 'bureaucrats')?*

Austria	There is no systematic evidence about this point mainly due to lack of data.
Belgium	There is no systematic evidence about this point mainly due to lack of data.
Germany	Empirical analysis of the pay–performance relation is difficult in Germany because only aggregate, as opposed to individual compensation, is disclosed. Different samples and methodologies yield diverging estimates.
France	This question has not been answered in France because of the insufficient availability of data. Many large companies have set up compensation systems for their top managers relating their compensation to the performance of the firm.
Italy	The very limited evidence (Brunello *et al.* 1997) suggests that pay–performance schemes are still uncommon. Also this is changing in large companies.
Japan	No systematic evidence exists as managers have been paid on a seniority basis so far. However, large companies are moving towards incentive pay systems.
The Netherlands	No studies/data available.
Spain	Crespí and Gispert (1998) find a positive relationship between total board compensation and company performance. This relationship is very weak for market performance measures and slightly stronger for accounting performance.
Turkey	There is no systematic evidence about this point mainly due to lack of data.
UK	Empirical evidence on the UK suggests that managerial compensation is not very sensitive to financial performance, but is highly sensitive to firm size. Similarly, there is no evidence of a link between top executive remuneration and ownership structure.
USA	While most authors find a positive association of pay and performance (e.g. Hall and Liebman 1997), the evidence concerning relative compensation schemes is on the negative side.

Note: The answers to the research questions reflect the opinions of the authors.

Question 5. *Does the identity of owners matter? Are institutional investors important?*

Austria	Institutional investors such as pension or mutual funds are unimportant to date; therefore, systematic evidence is lacking. Institutional investors will, however, gain in importance in Austria, too.
Belgium	Companies controlled by industrial companies (and families) are more closely monitored. Institutions do not directly interfere with governance actions. The presence of large holding companies in the ownership structure seems to have a detrimental effect on performance and is not related to any monitoring. (Renneboog 2000; Goergen and Renneboog 2000).
Germany	Too little evidence for a general statement.
France	The influence of the owner identity on performance is not clearly established. Results about differences between independent firms, group subsidiaries and heads of groups are mixed. However, there seems to be a positive influence of foreign shareholders.
Italy	The identity of owners matter, but not in a very significant way. Institutional investors still play a limited role.
Japan	A firm largely owned by the main bank and its member firms (*keiretsu*) enjoys more stable investment growth and financial resources. Yet, no evidence is found for a positive relationship between increasing foreign ownership and better performance. Control rights of institutional investors are constrained, so that their monitoring incentives are weak (Fukao 1997).
The Netherlands	No studies available.
Spain	The Spanish ownership structure has changed in composition rather than in concentration during the last years. Crespí and Garcia Cestona (1997) find substantial changes in ownership structures. The decrease of state participation, the growing importance of foreign companies as shareholders, and the listing of new companies need to be related to performance.
Turkey	Yurtoglu (1999) shows that business groups matter for investment decisions. Independent, younger, and smaller firms suffer from cash-constraints, whereas investment of firms belonging to a business group is less dependent on cash flow.
UK	Given the high dispersion of ownership in the UK, most studies focus on managerial ownership or use general indices of ownership concentration. Goergen (1998) focuses on the different types of shareholder, but does not find a link between performance and type of shareholder.
USA	The evidence is scarce as ownership concentration is much lower than in Continental Europe and identities of controlling owners cannot unambiguously be established. The evidence concerning the role of institutional investors is generally ambiguous reflecting principal–agent conflicts in these investors themselves.

Note: The answers to the research questions reflect the opinions of the authors.

Question 6. *Is there a relationship between board structure and performance?*

Austria	Nemec (1999) finds that 44.7% of the 47 listed Austrian firms in her sample have a bank member as chair or vice-chair of the supervisory board. Gugler *et al.* (2000) find oversized boards in state-owned firms. There are no studies relating board composition to performance.
Belgium	The role of the non-executive directors is important in the disciplining process: a high proportion of non-executive directors leads to increased executive board turnover. Furthermore, a higher probability of CEO replacement was found when the tasks of CEO ('delegated' director) and (non-executive) chairman are separated (Renneboog 2000; Goergen and Renneboog 2000).
Germany	Too little evidence exists to make a general statement. See, however, the answer to Question 1 regarding the findings of Franks and Mayer (1996*b*).
France	A significant link between the corporate governance system (board of directors vs. supervisory and management boards) and firm performance does not seem to exist (Shyy and Vijayraghavan 1996). Charreaux (1997) finds conflicting evidence on the relationship between the percentage of independent administrators and the performance of large companies.
Italy	There is no direct evidence on this issue since it is difficult to identify 'independent' directors. The effect of performance on board turnover is negative. Currently, there is a single-tier system in place, however, the proposed reform of company law will introduce the possibility of having also a two-tier system. There is no worker representation on the board.
Japan	No systematic evidence exists, since the Japanese board has been a management forum of insiders. Large companies recognize smaller board size with outside directors as an effective tool to control management.
The Netherlands	The effects of board size and the structured regime (a transfer of power from shareholders to supervisory board members) on firm performance are negative.
Spain	Fernandez *et al.* (1998) found a non-monotonically increasing relationship between board size and performance. Board composition through the monitoring of external board members influences company performance. Gispert (1998), however, finds that board composition does not explain the board turnover–poor performance relationship.
Turkey	The board of directors reflects the ownership structure, since boards are dominated by the owner family. Boards are in the first place an internal mechanism of control reinforcing the owners' influence on the company. Given that board structure and board size are endogenously determined, they are expected to have a similar impact on performance as variables that reflect the power of the ultimate owners.
UK	Lai and Sudarsanam (1997) find that there is a link between board structure and the incidence of certain types of corporate recovery actions. Peasnell *et al.* (1999) find that the higher the proportion of outside directors on the board the lower will be the use of earnings management to disguise losses or reduced earnings.
USA	There is no convincing evidence that greater board independence correlates with greater firm profitability or faster growth (Bhagat and Black 1998).

Note: The answers to the research questions reflect the opinions of the authors.

Question 7. *What is the major conflict: owner vs. managers or large vs. small shareholders?*

Austria	Both are present. The owner–manager conflict predominantly in state-controlled firms or in 'ownerless' legal forms, the large–small shareholder conflict when ownership concentration leads to rent extraction.
Belgium	There is substantial legal shareholder minorities protection, although there has been some evidence of (controlling) shareholder groups developing (or failing to develop) a long-term corporate strategy. The major agency problem is between large and small shareholders.
Germany	While the owner–manager conflict is likely to be present in some firms, the conflict between small and large shareholders appears to be much more important. Reasons include the predominance of large shareholders in most public firms, weak minority protection, partially ineffective disclosure regulations, and potential collusion among large shareholders.
France	It is likely that both exist in large companies in which a significant part of ownership is highly dispersed.
Italy	Until recently only the second was relevant. Privatization of very large companies is also introducing the first.
Japan	Until recently the former conflict was irrelevant as there was an implicit understanding between managers and owners to share control. With an increase in foreign and individual shareholders, the owner–manager conflict becomes more prominent.
The Netherlands	Both problems seem relevant. However, empirical examination is absent.
Spain	The primary conflict is between majority vs. minority shareholders. In a context of concentrated ownership the monitoring problem of managers by shareholders is not the main issue: there are no incentives to free ride. Precise knowledge about the ways of rent expropriation is needed.
Turkey	The main conflict is between small and large shareholders mainly in firms with pyramidal ownership structures and cross-shareholdings. More research is necessary to study the owner–manager conflict.
UK	The classic owner–manager conflict is the major concern.
USA	The classic owner–manager conflict is the major concern.

Note: The answers to the research questions reflect the opinions of the authors.

References for Chapter 17

Asako, K., M. Kunanori, T. Inoue, and H. Murase (1991), 'Fixed Investment Financing (Setsubitoshi to shikinchotatsu), *Economics Today*, 11/4. Japan Development Bank's Research Institute of Fixed Investment.

Bhagat, Sanjai and Bernard Black (1998), 'The Uncertain Relationship Between Board Composition and Firm Performance', in Klaus Hopt, Mark Roe, and Eddy Wymeersch, eds., *Corporate Governance: The State of the Art and Emerging Research*, Oxford: Oxford University Press.

Bianco, M., and P. Casavola (1999), 'Italian Corporate Governance: Effects on Financial Structure and Performance', *European Economic Review*, 43/4–6 (April), 1057–69.

—— —— and A. Ferrando (1997), 'Pyramidal Groups and External Finance: An Empirical Investigation', Fondazione Eni Enrico Mattei, Working paper n. 61/97.

Bosveld, R. and A.M. Goedbloed (1997), 'Effecten van beschermingsconstructies op aandelenkoersen', *Maandblad voor Accountancy en Bedrijfseconomie*, 70 (May), 261–70.

Brunello, G., C. Graziani, and B. Parigi (forthcoming) (1999), 'Executive Compensation and Firm Performance in Italy', *International Journal of Industrial Organization*.

Caprio, L. and A. Floreani (1996), 'Transfer of Control of Listed Companies in Italy: An Empirical Analysis', Fondazione Eni Enrico Mattei, Working paper n. 8/96.

Charreaux Gérard (1997), 'Structure de propriété, relation d'agence, et performance financière', in G. Charreaux (ed.), 'Le Gouvernement des Entreprises, Corporate Governance, Théorie et Faits', Paris: MEDEF, 55–85.

Crespí-Cladera, R. and M. A. Cestona, (1997), 'Ownership and Control of the Spanish Listed Firms', in *The Separation of Ownership and Control: A Survey of 7 European Countries*, Preliminary Report to the European Commission.

—— and C. Gispert-Pellicer (1998), 'Board Remuneration, Performance, and Corporate Governance in Large Spanish Companies', Workshop on Corporate Governance; Contracts and Managerial Incentives, Berlin (July).

Fernández Alvarez, A., S. Gómez Ansón, and C. Fernández Méndez (1998), 'The Effect of Board Size and Composition on Corporate Performance', in Balling *et al.* (eds.), *Corporate Governance, Financial Markets and Global Convergence*, Boston: Kluwer Academic Press, 1–14.

Franks J. and C. Mayer (1996*a*), 'Hostile Takeovers and the Correction of Managerial Failure', *Journal of Financial Economics*, 40: 163–81.

—— —— (1996*b*), 'Ownership, Control, and the Performance of German Corporations', Working paper, London Business School.

—— —— and L. Renneboog (1998), 'Who Disciplines Bad Management?', Discussion paper, 98130, CentER, Tilburg University.

Fukao, Mitsuhiro (1997), 'The Japanese Financial System and the Prospect for Structure of Corporate Governance' (Nihon no Kinnyu Sisutemu to Corporate Governance Kouzou no Tennbou), rev. report submitted 17 Feb. 1997 to the Third Research Group, Institute of International Trade and Industry, MITI, 22 June.

Galve Gorriz, C. and V. Salas Fumas (1993), 'Propiedad y resultados de la gran empresa española', *Investigaciones Económicas*, 27/2: 207–38

Gispert, Carles (forthcoming), 'Board Turnover and Firm Performance in Spanish Companies'. *Investigaciones Económicas*.

Goergen, M. (1998), *Corporate Governance and Financial Performance: A Study of German and UK Initial Public Offerings*, Cheltenham: Edward Elgar.

—— and L. Renneboog (2000), 'Insider Control by Large Investor Groups and Managerial Disciplining in Belgian Listed Companies', *Managerial Finance*, 26/10: 22–41.

Guelpa, F. (1992), *Crescita esterna e performance competitive*, Nuova Italia Scientifica: Roma.

Gugler, K. (1998), 'Corporate Ownership Structure in Austria', *Empirica*, 25: 285–307.

—— A. Stomper, and J. Zechner (2000), 'Corporate Governance, Ownership, and Board Structure in Austria', *Zeitschrift für Betriebswirtschaft*, Supplement (Jan.). 23–43.

Hall, B. and J. Liebman (1997), 'Are CEOs Really Paid Like Bureucrats?', NBER, Working paper no. 6213.

Hoshi, Takeo, and Takatoshi, Itoh (1991), 'Measuring Coherence of Japanese Enterprise Groups', paper prepared for TCER Finance Conference, 21–2 March.

—— A. Kashyap, and D. Sharfstein (1991), 'The Role of Banks in Reducing the Costs of Financial Distress in Japan', *Journal of Financial Economics*, 27: 67–88.

Kabir, R. D. Cantrijn, and A. Jeunink (1997), 'Takeover Defences, Ownership Structure and Stock Returns in the Netherlands: An Empirical Analysis', *Strategic Management Journal*, 18/2: 97–109.

Kremp, Elizabeth and Patrick Sevestre (2000), 'Ownership Concentration and Corporate Performance : Some New Evidence for France', *Research in International Business and Finance*, special issue (June).

Lai, J. and S. Sudarsanam (1997), 'Corporate Restructuring in Response to Performance Decline: Impact of Ownership, Governance and Lenders', *European Finance Review*, 1: 197–233.

La Porta, R. F. Lopez-de-Silanes, A. Shleifer, and R. W. Vishny (1997), 'Legal Determinants of External Finance', *Journal of Finance*, 52/3: 1131–50.

Morck, R., A. Shleifer, and R. W. Vishny (1988*a*), 'Management Ownership and Market Valuation: An Empirical Analysis', *Journal of Financial Economics*, 20: 293–315.

Nakatani, Iwao (1984), 'The Economic Role of Financial Corporate Grouping', in M. Aoki (ed.) *The Economic Analysis of the Japanese Firm*, Amsterdam: North-Holland, 27–258.

Nemec, E. A. (1999), 'The Two Faces of Debtholder Control in Bank-Oriented Covernance Systems: Evidence from German Speaking Countries', Vienna University of Economics and Business Administration, Working paper.

Okazaki, T. and A. Horiuchi (1992), 'Corporate Fixed Investment and Main Bank Relationships (Kigyo no setsubioshi to mainbanku kankei), *Finance Today,* Bank of Japan's Research Institute of Finance.

Paquerot, Mathieu (1997), Stratégie d'enracinement des dirigeants, performance de la firme et structure de contrôle, in Charreaux (ed.), *Le Gouvernement des Entreprises, Corporate Governance, Théorie et Faits*, 105–38.

Peasnell K., P. Pope, and S. Young (1999), 'Board Composition and Earnings Management: Do Outside Directors Constrain Abnormal Accruals?', Working paper 99/006, University of Lancaster.

Pistor, K. (1998), 'Co-determination in Germany: A Socio-Political Model with Governance Externalities', The Sloan Project on Corporate Governance at Columbia Law School, May.

Prowse, Stephen D. (1992), 'The Structure of Corporate Ownership in Japan', *Journal of Finance*, 47/3: 1121–40.

Renneboog, L. (forthcoming), 'Ownership, Managerial Control and the Governance of Poorly Performing Companies Listed on the Brussels Stock Exchange', *Journal of Banking and Finance.*

Roe, M. (1998), 'German Co-determination and German Securities Markets', *Columbia Business Law Review*, 5: 199–211.

Romieu, Nathalie and Najib Sassenou (1996), Quels liens établir entre la structure de l'actionnariat de la firme et ses performances économiques et financières?, *CDC Marché*, Flash no. 96-01, 5 Jan.

Shyy, Gang and Vijayraghavan Vasumathi (1996), 'Is a Supervisory Board Valuable? The French Evidence', Paper presented to the Second Annual Conference of the American Institute for Contemporary German Studies, 'Which Way Ahead for European Financial Markets?', June 10–11.

Van Kampen, M. W. J. M and B. P. J. van de Kraats (1995), 'Grootaandeelhouderschap en aandelenrendement', *Economisch Statistische Berichten* (June 7), 534–7.

Viénot, Marc (1999), *Rapport du comité sur le gouvernement d'entreprise*, Paris: AFEP, MEDEF.

Weinstein, David and Yishay Yafeh (1998), 'On the Costs of a Bank-Centered Financial System: Evidence From the Changing Main Bank Relations in Japan', *Journal of Finance*, 53/2: 635–72.

Yurtoglu, B. B. (1999), 'Business Groups, Liquidity and Investment: Evidence from Turkey', Working paper, University of Vienna.

—— (2000). Ownership, Control and Performance of Turkish Listed Companies', *Empirica*, 27: 193–222.

Zingales, L. (1994), 'The Value of Voting Right: A Study of the Milan Stock Exchange Experience', *Review of Financial Studies*, 7: 125–48.

Index